Party Competition and Responsible Party Government

Party Competition and Responsible Party Government

A Theory of Spatial Competition
Based upon Insights from
Behavioral Voting Research

James Adams

Ann Arbor

THE UNIVERSITY OF MICHIGAN PRESS

2004   2003   2002   2001   4   3   2   1

A CIP catalog record for this book is available from the British Library.

Library of Congress Cataloging-in-Publication Data

Adams, James, 1962–
    Party competition and responsible party government : a theory of spatial
competition based upon insights from behavioral voting research / James
Adams.
        p.   cm.
    Includes bibliographical references and index.
    ISBN 0-472-11201-5 (cloth : alk. paper) — ISBN 0-472-08767-3
(pbk. : alk. paper)
    1. Political parties.   2. Democracy.   3. Voting research.   I. Title.

    JF2051 .A33   2001
    324.2′01—dc21   2001034778

ISBN13 978-0-472-11201-2 (cloth)
ISBN13 978-0-472-08767-9 (paper)
ISBN13 978-0-472-02718-7 (electronic)

Paperback ISBN: 978-0-472-08767-9

To Dorothy Adams

Contents

Appendixes

Figures

Tables

Acknowledgments

The material in this book was developed over the past three years, and has, during that period, been greatly improved by comments and suggestions provided by Ernest Adams, Bill Adams, Ian Budge, Dieter Burrell, Seth DeFilippis, Bernie Grofman, Kent Jennings, David Lazer, David McKay, Nicholas Miller, Gordon Tullock, Eric Smith, and John Woolley. I also note that, in addition to drawing heavily from both the basic Downsian framework and the vast behavioral literature on voting behavior, much of this work was directly inspired by Feld and Grofman's (1991) insight that voter biases arising from non-policy-related considerations have fundamental implications for parties' policy strategies. In addition, the sections of this book that consider parties' cross-time policy strategies were inspired by Ian Budge's (1994) study of this same topic.

I particularly thank Samuel Merrill III and Roy Pierce for their detailed and insightful comments on large portions of the manuscript. Samuel Merrill kindly gave his permission to include a summary of joint work in progress.

The data sets used in this study were made available through the Inter-university Consortium for Political and Social Research (ICPSR), Ann Arbor, and are gratefully acknowledged.

Chapter 2 is based in part on ideas presented in Adams 1998, while chapters 3–5 draw from Adams (forthcoming).

I also extend special appreciation to my father Ernest Adams, my mother Anne, and my brother Bill for their support and encouragement during this enterprise.

Finally, I gratefully acknowledge my wife Dorothy Adams, whose love and support made this book possible.

PART I
Party Competition
under the Basic Partisan
Spatial Model

CHAPTER 1

Political Representation
and Responsible Party Government

1.1. Introduction

The linkage between the mass public and political decision makers is one of the central topics in the study of contemporary democracies (Dalton 1996). The study of political representation has stimulated extensive theoretical and empirical work concerning both the *process* through which citizens can influence the decisions of political elites and the *degree* to which they exercise such influence.

While research focusing on American politics has frequently conceptualized the representation process as one based upon the connections between the opinions of individual legislators and the policy preferences of the geographically based constituencies they represent (see, e.g., Miller and Stokes 1963; Achen 1975, 1978; and Page et al. 1988), political scientists working in non-American settings have increasingly focused on a theoretical model of representation based upon political parties as collectives. According to this *responsible party government* model of representation, it is political parties, not individual legislators, that are the primary vehicles that articulate citizens' policy beliefs and convert them into public policies. This notion of political representation appears to be appropriate outside of the United States because in non-American settings the members of each party's parliamentary delegation typically act in unison (see, e.g., Harmel and Janda 1982; and Thomassen 1994) so that it makes sense to focus on political parties as collectives, rather than on the behavior of individual parliamentary representatives.[1] Thus, Giovanni Sartori maintains that "citizens in Western democracies are represented *through* and *by* parties. This is inevitable" (1968, 471, italics original; also quoted in Dalton 1996).

Indeed, important elements of the responsible party model of political representation may even apply to the United States. Some scholars argue that the policy link between party elites and their supporters is relevant to policy representation in the United States (see, e.g., Backstrom 1977; Bishop and Frankovic 1981; and Herrera, Herrera, and Smith 1992) or even that in practice policy representation in the United States revolves around parties, not individual legislators (see Ansolabehere, Snyder, and Stewart 1999).

The responsible party government model has inspired extensive theorizing about the necessary conditions that would make it possible for citizens to select parties that represent their policy beliefs and for parties' parliamentary delegations in turn to represent their supporters' preferences (Dalton 1985; Powell 1982, 1989; Iversen 1994a, 1994b; Ranney 1962). While many such preconditions have been proposed, three requirements relating to the behavior of mass electorates and the behavior of party elites appear especially crucial for responsible party government.[2]

1. Policy divergence among the parties contesting the election. Elections should involve competition between parties that offer divergent policy visions so that voters have meaningful electoral choices (Dalton 1985; Powell 1989). Without such policy divergence, electors have little opportunity to influence government policies through their votes. Furthermore, policy convergence among the competing parties may well leave large portions of the electorate without an attractive party for which to vote, in which case there is little reason to expect agreement between the policies proposed by party elites and the policy preferences of their supporters.

2. Policy stability on the part of the parties contesting the election. Parties should present reasonably stable policies over time, first, because drastic policy shifts may leave voters confused concerning what the party actually stands for (Bartels 1986), which in turn impairs the electorate's ability to influence government policy through its votes. Second, even when voters are well informed about the parties' current policies, they will have difficulty translating their own preferences into votes if they perceive a high probability that the parties will change their policy positions.[3]

When these requirements on the behavior of party elites are satisfied—and when additionally parties vote as a bloc in parliament, as is typically the case outside the United States—then voters' choices of parties provide them with a method of exercising control over the actions of individual legislators and through these over the affairs of government (Dalton 1996, chap. 11). However, there is an additional condition the *electorate* must satisfy in order to exercise this policy control.

3. Policy-voting on the part of the electorate. Voters must base their decisions at least in part on comparative evaluations of the competing parties' policy programmes in order to directly influence government policy outputs.[4] Without such policy voting, election results do not provide a meaningful referendum on the competing policy visions the parties propose. Furthermore, if voters are not motivated by policy considerations there is little reason to expect a close match between the policies parties propose and the beliefs of their supporters, and thus the citizen-elite policy linkage that underpins the responsible party model is jeopardized.

Of course, each of the above desirata—policy divergence and stability on the part of political parties and policy voting on the part of the electorate—need not be "completely" satisfied in order to ensure responsible party government. Parties may alter their policies to some extent without unduly confusing the electorate, in addition to which the emergence of new policy issues typically requires some change in parties' policy images. With respect to policy voting, voters may be swayed to some degree by factors not directly related to policies, such as comparative evaluations of party leaders' competence and integrity, without completely severing the connection between the policies parties propose and the views of their supporters.[5] However, it seems plausible that the more closely the behavior of parties and voters approximates the three conditions just outlined the better the prospects are for responsible party government.

In summary, the responsible party government model directs scholars' attention to the links between political parties and the electorate. In particular, it suggests that, to the extent that competing parties present divergent, stable policies and citizens use these policies as the basis for their voting decisions, parties provide effective vehicles for representing the electorate's political beliefs. According to this model, an important criterion for assessing the degree to which parties provide faithful representation is to compare the "dyadic correspondence" between the policy positions a given party proposes, on the one hand, and the beliefs of the party's supporters on the other.[6] When the conditions outlined above are met, the degree of dyadic correspondence should be high.

1.2. The Problem

In the decades following World War II, political scientists operating from two different research perspectives argued for disturbing conclusions, suggesting that the conditions for responsible party government would *not* be satisfied in most contemporary democracies. One approach, dating back to Anthony Downs's (1957) *An Economic Theory of Democracy,* involves spatial models of party competition. Using the assumption of a policy-oriented electorate, spatial modelers attempt to deduce the policy programmes that political parties will present in order to win elections.[7] The second approach, dating back to *The American Voter* (Campbell et al. 1960) and before, is behavioral research. Behaviorists emphasize the empirical study of voting behavior, and they typically analyze a variety of voter motivations in addition to policy voting such as party identification; group loyalties rooted in class, religion, or ethnic identities; comparative judgments of party leaders; and retrospective evaluations of incumbent performance.

Departing from quite different perspectives on how voters decide, each research tradition has produced results that call the preconditions for responsible party government into question. In the case of spatial modeling, the most basic result is the median voter theorem—that in elections involving exactly two parties competing over a single policy dimension the parties will converge to the position of the median voter. This result implies that the parties will present stable policies in that the parties reach an equilibrium—that is, a policy configuration such that neither party has incentives to change its position. However, this two-party equilibrium also entails policy similarity in that the parties present identical policies and thus fail to offer the electorate divergent positions that provide voters with meaningful choices. And, while results are somewhat different in two-party competition over multiple policy dimensions, recent theoretical work suggests that in these situations vote-seeking parties can again be expected to converge toward extremely similar, centrist positions.[8] In toto, the literature on two-party competition suggests that vote-seeking parties will present similar positions that deny the electorate a meaningful choice between distinct policy visions, which is a prerequisite for responsible party government.

Although early spatial modeling results applied almost exclusively to two-party elections (but see Downs 1957, 122–32), the theoretical prediction that vote-seeking parties will present similar positions extends to three-party competition. Furthermore, such multiparty elections also encourage a high degree of policy instability in the sense that the parties have electoral incentives to continually leapfrog their competitors. A simple example illustrates these points. Consider the scenario illustrated in figure 1.1A, which shows three parties A, B, and C, located along a single policy dimension, which for convenience I label the Left-Right dimension. Under the standard Downsian logic, parties A and C are motivated to converge toward the center (fig. 1.1B), thereby "squeezing" party B because this centrist positioning gains additional support from Center-Left voters (who switch their support from B to A) and Center-Right voters (who switch their support from B to C). However, when party B is squeezed between A and C, then B is motivated to leapfrog one of its competitors, thus locating either to A's immediate left or C's immediate right (fig. 1.1C illustrates the situation in which B leapfrogs A). However, if B leapfrogs party A, then A is squeezed between B and C and is motivated to leapfrog one of its competitors in turn. This process can be expected to continue indefinitely, with the parties continually leapfrogging but always locating near the center of the policy space. Thus, in three-party elections spatial theory predicts that, from the perspective of responsible party government, the parties' behavior offers voters the worst of both worlds, namely, a scenario in which the parties' positions are unstable (in the sense that they consistently leapfrog) but they nonetheless present extremely similar, centrist positions that deny the electorate the choice between distinct policy alternatives. While results differ somewhat when four or more parties compete—roughly speaking, the problem of policy instability grows more severe and the problem of similarity somewhat less severe—the central

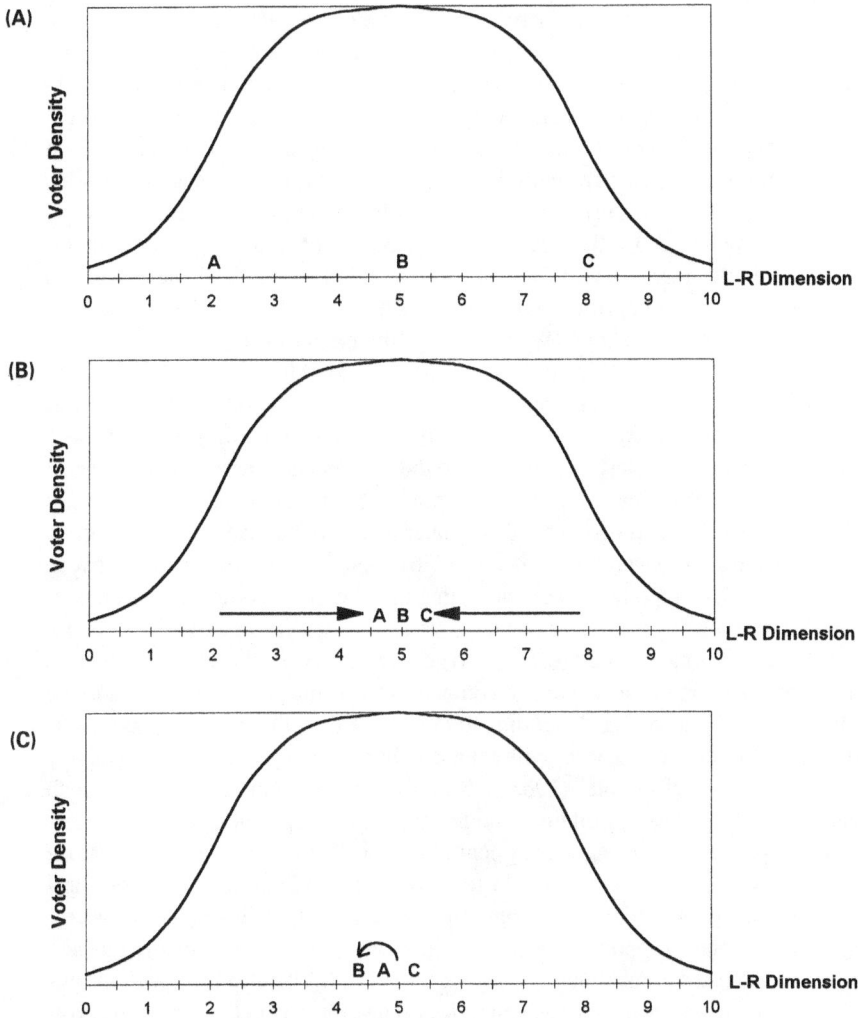

Fig. 1.1. Three-party spatial competition for the standard Downsian model. (A) Parties' initial Left-Right locations; (B) Policy convergence by A and C; (C) Leapfrogging behavior by party B.

intuitions developed here, that parties' policies will be *unstable*,[9] in that they will continually leapfrog, and that rival parties' policies will be *similar*, typically extend to systems with any number of parties.[10]

From their individual-level perspective, behavioral researchers' empirical findings call into question the requirement for policy voting on the part of the electorate, which appears to be essential for the party-voter policy linkage that underlies responsible party government. Behaviorists' results suggest that, although policies matter at least to some voters, their decisions are also readily swayed by considerations such as comparative evaluations of the party leaders' competence and integrity, economic conditions, group loyalties based upon class, religion, geography, and ethnicity, party identification, and so on. This conclusion, which was originally reached with respect to American voters (see, e.g., Campbell et al. 1960; Fiorina 1981; and Key 1966), has been extended outward over the past 30 years to encompass the electorates of most Western democracies (Alvarez, Bowler, and Nagler 1996; Butler and Stokes 1969; Converse and Pierce 1986; Dow 1997b, 1997c; Klingemann et al. 1994; Lewis-Beck 1988; Listhaug 1989; Pierce 1995; Rose and McAllister 1990; Strøm and Svåsand 1997; Whitten and Palmer 1996). Although, as I outline in chapter 2, the relative electoral impact of policy motivations and nonpolicy influences is a matter of heated scholarly debate, in toto the studies cited here strongly suggest that the cumulative impact of voters' nonpolicy motivations upon the vote is at least as great as—and perhaps much greater than—the impact of policy voting.

As I shall emphasize in greater detail in chapter two, the distinction between voting based upon policy issues and voting based on non-policy-related motivations is not always clear. For instance, voters' retrospective evaluations of incumbent performance, their reactions to government scandals, and their comparative evaluations of party leaders' competence and integrity can reasonably be described as issue voting. According to Donald Stokes, these *valence issues* "involve the linking of the parties with some condition that is positively or negatively evaluated by the electorate" (1963, 373). This contrasts with *position issues* such as Left-Right ideology, welfare spending, and the death penalty, upon which voters (and parties) may disagree. My central point is that when voters deemphasize position issues election outcomes do not provide referendums on the parties' competing (positional) policy visions and, furthermore, that the link between parties' policies and their supporters' beliefs—which are assessed by comparing dyadic correspondence on positional issues—is threatened. Therefore, throughout this book I refer to valence issues as nonpolicy related, reserving the term *policy voting* for voting over positional issues.

This result suggests that it may be impossible to simultaneously satisfy the requirements of policy stability and policy divergence on the part of political parties, and of policy voting on the part of the electorate, that are central to responsible party government. If voters are policy oriented, as spatial modelers assume, then (with the exception of two-party competition along a single policy dimension) parties' policies are likely to be *unstable* in the sense that the parties continually leapfrog, and their policies will also be *similar,* so that voters are not afforded the option of choosing between truly distinct policy visions. If voters deemphasize policies, as behavioral researchers suggest, then parties' policies may not be *representative* of their supporters' beliefs since policies are not the primary basis of these supporters' party preferences.

1.3. The Puzzle

The findings of spatial modelers and behavioral researchers suggest that political representation through responsible party government is unattainable because the preconditions for responsible party government outlined in section 1.1 are not met in most Western democracies. Yet, in surveying the polities of Western Europe and North America, what is striking is the extent to which this prediction is *not* borne out by empirical observation. Contrary to spatial modelers' predictions of policy instability and policy similarity, empirical studies conclude that political parties present relatively stable policy programmes over time while rarely leapfrogging each other (see, e.g., Budge 1994) and furthermore that parties differentiate their policies, thereby presenting voters with a wide range of alternatives (Castles and Mair 1984; Huber and Inglehart 1995; Laver and Budge 1992). Thus, party systems are characterized by *policy stability* and *policy divergence.* And, while the behavioralists' finding that voters are motivated in large part by nonpolicy considerations seems to emperil mass-elite policy linkages, comparative research supports the proposition that in most party systems political parties provide reasonably faithful *policy representation* in that the policies parties propose reflect the views of their supporters (see, e.g., Dalton 1985; Holmberg 1989; Iversen 1994b; and Jennings 1992).

   While I present data in subsequent chapters on empirical findings of policy divergence, policy stability, and policy representation, it is worth briefly surveying some of this evidence here. With respect to policy divergence, table 1.1 reproduces results reported by Huber and Inglehart (1995, app. 2) on the mean Left-Right positions that expert observers assigned to the major political parties in several Western European party systems and the United States as of 1993. The results indicate that experts perceive that each party system presents its voters with a wide range of ideological options. Alternative methodologies for estimating party positions, such as analyses of roll call voting, studies of party manifestos, and opinion surveys of party elites, confirm these experts' perceptions that party systems in most Western democracies are characterized by policy divergence not policy similarity (see, e.g., Budge 1994; Budge et al. 1987; Castles and Mair 1984; Dodd 1976; Inglehart and Klingeman 1987; and Sani and Sartori 1983).

   With respect to policy stability, the most comprehensive empirical study of the evolution of party policies in postwar democracies has been conducted by Ian Budge and his colleagues at the Manifesto Research Group (MRG) (Klingemann et al. 1994; Laver and Budge 1992; Budge et al. 1987). Through

TABLE 1.1.   Experts' Mean Party Placements for Eight Western European Democracies, in 1993

Country	Mean Position	Country	Mean Position
Austria		*France*	
Green Alternative	2.86	Communists	2.25
Socialists	4.75	Socialists	4.13
People's Party	6.25	French Democratic Union (UDF)	6.67
Liberal Forum	6.33	Rally for the Republic (RPR)	7.88
Freedom Party	8.63	National Front	10.0
Belgium		*Germany*	
Ecologist	3.40	Green	2.91
Socialist	4.00	Social Democrat	3.83
Christian-Social	5.71	Free Democrat	5.64
People's Union	6.50	Christian Democrat	6.42
Liberal	7.29	Republicaner	9.30
Britain		*Norway*	
Labour	4.43	Socialist	2.55
Liberal Democrats	5.21	Labor	4.13
Conservatives	7.71	Center	5.33
		Conservative	8.00
Denmark		Progress	9.18
Socialist People's	2.89		
Christian People's	6.22	*United States*	
Conservatives	7.56	Democrats	4.15
Liberal	8.11	Republicans	6.85
Progress	9.13		

Source: Huber and Inglehart 1995, app. 2.
Note: Parties are located on a 0–10 Left-Right scale.

comparative codings of the election programmes of the major parties in some 20 democracies during the postwar period the Manifesto Research Group has assigned positions to parties along a variety of policy dimensions, including an overall Left-Right summary (I review the details of the MRG's methodology in chapter 3). Table 1.2 reproduces the results of a temporal analysis of the MRG's codings reported by Budge (1994), which bears on policy stability in postwar democracies. Column 3 reports, for every postwar Western European democracy plus the United States, the proportions of party platforms that were coded as being outside the party's traditional "ideological area," defined as left of center for the Socialist, Communist, Labour, and Democratic Parties and as right of center for the Conservative, Christian Democratic, and Republican Parties. The results indicate that parties virtually never shift their Left-Right position outside their traditional ideological area. In addition, columns 1 and 2,

TABLE 1.2.   Incidence of Leapfrogging and Crossing Outside of Ideological Areas in 14 Postwar European Democracies and the United States

	Leapfrogging		Ideological Area
	Percentage of Cases That Involve Leapfrogging (1)	Percentage of Leapfrogs That Involve Contiguous Parties (2)	Percentage of Party Positions Falling Outside the Party's Traditional Ideological Area (3)
Ireland	15	75	19
United Kingdom	12	100	14
Spain	4	100	12
Italy	13	29	—
France (Fifth Republic)	7	80	6
Germany	12	100	—
Austria	13	75	9
Luxembourg	12	83	7
Belgium	5	100	9
Netherlands	3	100	—
Denmark	3	100	7
Norway	3	88	—
Sweden	8	67	12
Iceland	4	100	12
United States	0	—	13

Source: Budge 1994, 460 (United Kingdom results updated through 1997).

which report the frequency with which parties leapfrog each other—that is, the extent to which parties shift their Left-Right orientation relative to rival parties—show that leapfrogging has been rare and that when it occurs it usually involves parties that are contiguous along the Left-Right continuum. These results testify that throughout the postwar period political parties in Western democracies have presented remarkably stable policy images.

With respect to political representation, empirical studies suggest that parties typically take positions that are reasonably *representative* of their supporters' beliefs (see, e.g., Converse and Pierce 1986; Holmberg 1989; and Iversen 1994b). Figure 1.2 (reproduced from Iversen 1994b, fig. 2) compares the average Left-Right economic positions of party elites with the average positions of party voters from the 1979 European Parliament Study, in which both samples are aggregated by party. In these comparisons, which encompass seven countries (Belgium, Denmark, France, West Germany, Britain, Italy, and the Netherlands) and 34 party-elite dyads, the horizontal axis plots the average opinion of the party supporters, while the vertical axis plots the average opinions of the party elites;[11] the 45-degree line represents perfect representation, when the opinions of party elites and party voters exactly coincide. It is clear from the

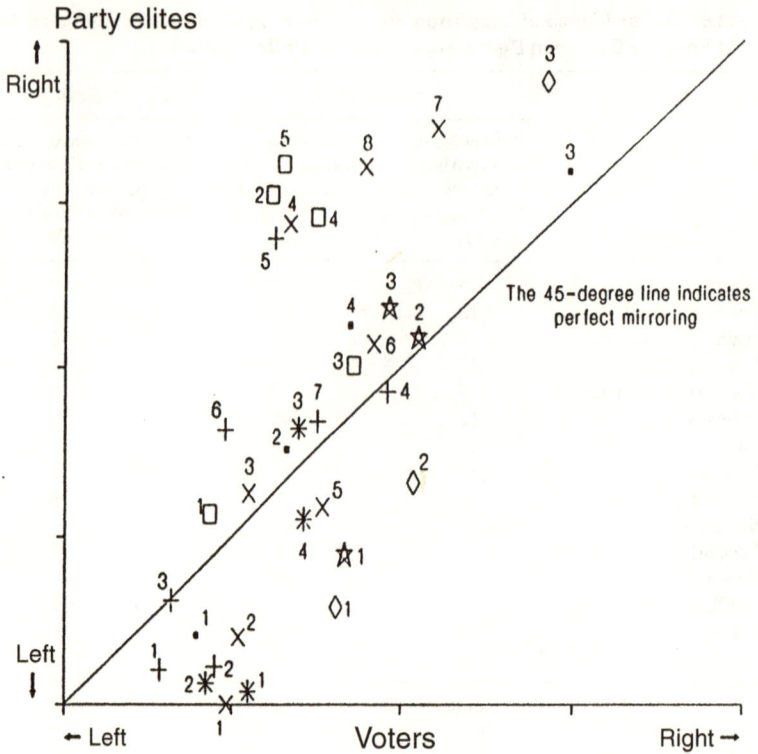

Party elites

Right

The 45-degree line indicates
perfect mirroring

Left

← Left   Voters   Right →

Key:

+	X	✳	☆	◇	☐	·
Belgium	**Denmark**	**France**	**Germany**	**Britain**	**Italy**	**Netherlands**
1 PCB/	1 SF	1 PSU	1 SPD	1 LAB	1 PSI	1 PvdA
· KPB	2 SD	2 PS	2 FDP	2 LIB	2 PSDI	2 D'66
2 PSB	3 RF	3 UDF	3 CDU/	3 CON	3 PLI	3 VVD
3 BSP	4 CD	4 RPR	CSU		4 DC	4 CDA
4 PRL	5 KrF				5 MSI	
5 PVV	6 V					
6 CVP	7 KF					
7 PSC	8 Frp					

Fig. 1.2. Mean locations of parties and voters along a Left-Right economic issue dimension. (Data from Rabier and Inglehart 1980 [*Eurobarometer II*].)

clustering around this 45-degree line that in 1979 party elites were reasonably representative of their parties' voters. And, while conclusions on the closeness of mass-elite linkages vary somewhat depending on the policy area under review, as well as the analyst's methodology, subsequent analyses (e.g., Adams and Merrill 1999a) suggest that this pattern of voter-elite linkage extends to more recent election periods.[12]

1.4. A Possible Solution

Why is the behavior of political parties in advanced industrial societies characterized by policy stability and policy divergence when spatial models built on the assumption of policy-oriented electorates imply the opposite conclusion? Why do parties provide reasonably faithful policy representations of their supporters' beliefs given behavioral researchers' finding that voters are motivated in large part by nonpolicy considerations? In short, why does responsible party government function reasonably well in contemporary Western democracies when results obtained by spatial modelers and behavioralists suggest that it should function poorly?

My central goal in this book is to sketch answers to these questions in the context of *multiparty democracies,* that is, polities that feature three or more major political parties (although I will also sketch an extension of my argument that applies to the American two-party system). The method I employ combines the perspectives of spatial modeling and behavioral research. Specifically, I take as a starting point the complex but realistic models of voting behavior developed by behavioralists and then deduce their implications for party policy strategies and political representation via the formal methods used by spatial modelers. I ask several questions. If voters are motivated by policies *as well as* by such non-policy-related considerations as party identification, group loyalties, and comparative evaluations of party leaders, then what kinds of policies will vote-seeking parties propose? Will these policies be stable? Will competing parties' policies diverge, and will the policies parties propose correspond to the views of the voters who support them?

The Strategic Implications of Biased Voters:
The Central Argument

I believe that an approach that integrates the behavioralists' empirically based voting models into the formal framework of spatial modeling can provide insights into empirical findings of policy stability, policy divergence, and policy representation that neither research tradition provides by itself. Although the critical role that measured nonpolicy motivations, which I label voter *biases,* can play in spatial modeling was recognized early by behavioral researchers—most notably in Donald Stokes's (1963) classic critique of the Downsian model—until quite recently the strategic implications of nonpolicy biases for parties' policy strategies have been virtually ignored by spatial modelers, at least in the context of multiparty competition.[13] This omission is unfortunate because we shall see that the logic of spatial competition in a biased electorate differs fundamentally from spatial competition under the "standard" Downsian model, which assumes unbiased voters. For multiparty competition, I argue that the fact of voter biases serves as a starting point for an explanation of the empirical findings of policy stability, policy divergence, and policy representation—in other words, that a "biased voting" model of spatial competition illuminates the reasons why responsible party government works in multiparty democracies.

To begin, let me briefly elaborate on the notion of voter bias and in particular upon those biases that originate in such voter characteristics as class, religion, party identification, and race. In stating that these characteristics have been found to bias individuals' vote choices, I mean that behavioral researchers find that these respondent characteristics influence the vote *independently* of policy positions, so that, for instance, a British working-class voter is more likely to vote Labour than is a middle-class voter, *even if both report identical policy views.* This is not to imply that policies do not influence the vote (or else I would hardly devote this book to spatial modeling!), nor that respondents' policy views are unconnected to their personal characteristics. Indeed, as I stress below, policy preferences and personal characteristics *are* connected, and I argue that this connection has crucial implications for the strategic dynamics of party competition. However, the central feature of voter biases is that they represent aspects of voters' party evaluations that do not depend on the parties' policy positions. Thus, in the example of class voting in Britain, while it is true that many—but not all—working-class voters favor the policies proposed by the Labour Party, behavioralists conclude that, this correlation between class and policy preferences notwithstanding, membership in the working class *in and of itself* enhances voters' evaluations of Labour, regardless of their policy views (see, e.g., Butler and Stokes 1969; Rose and McCallister 1990; and Bartle 1998).[14]

What is the nature of voter biases rooted in class, religion, or party identification? While the psychological bases of these voting influences are imperfectly understood, behavioralists typically conceptualize these motivations as containing an affective component that is independent of the voters' cognitive evaluations of the parties. According to the "Michigan model" of voting (Campbell et al. 1960), party identification represents a long-term, affective, psychological identification with one's preferred party that enhances voters' evaluations of their parties independently of these parties' policy images. This kind of affective identification may fall outside of the spatial modeler's focus on "rational" voting decisions.[15]

Although the logic of party competition in a biased electorate revolves around many strategic considerations, I argue that the central features of responsible party government can be understood by exploring the ramifications of two related aspects of voters' nonpolicy biases and parties' strategic motivations, one empirical and one theoretical. The empirical observation is:

OBSERVATION 1: *Many of the personal characteristics that motivate voter biases, such as party identification, social class, race, and religion, correlate with voters' policy preferences, so that, for instance, working-class voters and those identifying with Labor or Socialist Parties tend to take left-wing positions, while middle-class voters and Conservative Party partisans locate on the right.*[16]

This empirical observation, which I support with extensive survey data in chapters 2–4, has been confirmed in a variety of electoral settings (see, e.g., Adams and Merrill 1999a, 2000; Baker et al. 1981; Bartle 1998; and Dalton 1985). Indeed, to my knowledge the correlations between social class and policy preferences, and between partisanship and policy preferences, have been observed in every Western democracy for which survey research on voting is available (in chapter 2, I present evidence in support of this proposition). This implies that voter biases are not distributed randomly throughout the voting population but that, to the extent that such voter characteristics as partisanship and social class exercise independent influences on the vote, left-wing voters tend to be biased toward the Socialist and Labour Parties *in part for nonpolicy reasons* while right-wing voters display nonpolicy biases toward the Conservative and Christian Democratic Parties. The theoretical proposition is:

PROPOSITION 1: *In multiparty spatial competition, parties have electoral incentives to appeal on policy grounds to voters biased toward them for nonpolicy reasons.*

This strategic proposition, the logic of which I outline in chapter 2, appears to be counterintuitive, in that one might think that vote-seeking parties should target independent (i.e., unbiased) voters while taking their committed supporters "for granted." In fact, we shall see that this is not the case.

When proposition 1 is combined with observation 1, that the individual characteristics that influence voter biases correlate with voters' policy preferences, then three deductions concerning the dynamics of multiparty spatial competition immediately follow:

First, because groups of voters biased toward different parties tend to cluster in different areas of the policy space, the incentive for parties to appeal to their sympathizers—i.e., those voters who approve of the party on non-policy-related grounds—motivates *policy divergence* on the part of political parties.

Second, a corollary of proposition 1 is that parties risk severe electoral penalties if their policies diverge from their sympathizers' policy preferences.

Given that each party's sympathizers tend to cluster within relatively narrow regions of the policy space—because voter biases correlate with their policy preferences—this implies that each vote-seeking party is constrained to select its platform from among the circumscribed set of proposals acceptable to its sympathizers. This ensures considerable *policy stability* on the part of political parties.

Third, the proposition that vote-seeking parties are motivated to propose policies that reflect the policy preferences of their sympathizers implies that there will be a close correspondence between the policies parties espouse and the beliefs of their supporters because parties' supporters share the party's policy views *and* have non-policy-related biases toward the party. Thus, parties will provide their supporters with faithful policy representations, *even in situations in which these voters are motivated primarily by non-policy-related considerations.*

In summary, the proposition that vote-seeking parties should appeal on policy grounds to voters who are predisposed to support them in part for nonpolicy reasons can explain the empirical findings of policy stability, policy divergence, and policy representation in contemporary democracies. Of course, the logic of responsible party government does not revolve around voter bias alone; the outcomes of multiparty spatial competition depend on additional factors such as the number of parties, the distribution of voters' policy preferences, the number of policy dimensions, and so on. (And in chapter seven we shall see that many of these variables also shape the strategic logic of two-party competition under the biased voter spatial model.) Much of this book is devoted to exploring how party policy behavior responds to changes in these variables. Nonetheless, we shall see that while these factors influence party behavior and thus the functioning of responsible party government the central predictions arising from the biased spatial voting model—of policy divergence, policy stability, and policy representation—extend to virtually every possible scenario involving different numbers of parties, varying policy dimensions and voter distributions, and so on. And in all cases *voter bias is the engine that drives these results.*

1.5. The Empirical, Theoretical, Deductive, and Behavioral Focus

The Empirical Focus: Party Competition in Postwar Britain and France with an Extension to the United States

On the empirical side, I investigate the implications of the formal arguments developed above in the context of party competition in Britain and France (with some additional extensions to the United States, discussed below). Specifically,

I employ survey data drawn from national election studies in Britain and France to estimate the distributions of voters' policy preferences *and* the distributions of their non-policy-related biases, and I then investigate how these biases affect parties' policy strategies and in turn what this implies for responsible party government. For each country, I also compare my theoretical predictions against the parties' actual policy behavior during the postwar period.

The choice of Britain and France as the primary testing grounds for my formal arguments was motivated by both practical and theoretical considerations. The practical consideration is that the only viable data sources that combine information on the distributions of voters' policy preferences along with data relevant to their nonpolicy biases are national election studies; therefore, in conducting empirical applications of the biased spatial voting model I am restricted to the relatively small population of countries for which such studies are available. The decision to select Britain and France from among this reduced population stems from my desire to apply and test my formal arguments in diverse settings. Britain and France differ along a variety of important dimensions, including their institutional features, electoral laws, the number of major parties, and the party composition of their governments. With respect to constitutional features, Britain features a parliamentary democracy while France has a mixed presidential-parliamentary system. With regard to the selection of parliamentary representatives, British members of Parliament (MPs) are selected from single-member districts via a one-stage plurality system, while representatives in the French National Assembly are selected from single-member districts but via a two-stage plurality system. With respect to the number of parties, during the postwar era British politics has been characterized as a "two and a half" party system—in which the Liberals (and in later years the Liberal–Social Democratic Alliance and then the Liberal Democrats) have competed against the dominant Labour and Conservative Parties—while France since the 1960s has featured at least four major parties. Finally, a factor related to party system size is that British elections virtually always award a parliamentary majority to a single party, which thereby controls the government. By contrast, French parliamentary elections since the late 1970s have produced more splintered seat distributions, resulting in the formation of coalition governments. By exploring the implications of the biased spatial voting model in these diverse settings, I hope to demonstrate that this approach can provide a general explanation for party behavior and mass-elite policy linkages in multiparty systems and for the functioning of responsible party government.

Finally, although the central focus of this book is on the strategic dynamics of multiparty elections, the question naturally arises: Can the biased spatial voting model similarly illuminate the dynamics of two-party elections such as those that occur in the United States? In the final substantive chapter of this book, I show that the answer to this question is no; however, I then sketch an amended version of the biased spatial model that incorporates voter turnout, and I show that this expanded model provides important insights into party strategies in American elections. As noted earlier, it is unclear whether the responsible party model is relevant to political representation in the United Sates, and hence I do not claim that this extension provides additional illumination into the working of responsible party government. However, my results do suggest that a spatial model that incorporates voters' nonpolicy biases may capture the logic of parties' policy strategies in both two-party *and* multiparty systems.

The Theoretical Perspective: A "Simple" Model of Party Behavior, but a Dynamic Conception of Policy Stability

Although I develop a spatial model that is complex in the sense that it assigns voters a mixture of policy-related and non-policy-related motivations, it is simple in that throughout this book I assume that parties maximize votes. This focus on single-mindedly vote-seeking parties contrasts with the party motivations spatial modelers have explored in a number of recent multiparty models; these include the goal of discouraging entry into the political system by new parties (Palfrey 1984), parties' calculations concerning postelection coalition negotiations in parliamentary democracies (Austen-Smith and Banks 1988; Banks and Duggan 1998), and party leaders' policy motivations (Cox 1984; Schofield and Parks 1997; Schofield and Sened 1998; Wittman 1973, 1983). Since, as I outline in chapter 2, spatial modelers have shown that these party motivations can motivate a dispersed policy equilibrium—that is, they imply the features of policy divergence and stability that I seek to explain—the question arises, why limit my focus to the "simple" assumption of vote-maximizing parties?

My first answer is that I show that in the context of the biased voting model the vote-maximization assumption by itself can illuminate the empirical findings of political parties' policy stability, divergence, and representation. Hence, my explanations for these empirical phenomena need not invoke more complex party objectives. Second, as I discuss in chapter 2, each of the studies summarized above invokes party motivations that appear plausible only in quite specific—hence limited—competitive scenarios such as elections involving exactly three parties, electoral competition under proportional representation, party competition in parliamentary democracies with coalition governments, and so on. While such studies provide valuable insights into the strategic implications of varying competitive contexts, any such study by itself obviously cannot explain the range of empirical findings on party behavior summarized above. What I propose here is a *general* perspective on the strategic logic of party behavior, one that illuminates the empirical findings of policy divergence, stability, and representation across a variety of party systems and constitutional settings. In search of such a general explanation, I employ the most general model of party motivations, namely, that parties maximize votes.

Although I employ a simple model of party motivations, the conception of policy stability I explore is in some ways more complex than that usually studied by spatial modelers, who typically define stability in terms of the existence of a policy equilibrium for a single election period, that is, a configuration of policies such that no party has incentives to change its position. I present such equilibrium analyses in chapters 2 and 6. However, in chapters 3–5 and 7, I explore the *temporal* aspects of policy stability by asking the question: Under the biased voting model of spatial competition, how will parties' policies evolve over a series of elections? My central argument is that even in situations for which equilibria do not exist for a single election period, over time parties will vary their policies—but only within certain "ideologically delimited" areas of the policy space—and, moreover, parties will rarely leapfrog. These results on the dynamic aspects of spatial competition illuminate how party policies can be relatively stable over *time,* even in the absence of a single-election policy equilibrium.

Deductive Perspective: A Mixture of Deductive and Inductive Logic

In exploring the twin concepts of policy stability defined in terms of party equilibrium in a single election period, and stability defined cross-time, I employ a mixture of deductive and inductive logic. In analyzing single election periods, I deduce theorems on the existence of party policy equilibria as well as the specific equilibrium policies the competing parties will propose. These equilibrium results, which I present in chapters 2, 6, and 7, rely on the kind of deductive arguments favored by spatial modelers.

In contrast to my equilibrium analyses, my study of parties' cross-time policy trajectories is primarily inductive in that I base my conclusions on the results of a series of computer-simulated elections carried out using British, French, and American voting data. I also support these conclusions, which are reported in chapters 3–7, by presenting illustrative arguments designed to highlight the strategic logic that drives parties' behavior. I employ this inductive approach because I have found, like prior spatial modelers interested in the trajectory of parties' platforms over a series of elections (e.g., Jackson 1990; Kollman et al. 1992; Lomborg 1996; but see Merrill and Grofman 1999, chap. 9), that the study of parties' cross-time policy trajectories presents complications that do not readily admit analytical results. However, I note that my inductive conclusions are strengthened because I find that the strategic logic that drives party behavior as the parties adjust their policies across time is the same logic that motivates single-election policy equilibrium, namely, that vote-seeking parties are motivated to present policies that appeal to voters biased toward them for nonpolicy reasons.

The Behavioral Focus: A Simple Partisan Voting Model and Its Implications for Behavioralists' Empirical Debates

To this point, I have discussed the strategic implications of voter biases rooted in group loyalties arising from social class, religion, race, party identification, and so on. Behavioralists' empirical vote models typically account for all of these influences in addition to policy motivations (see, e.g., Alvarez, Bowler, and Nagler 1998; Bartle 1998; Campbell et al. 1960; Dow 1997a, 1997b; Markus and Converse 1979; Pierce 1995; and Whitten and Palmer 1996). Although I explore the implications of such fully specified voting models in chapter 6, most of my analysis assumes a far simpler model, in which voters' decisions rest entirely on a combination of *policy voting* and *party identification.* This simple partisan voting model is useful partly as a heuristic device, which allows me to clearly present the logic of spatial competition in a biased electorate. However, two additional advantages of this simple model are, first, that there is extensive empirical evidence that respondents' expressed party identifications serve as surrogates for biases arising from other types of group loyalties when the latter are omitted from the behaviorist's empirical model (I review this evidence in chapter 2). To the extent that this is true, then, in incorporating party identification I indirectly control for such factors as social class, race, and religion as well.[17]

Second, as I outline in chapter 2, the electoral impact of party identification is the subject of heated scholarly debate, with some scholars arguing that voters' long-term psychological identifications with political parties outweigh their policy motivations and others arguing that the electoral impact of policies greatly exceeds that of partisanship. I show that this debate is crucial for multiparty spatial competition, in that the extent to which parties are motivated to propose policies that appeal to their partisans varies with the *strength of party identification,* that is, with the electoral impact of partisan bias. If partisanship has the potent electoral impact that certain scholars attribute to it, then the partisan vote model can indeed account for the empirical phenomena of policy divergence, stability, and representation on the part of political parties. If partisanship exercises a weak or even nonexistent impact on voting, as other scholars argue, then the partisan voting model cannot account for these features of responsible party government. Although I conclude that the partisan voting model motivates policy divergence, stability, and representation over a wide range of assumptions about the strength of partisanship—including most "realistic" partisan parameters, as estimated in empirical voting studies—it is still the case that the empirical fit between the predictions on party behavior I generate from the partisan vote model and parties' actual behavior in historical elections improves with the strength of partisanship I assume in the electorate. Hence, my focus on party identification highlights the importance of the behavioralists' debates about the electoral impact of partisanship versus policies.

1.6. Plan of the Book

This book is divided into two parts, which explore the implications for responsible party government of two versions of the biased vote model. Part I, which encompasses chapters 1–4, explores the logic of multiparty competition for the simplest possible model of biased voting, one in which voters are swayed by a combination of partisanship and their evaluations of parties' policies along a unidimensional continuum. Exploring the implications of this *basic partisan vote model* allows me to illuminate the central strategic logic of spatial competition, when parties seek votes from a partisan electorate. In addition, while this model abstracts from many complexities of real world voters' decision processes, it is arguably defensible in the context of British postwar politics as well as certain periods of French postwar politics in which policy debates largely revolved around issues related to the Left-Right economic dimension. Part II, which consists of chapters 5 through 8, considers several complicating factors excluded from the basic partisan vote model. These include: the introduction of multiple policy dimensions; voter biases arising from group-oriented loyalties rooted in class, religion, and union membership; the implications of *unmeasured* influences upon the vote that render voters' choices probabilistic from the parties' perspectives; and the implications of variable voter turnout.

Chapter 2 reviews behavioralists' findings concerning nonpolicy voting influences—with particular focus on the theoretical status of party identification—and then develops a basic partisan voting model in which voters are swayed by partisanship and policy motivations along a single underlying dimension.[18] I present heuristic arguments and formal results on the central intuition developed in this book: that in multiparty elections parties have electoral incentives to appeal on policy grounds to voters biased toward them for nonpolicy reasons. I show how this strategic consideration can motivate a three-party equilibrium and illustrate and test these results against empirical voting data from Britain. The results show that multiparty equilibria exist over a wide range of assumptions about the electoral impact of partisanship and that, moreover, at equilibrium parties present divergent sets of policies that reflect the preferences of their partisans.

Chapters 3 and 4 extend the insights developed in chapter 2 in two directions.[19] Chapter 3 presents heuristic arguments about how the basic partisan vote model can illuminate the *temporal* aspects of parties' policies in three-party systems, in that over time parties present divergent sets of policies that are relatively *stable* but not *static,* that is, that parties vary their policies between elections but only within ideologically delimited areas of the policy space, so that they do not leapfrog. The central insight arising from this analysis is that, even in the absence of policy equilibrium for a single election period, spatial competition under the basic partisan vote model nonetheless motivates policy stability, divergence, and representation on the part of political parties. I present applications to empirical voting data from Britain, which support the intuitions arising from these heuristic arguments. In addition, I show that the predictions I generate on parties' policy trajectories closely match the British parties' actual behavior during the postwar period, as measured via the spatial "maps" of parties' policies in postwar elections that have been published by the Manifesto Research Group.

Chapter 4 extends the arguments developed in chapter 3 to elections involving more than three parties. I present examples that suggest that the central strategic logic of three-party competition in a partisan electorate, that parties are motivated to present policies that appeal to voters biased toward them for nonpolicy reasons, extends to elections involving larger numbers of parties. As a result, parties in any multiparty system are motivated to present stable, divergent, and representative policies. I then report empirical applications to French voting data that support these conclusions, and I also show that French parties' predicted policy behavior under the basic partisan vote model matches the actual behavior of French postwar parties, as measured by the Manifesto Research Group.

In part II of the book I shift my focus to more complex models of voter choice. In chapter 5, I explore two aspects of French voters' decision making that are not captured in the basic partisan vote model. The first is the rise in importance of policy debates relating to immigration, an issue that plausibly crosscuts the traditional Left-Right economic dimension. The second is the possibility that, due to the system of party alliances that occurs in parliamentary elections, French voters' sense of party identification extends not simply to a single party but to their party's coalition partner. In chapter 6, I extend this analysis to encompass several additional complicating factors, including probabilistic voting models and the influences of group-oriented biases rooted in class, union membership, and religion.[20] In both chapters, I present theoretical arguments that the central results on policy stability, divergence, and representation obtained for the basic partisan voting model analyzed in chapters 2–4 will generalize to these more complex voter decision models. I also present empirical applications to Britain and France that support these conclusions.

Chapter 7 sketches a possible extension of the basic partisan spatial model that applies to two-party competition in the United States. I present illustrative arguments and a theorem, which suggest that by expanding the model to incorporate the possibility that voters abstain if neither party is sufficiently attractive (i.e., that *voters abstain due to alienation*) then vote-seeking parties in two-party systems have the same strategic motivations as the parties in multiparty systems do under the full-turnout version of the biased voter model, namely, that parties have incentives to present divergent policies that reflect the beliefs of their partisan constituencies. I then present empirical applications of this turnout-based version of the model to voter distributions derived from American National Election Study data, which suggest that this model illuminates American parties' policy strategies. Chapter 8 briefly summarizes my central findings and discusses directions for future research.

1.7. Summary

Scholars of political representation have long emphasized that responsible party government requires that political parties present divergent and stable policy positions to a policy-oriented electorate. Unfortunately, the results developed by spatial modelers and behavioral researchers suggest that these requirements cannot be satisfied—spatial modelers because a policy-oriented electorate motivates policy similarity and instability (in the form of leapfrogging behavior) on the part of vote-seeking parties and behavioralists because their empirical studies suggest that voters are largely motivated by nonpolicy considerations. Yet in surveying politics in most Western democracies it appears that responsible party government does in fact function reasonably well in that parties present divergent, stable policy images that reflect the beliefs of their supporters.

This book represents an attempt to resolve this paradox by combining the perspectives of spatial modeling and behavioral research. From spatial modeling, I adopt the perspective that parties manipulate their policy images in an effort to attract support from a policy-oriented electorate. From behavioral research, I incorporate the finding that in addition to policies voters are motivated by group loyalties rooted in social class, religion, race, and especially party identification. I argue that when vote-seeking parties account for these nonpolicy biases the likely outcomes of multiparty spatial competition are fundamentally changed compared to outcomes of the basic Downsian model. Specifically, political parties that compete for votes from a biased electorate are motivated to present stable, divergent policy images that reflect the beliefs of voters attached to them for nonpolicy reasons. The central logic that drives these outcomes emerges from two related observations: that voters' nonpolicy biases correlate with their policy beliefs and that vote-seeking parties are motivated to appeal on policy grounds to voters sympathetic toward them for nonpolicy reasons. Using these two observations, I intend to show that the combined perspectives of spatial modeling and behavioral research can furnish a parsimonious, general explanation for the functioning of responsible party government, that this approach can account for political parties' actual behavior in postwar Britain and France, and that a plausible extension of this approach illuminates party policies in the United States.

CHAPTER 2

Policy Stability, Policy Divergence, and the Pressure for Responsible Parties in a Three-Party System: The Case of Britain

2.1. Introduction

As discussed in chapter 1, my goal in this book is to sketch an explanation for why responsible party government functions well in most Western democracies when the results reported by spatial modelers and behavioralists call the underpinnings of this representation model into question. My approach combines the perspectives of spatial modeling and behavioral research in that I take as a starting point the complex but realistic models of voting behavior developed by behavioralists and then deduce these models' implications for party policy strategies via spatial modeling techniques. I argue that the combined perspectives of behavioral research and spatial modeling illuminate the empirical findings that political parties in contemporary democracies present stable, divergent, policy programmes and that these programmes reflect their supporters' beliefs.

In this chapter, I outline the strategic logic that motivates policy stability, divergence, and representation by political parties in the simplest possible multiparty context, that of a three-party election in which the parties compete for votes along a unidimensional (Left-Right) policy continuum. I further assume a simplified version of the behaviorist's vote model, in which voters are motivated solely by party identification in addition to policies. In chapters 3–7, I generalize these arguments to elections involving different numbers of parties, to multiple policy dimensions, and to more complex decision rules on the part of voters. However, while these added complications create additional analytical difficulties, I emphasize that the logic that drives my results for three-party, unidimensional policy competition extends to each of these more complex electoral environments. The central strategic motivation that underlies this logic is easily stated: *in multiparty elections, parties are motivated to appeal on policy grounds to voters who are biased toward them for nonpolicy reasons.*

I begin in section 2.2 by reviewing the explanations for policy stability and divergence that spatial modelers have proposed, and I argue that, although these models offer valuable insights into parties' policies in specific constitutional and electoral contexts, they do not provide a general explanation for the successful functioning of responsible party government. Section 2.3 develops a behavioral model of the vote that incorporates the policy motivations that spatial modelers emphasize as well as party identification. I review the scholarly debate over the electoral impact of partisanship, and I show empirically that partisanship correlates with voters' policy preferences. In section 2.4, for a simple partisan voting model that incorporates only Left-Right policies in addition to partisanship I explore the strategic logic of three-party policy competition and present theoretical results on party equilibria. I show that when voters' partisanship correlates with their policy preferences and when equilibria exist the competing parties will present divergent policies that appeal to voters who are biased toward them for nonpolicy reasons. Section 2.5 presents empirical applications to British politics. I report equilibrium analyses for three-party competition involving the Conservatives, Labour, and the Liberal–Social Democrat Alliance using data from the 1987 British General Election Study. For a wide range of assumptions concerning the electoral impact of partisanship, I find that party equilibria exist and that these equilibria invariably locate the parties near those voters who display partisan biases in their direction. Thus, in the case of the 1987 British general election a simple partisan voting model illuminates the empirical findings of policy divergence, stability, and representation.

2.2. Spatial Modeling Explanations for Policy Divergence and Stability in Multiparty Systems

As noted in chapter 1, scholars focusing on multiparty spatial competition have concluded that under the Downsian spatial model, in which parties maximize votes and voters vote sincerely, parties' policies will be unstable, in that the parties will continually leapfrog without reaching a policy equilibrium, and furthermore that parties' policies will be similar in that parties have incentives to move towards each other in the policy space (see Eaton and Lipsey 1975 and Hermsen and Verbeek 1992). These results violate the requirement for responsible party government (developed in chapter 1) that parties present stable and divergent policy images. As was also noted in chapter 1 (see section 1.3), these predictions also conflict with empirical observations of parties' behavior. The divergence between theoretical results and empirical outcomes has motivated spatial modelers to propose various modifications to the basic Downsian model in an effort to explain policy stability and divergence. These modifications include:[1]

1. That equilibria are driven by the fact that parties are motivated not simply to maximize votes but to discourage entry into the party system by new competitors. Thus, in Palfrey's (1984) model an equilibrium can exist in which two established parties locate on either side of an entering party, which in turn locates at the position of the median voter. At equilibrium, the entering party loses the election.

2. That voters associate differing levels of uncertainty with the policy positions different parties will adopt once elected. Hug (1995) shows that under this scenario three-party equilibria can exist in which the least "risky" party invariably locates between the two riskier ones and wins the election.[2]

3. That sophisticated behavior by voters can drive multiparty equilibria. Under plurality, it has been shown that sophisticated voting can drive all parties to locate at the position of the median voter (Feddersen, Sened, and Wright 1990). At this equilibrium, all parties receive equal expected vote shares, and all parties are equally likely to win the election. Under proportional representation (PR), Austen-Smith and Banks (1988) argue that multiparty equilibria are possible because voters explicitly consider the coalition-bargaining stage in their voting decisions. At the Austin-Smith and Banks three-party equilibrium, the center party locates at the position of the median voter and receives fewer votes than its rivals.

4. That voting is "probabilistic," in that parties cannot predict voters' decisions with certainty based on their policy preferences. Adams (1999a), Lin et al. (1999), de Palma et al. (1990), and Schofield et al. (1998a), derive equilibria for situations in which voters' party evaluations are perturbed by unobserved components that render their decisions probabilistic from the parties' perspectives.[3] When the variance of the unobserved components is sufficiently high, the equilibrium locates all parties at the "minimum sum point" (Lin et al. 1999), which minimizes policy losses over the entire electorate, and all parties receive equal expected vote shares. For lower variances, equilibrium becomes more problematic; however, when such equilibria exist parties typically display considerable policy similarity in that they coalesce into a limited number of "blocs," each representing two or more parties that present identical policy programmes (see, e.g., de Palma et al. 1990, figs. 2–8; and Schofield et al. 1998a).

5. That parties are motivated at least in part by policy considerations and this, combined with their calculations about postelection coalition negotiations, can motivate a divergent policy equilibrium. Schofield and Sened (1998) and Schofield and Parks (1997) have shown how such a model can accommodate a policy equilibrium and that at equilibrium parties tend to locate in the direction of their preferred policies.[4]

Each of these explanations provides important intuitions about the strategic logic of multiparty competition. However, as the authors of these studies recognize, most of their explanations are to some extent "context specific," that is, they illuminate multiparty strategies only under specified conditions. Examples of these context-specific explanations include: studies focusing exclusively on electoral competition under proportional representation (Austen-Smith and Banks 1988), studies limited to plurality elections (Feddersen et al. 1990), analyses of elections that result in coalition governments in parliamentary democracies (Austen-Smith and Banks 1988; Schofield and Sened 1998), and elections involving exactly three parties (Austen-Smith and Banks 1988; Hug 1995; Palfrey 1984). In addition, many of these models imply specific electoral consequences such as that the center party receives the largest vote share (Hug 1995), that the center party receives the fewest votes (Palfrey 1984; Austen-Smith and Banks 1988), and that all parties receive equal vote shares (Feddersen et al. 1990; Adams 1999a; Lin et al. 1999).[5]

These considerations suggest that none of the above approaches by themselves provide a *general* explanation for why responsible party government functions in diverse electoral and constitutional settings, including among polities that employ proportional representation and those that feature plurality, party systems that feature single-party majority governments as well as those that feature coalition governments, and elections in which centrist parties are electorally successful as well as elections in which centrist parties fare poorly. Below I propose such an explanation, which abstracts from restrictive assumptions related to a given polity's constitutional and institutional features, resting instead on the basic Downsian logic that parties seek votes while voters vote sincerely. With respect to voting behavior, this model incorporates the policy motivations that spatial modelers emphasize, but it also incorporates the non-policy-related motivations or biases that behavioral researchers emphasize. I show that when voters' biases correlate with their policy preferences—an assumption that is supported by extensive empirical research—then a biased spatial voting model of multiparty competition can provide a general explanation for policy stability, divergence, and representation. This chapter provides such an analysis for a three-party election in which parties compete on Left-Right policies and voters choose according to a very simplified behavioral voting model that includes only party identification as a nonpolicy bias. Subsequent chapters extend this argument to more general settings.

2.3. A Spatial Voting Model with Partisan Bias

Spatial modelers generally represent the vote as a function of proximity, with voters preferring parties whose policies or ideologies are similar to their own preferences. More specifically, in the basic version of the Downsian model voters and parties are arrayed along a unidimensional continuum, which I label

Left-Right. Specifically, I assume that voters' and parties' Left-Right positions represent summary measures of their political ideologies, which are associated with their preferences on specific questions of public policy. Therefore, I will sometimes refer to voters' "policy motivations" when discussing the influence of Left-Right ideology on the vote. Following the convention typically employed in both behavioral research and spatial modeling, I represent each voter i's policy losses, L_{iK}, with respect to each party, K, by quadratic losses:

$$L_{iK} = -(x_i - k)^2 \qquad (2.1)$$

where x_i represents i's preferred Left-Right policy position and k the position of party K.

In contrast to spatial modelers, behavioralists view the vote choice as influenced in large part by non-policy-related considerations. Of these factors, perhaps the most widely studied is *party identification.* According to the "Michigan model" of voting (Campbell et al. 1960), partisan loyalties are a central element in voters' belief systems, which represent long-term, affective, psychological identifications with one's preferred party (Dalton 1996).[6] Behavioralists find that partisanship predisposes voters to support the parties with which they identify independently of ideology (Campbell et al. 1960; Butler and Stokes 1969; Converse and Pierce 1986, 1993).[7] I modify the basic policy voting model to incorporate voter i's partisanship p_{iK} into his or her utility calculus:

$$U_i(K) = p_{iK} + L_{iK} \qquad (2.2)$$

where p_{iK} is a dummy variable that equals b if voter i identifies with party K and equals zero otherwise; b is defined as the *strength of partisan attachment* relative to ideology. For this *partisan voting model,* the magnitude of b indicates the importance of voters' partisan attachments relative to Left-Right ideology. When b is large, voters are influenced primarily by partisanship; when b is small, voters are mostly policy oriented, as in the standard Downsian model. Although this model simplifies the voting decision by omitting the reciprocal effects of partisanship upon ideology (see below), the specification in equation 2.2 represents the standard behavioral specification for how ideology and partisanship influence the vote (but see Markus and Converse 1979; Page and Jones 1979; and Fleury and Lewis-Beck 1993). Note that in the discussion that follows I will sometimes state that a voter is "attached" to a party to indicate that he or she identifies with the party.

Equation 2.2 represents an extremely simplified behavioral model of the vote in which the voter's decision is a deterministic function of his or her partisanship and policy preferences. As in most behavioral models (but see Rivers

1988 and Glasgow 1999 for exceptions), I assume a "homogeneous" decision calculus throughout the voting population in that all voters assign the same relative importance to policy vis-à-vis partisanship. Note also that this simple model assumes that the strength of partisan attachment is identical for partisans of different parties. In subsequent chapters, I relax these strong assumptions and also generalize the model to include multiple policy dimensions, additional measured nonpolicy motivations, voters' turnout decisions, and the unmeasured motivations that render voters' decisions probabilistic from the analyst's perspective.

Anchoring Contemporary Voters: Partisanship versus Ideology

In exploring the implications of the partisan voting model for multiparty spatial competition, an obvious first question is: in realworld elections what are realistic parameters for b, the strength of partisan attachment relative to Left-Right ideology? One of the central controversies in the behavioral literature revolves around this question. While fully summarizing the methodological and conceptual issues involved in this debate is beyond the scope of this book, it is worth looking at one or two of them in some detail.

One factor that complicates empirical analyses of the electoral impact of partisanship relative to ideology is that, as indicated above, ideology and partisanship not only influence the vote but plausibly influence each other. In other words, citizens holding left-wing views are motivated to identify with leftist parties *and* to vote for these parties, while citizens who identify with right-wing parties are motivated to vote for these parties *and* may be persuaded to adopt these parties' ideologies (see fig. 2.1). If such a nonrecursive model correctly specifies the voting decision, then party identification and ideology are both highly endogenous. While this complication could conceivably be overcome by estimating simultaneous equation models, such models entail a host of con-

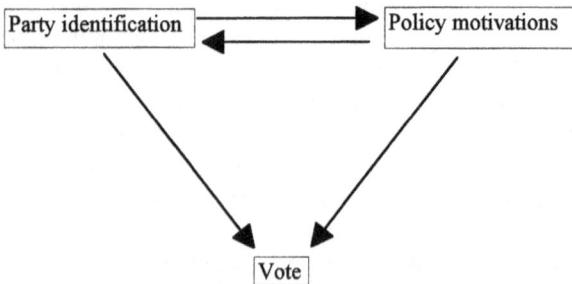

Fig. 2.1.   A model of the voting decision

straining assumptions, many of which lack plausibility or the hope of valida-
tion (see, e.g., Bartle 1998; Converse and Pierce 1993; and Shanks and Miller
1990, 1991). It is not surprising, therefore, that studies that attempt to estimate
such nonrecursive models from empirical voting data reach conflicting conclusions concerning the relative importance of ideology and partisanship (see, e.g.,
Markus and Converse 1979 and Page and Jones 1979; also see the exchange
between Fleury and Lewis-Beck [1993] and Converse and Pierce [1993]).

Another factor that complicates investigations of the electoral impact of
partisanship, especially outside the United States, revolves around the wording
of survey questions designed to elicit respondents' party identifications. Some
scholars have argued that outside the United States these items actually tap current voting preferences, thereby rendering them useless for explaining the vote
choice (Brynan and Sanders 1997; Butler and Stokes 1969; Kaase 1976; Rose
and McCallister 1990, 155–56). Other scholars have used the high correlation
between respondents' reported partisanship and their current vote intention, to-
gether with the rather high levels of instability in responses to party identification items reported in panel surveys outside the United States, to argue that
abiding partisan attachments did not develop in Europe or at least could not be
measured (Budge et al. 1976; Kaase 1976). However, this conclusion has been
challenged by other scholars, who argue that in toto survey results strongly support the inference that partisanship significantly influences the vote and that in
some polities this influence exceeds the electoral impact of ideology (Converse
and Pierce 1986, 1992a, 1993).

In summary, there exists no scholarly consensus about the relative impact
of partisanship and Left-Right ideology upon the vote, particularly in elections
held outside the United States.[8] Some scholars argue that partisanship exceeds
ideology in its electoral impact; others argue that the electoral impact of ideology exceeds that of partisanship. Given this controversy, it is important that any
explanation for responsible party government that invokes the partisan vote
model be shown to apply given a wide range of assumptions about the electoral
impact of partisanship relative to ideology. This is what I demonstrate below
with respect to British politics.

The Correlation between Partisanship and Ideology

Although the electoral impact of partisanship is the subject of heated debate,
there is a scholarly consensus that in Western party systems voters' party identifications correlate with their political ideologies, so that, for instance, leftist
voters tend to be partisans of Socialist, Labour, Social Democratic, and Communist parties, while right-wing voters tend to identify with Conservative and
Christian Democratic parties. This correlation has been observed in over a
dozen electorates, and indeed to my knowledge it extends to every party sys-

tem for which survey research on voter partisanship and ideology is available (see Dalton 1985 and Iversen 1994b).

Figure 2.2 presents the mean ideological self-placements of the respondents in recent national election surveys conducted in Britain, France, and Norway, stratified according to the respondents' reported party identifications; also given are the mean placements for independent voters, that is, those who indicated that they did not feel close to any party, and the number of respondents in each group.[9] For France and Norway, the scale represents voters' Left-Right self-placements; for Britain, for which the Left-Right item is not available, the

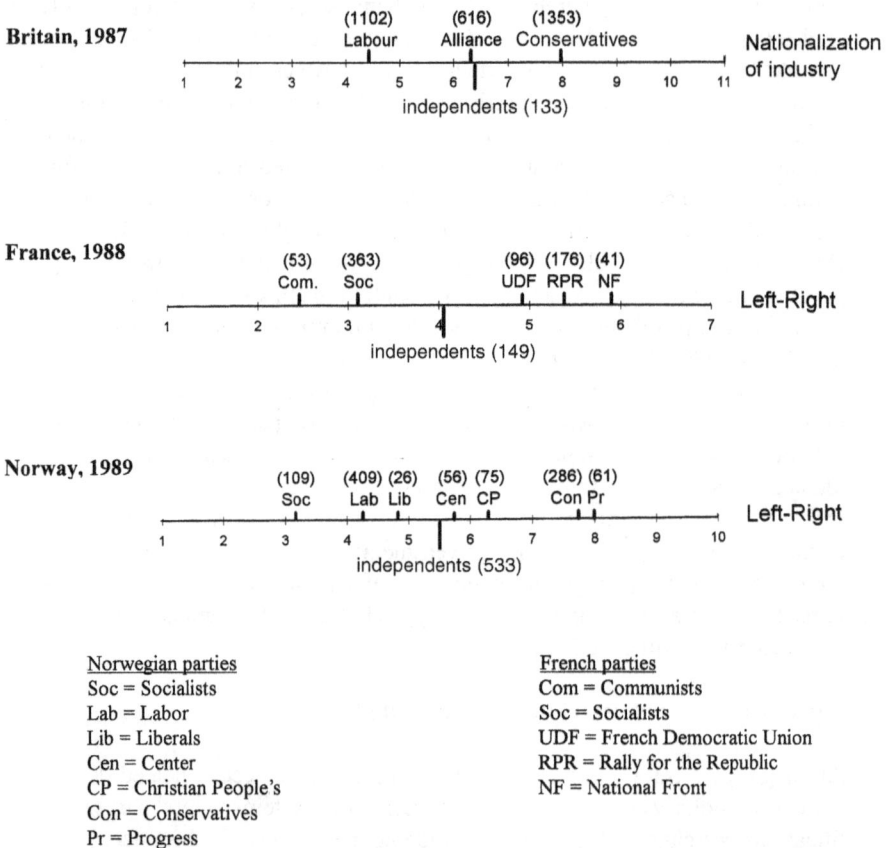

Britain, 1987

```
                        (1102)      (616)    (1353)
                        Labour    Alliance Conservatives      Nationalization
      |---|---|---|---|---|---|---|---|---|---|         of industry
      1   2   3   4   5   6 | 7   8   9   10  11
                      independents (133)
```

France, 1988

```
                    (53)   (363)        (96) (176) (41)
                    Com.    Soc         UDF  RPR  NF
        |-------|-------|-------|-------|-------|-------|    Left-Right
        1       2       3      4|       5       6       7
                      independents (149)
```

Norway, 1989

```
                  (109)  (409) (26) (56) (75)    (286) (61)
                   Soc   Lab   Lib  Cen  CP      Con   Pr
      |---|---|---|---|---|---|---|---|---|---|     Left-Right
      1   2   3   4   5 | 6   7   8   9   10
                   independents (533)
```

Norwegian parties
Soc = Socialists
Lab = Labor
Lib = Liberals
Cen = Center
CP = Christian People's
Con = Conservatives
Pr = Progress

French parties
Com = Communists
Soc = Socialists
UDF = French Democratic Union
RPR = Rally for the Republic
NF = National Front

Fig. 2.2. Mean positions of party identifiers and independents in Britain, France, and Norway. (Data from 1987 British General Election Study, 1988 French Presidential Election Study, and 1989 Norwegian Election Study.)

scale represents voters' self-placements on nationalization of industry, an issue that has been central to British politics during much of the postwar period and that presumably taps underlying Left-Right orientations (see, e.g., Butler and Stokes 1969 and Rose and McCallister 1990). In each country, the partisans of the traditional leftist parties (Labour in Britain, the Communists and Socialists in France, and the Socialists and Labor in Norway) locate on the left, on average, while voters who identify with traditional right-wing parties (the British Conservatives, the French RPR, and the Norwegian Christian People's Party and the Conservatives) tend to locate on the right. Furthermore, partisans of the newly emerged, Far Right parties in France (the National Front) and Norway (Progress) tend to take extreme right-wing positions. In addition, note that in each survey the total number of party identifiers is much greater than the number of independents.[10]

Of course, the observed correlation between partisanship and ideology is predictable, given the empirical findings described above, on the reciprocal influences of ideology and partisanship. However, given the research summarized earlier, which suggests that partisanship encompasses an affective component that exercises an independent influence on the vote, this correlation implies that left-wing voters tend to be biased toward left-wing parties *in part for nonpolicy reasons,* while right-wing voters have partisan biases toward right-wing parties. As I argue below, the empirical finding that voters' partisan attachments correlate with their political ideologies has important implications for party policy strategies.

2.4. The Logic of Multiparty Spatial Competition under the Partisan Vote Model: A Stylized Analysis of Three-Party Elections

To explicate the logic of party strategies when voters' partisan attachments correlate with their policy preferences, I assume that three parties, labeled L, C, and R, compete for votes from an electorate that is motivated by both partisanship and Left-Right ideology. A hypothetical distribution of voters' policy preferences and partisan attachments is given in figure 2.3A, in which voters' Left-Right positions are distributed along a 1–11 scale and correlate with their party identifications: all voters in the policy interval [1,4] on the left are assumed to identify with party L, those located in the central interval [4,6.5] identify with C, and voters located to the right of 6.5 are attached to R (the strength, b, of voters' partisan attachments is specified below). The voter distribution is approximately normal, although it is slightly denser to the left of center, which, as we shall see in subsequent chapters, reflects the distributions of voters' ideologies in several contemporary electorates. Parties L, C, and R locate initially at $l =$

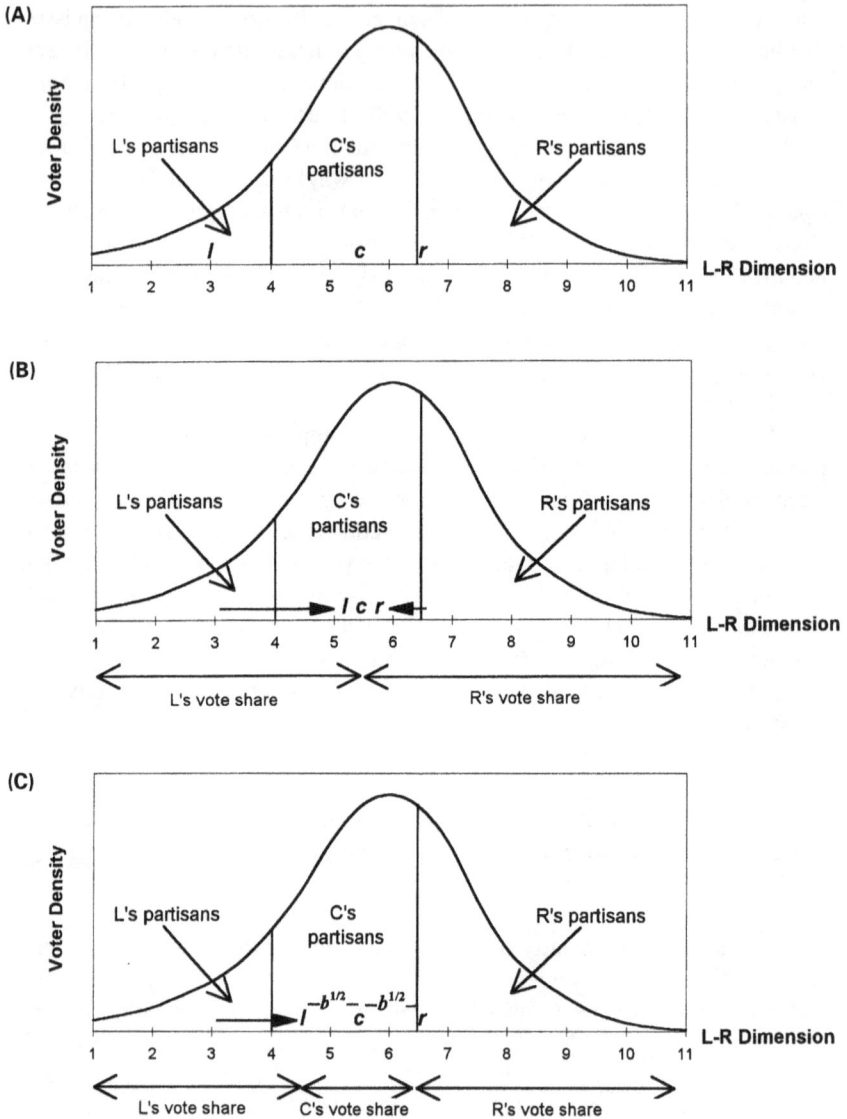

(A)

Voter Density

L's partisans

C's partisans

R's partisans

l

c   *r*

L-R Dimension

1   2   3   4   5   6   7   8   9   10   11

(B)

Voter Density

L's partisans

C's partisans

R's partisans

l c r

L-R Dimension

1   2   3   4   5   6   7   8   9   10   11

L's vote share   R's vote share

(C)

Voter Density

L's partisans

C's partisans

R's partisans

$l \overset{-b^{1/2}-}{c} -b^{1/2}- r$

L-R Dimension

1   2   3   4   5   6   7   8   9   10   11

L's vote share   C's vote share   R's vote share

Fig. 2.3. Spatial competition under the partisan vote model: The pressure for policy divergence when partisanship correlates with Left-Right position. (*A*) Initial policy distribution of voters and parties L, C, and R; (*B*) policy convergence for $b = 0$; (*C*) policy divergence for $b = 1$.

3.0, $c = 5.5$, and $r = 6.5$, respectively; note, however, that the party labels L, C, and R refer to the locations of the rival party's partisans rather than the locations of the parties themselves; it is possible, for instance, that party L could be motivated to locate on the far right, that C could shift to the left, and so on. As is usual in spatial modeling, I conceptualize the parties as unitary actors that possess full information about the distributions of voters' policy preferences and the policies proposed by their competitors. I also assume that all three parties maximize votes and that voters vote sincerely for the party that maximizes their utilities, which are computed using the specification given in equation 2.2.

Note that in this hypothetical example all voters are assumed to be partisan and the policy preferences of rival parties' partisans do not overlap. While these assumptions—which apply to all of the analyses presented in this section—are stylized, they reflect the empirical findings, summarized above, that most voters report a partisan attachment in a developed party system (see also Dalton 1996, chap. 9; and Converse 1969) and that partisanship correlates with voters' ideologies. In section 2.5 and subsequent chapters, I show that the strategic logic of party competition I develop for this stylized distribution extends to empirical voter distributions that relax these strong assumptions.

Voter Partisanship and the Pressure for Policy Divergence

To begin, consider how voter partisanship alters parties' strategic calculus for the partisan distribution pictured in figure 2.3A. Under the standard Downsian model, which ignores partisanship (i.e., when the strength of party attachment b is set to zero in eq. 2.2), parties L and R converge toward the center and thereby "squeeze" party C, so that R attracts support from all right-wing voters, including C's right-of-center partisans, while L is supported by all voters on the left (fig. 2.3B). However, this motivation for policy convergence is mitigated when voters display partisan biases. This is illustrated in figure 2.3C, which shows the situation in which b is set at 1.0. For this degree of partisan bias, party L would be ill advised to converge to the immediate left of C because leftist partisans of C would then be nearly indifferent between the parties on ideological grounds and hence would vote for C on the basis of their partisan attachments. Party L can attract these partisans' support only by differentiating itself from C. Specifically, L maximizes votes by locating at $l = 4.5$, at a distance of one policy unit to the left of party C's position, c; in so doing, L attracts support from all voters, including C's partisans, located to the left of 4.5. This is because, when $l = 4.5$, for any voter, i, to the left of 4.5, i's comparative ideological preference for L over C, $[L_{iL} - L_{iC}]$, will outweigh his or her partisan attachments, $b = 1$, to party C.[11] Note that this analysis shows that L can attract voters among those who identify with C. Just as in actual elections, voters with long-standing partisan attachments may temporarily "defect" to a rival party.

In addition, note that when $b = 1$ party R has no electoral incentive to converge toward C because, given C's centrist location, the right-of-center partisans in the policy interval [5.5,6.5] will vote for C regardless of R's position. This is because these voters approve of C's ideology *and* support C for nonpolicy reasons, so that there is literally no political ideology R can propose that would induce C's partisans to desert their party. Therefore, the ideological interval [4.5,6.5] represents the "region of invulnerability" for party C since there is no ideology that L and R can propose that attracts support from voters located in this interval.

More generally, when parties seek support from rival parties' partisans they will typically propose a position that differs from the rival party's position by a policy distance of at least $b^{1/2}$.[12] This is because it is impossible to win the support of a rival party's partisan if the policy distance between this partisan's position and the position of his or her party is *less* than $b^{1/2}$. To see that any party F (whose ideological position is denoted f) must invariably attract support from all of its partisans located in the policy interval $[f - b^{1/2}, f + b^{1/2}]$— and hence that this interval represents party F's "region of invulnerability"— note that, for a voter i who is a partisan of F, i's utility differential for F versus party G (whose ideological position is denoted g) is

$$U_i(F) - U_i(G) = (b + L_{iF}) - L_{iG}$$

$$= b - (x_i - f)^2 - [-(x_i - g)^2]$$

In the case in which party G proposes the voter i's preferred policy (i.e., $g = x_i$), the utility differential $[U_i(F) - U_i(G)]$ simplifies to

$$U_i(F) - U_i(G) = b - (x_i - f)^2$$

so that voter i prefers party F to party G whenever $[b - (x_i - f)^2]$ is positive:

$$U_i(F) - U_i(G) > 0 \Rightarrow b - (x_i - f)^2 > 0$$

$$\Rightarrow b^{1/2} > |x_i - f|$$

$$\Rightarrow x_i \in [f - b^{1/2}, f + b^{1/2}]$$

For this reason, in the illustrative examples presented below the parties' optimal positions will frequently be separated from their nearest competitor's positions by a policy distance of exactly $b^{1/2}$ (this is the case in the example illustrated in fig. 2.3, in which the parties L and R locate at policy distances of $b^{1/2} = 1$ to the left and the right of party C, respectively). In order to simplify the presentation of my arguments, I will therefore express the strength of partisan bias in terms of the square root of b (i.e., I will write $b^{1/2} = 2$ for $b = 4$).

The example illustrated in figure 2.3 shows how voters' partisan attachments alter the logic of the standard Downsian model in that parties no longer have electoral incentives to co-opt rival parties' policies. This is because parties cannot pry loose support from a rival party's partisans by mimicking this rival's ideology. Instead, they must present policies that are significantly more attractive than—hence different from—these rivals' positions. In this way, partisanship encourages *policy divergence* on the part of competing parties.

Voter Partisanship and the Pressure for Policy Stability

While partisanship can motivate policy divergence, at first glance one might think that spatial competition under the partisan voting model may promote policy instability in that no policy equilibrium is likely to exist. For the voter and party configuration given in figure 2.4 (which is identical to fig. 2.3C, with the strength of partisan attachment again set at $b^{1/2} = 1.0$), for instance, note that party R's vote share is larger than that of party L and furthermore that all voters who support R are located to R's right (the significance of the policy position l' is discussed below). This being the case, one might expect that L has electoral incentives to leapfrog R.

In fact, due to voters' partisan motivations, *the party configuration pictured in figure 2.4 represents an equilibrium in vote-maximizing strategies.* To

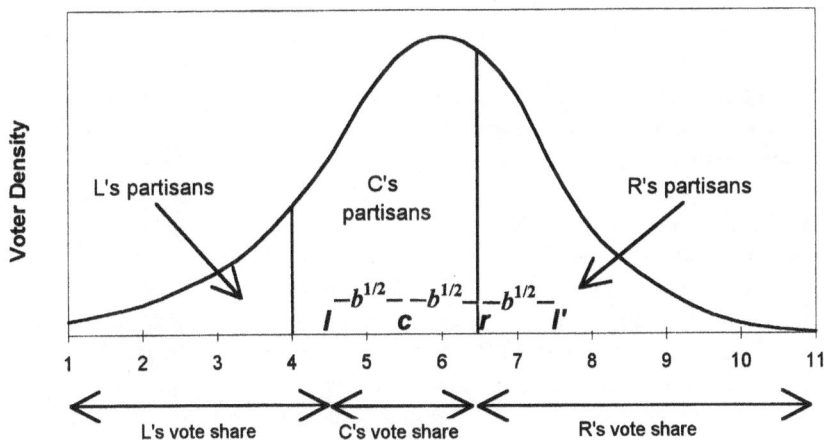

Fig. 2.4.   Equilibrium configuration for $b = 1$

grasp the logic that underlies this equilibrium, note first that L cannot capture R's vote by leapfrogging to a position just to the right of its rival. In this case, L receives no support from R's partisans because these voters' partisan attachments to R will outweigh their (slight) policy preferences for L. In order for either peripheral party to capture some portion of the other peripheral party's supporters, it must offer a more extreme position that can differentiate it from its rival. Thus, for L to maximize its share of votes on the right it must locate at $l' = 7.5$, at a distance $b^{1/2} = 1$ to R's right. However, at l', party L attracts support only from those voters located to the right of $l' = 7.5$, that is, the voters located in the policy interval [7.5,11]; by inspection, this constitutes a smaller constituency then L wins when it is located at its equilibrium location, $l = 4.5$.

With respect to the logic that motivates C to present a stable policy, note first that, because voter partisanship motivates L and R to differentiate themselves from C, C is not tightly "squeezed" and therefore lacks the compelling motivation to leapfrog its opponents that obtains for centrist parties under the standard Downsian model. In addition, were C to leapfrog it would face the same dilemma that precludes the two peripheral parties from capturing each other's votes: it must offer a rather extreme left- or right-wing position in order to capture rival parties' partisans. Thus, the existence of rival partisans renders the periphery unattractive to C. More generally, when partisanship correlates with ideology *the fact of voter partisanship typically forces leapfrogging parties to present policies significantly more extreme than those of their rivals, which are likely to prove electorally unattractive.*

Note that the equilibrium pictured in figure 2.4 is stable in the face of quite dramatic changes in the voter distribution such as those that occur when some voting group is newly enfranchised or, less dramatically, as a result of population replacement. To see this, suppose that a large bloc of center-right voters, who are all partisans of R, enter the electorate at a point slightly to the right of R's policy position (fig. 2.5). This additional support boosts R's vote share above that of party C but leaves unchanged the equilibrium configuration because these new voters are located within R's "region of invulnerability" and hence cannot be captured by a rival party.[13]

One other aspect of the equilibrium configurations pictured in figures 2.4 and 2.5 deserves comment. Note that in figure 2.4 the center party, C, wins a plurality of the vote, but for the voter distribution pictured in figure 2.5 it is party R that wins an electoral plurality. This shows that a spatial model with partisan voting can accommodate equilibria in which the center party either "wins" or "loses" the election. (The partisan vote model can also accommodate "ties," as illustrated in fig. 2.6). This diversity of electoral outcomes corresponds to the range of real world elections, which include elections in which centrist parties attract modest support (such as elections involving the British Liberal Democrats and the German Free Democratic Party [FDP]) as well as

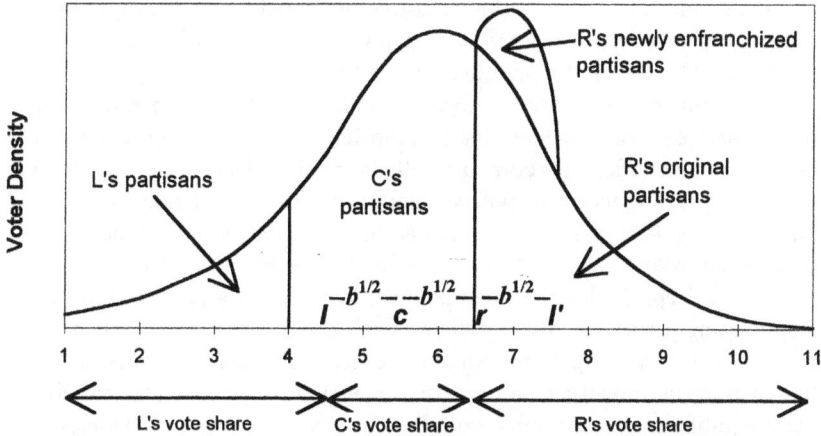

Fig. 2.5. Equilibrium configuration when a new voting constituency enters the electorate ($b = 1$)

elections in which centrist parties are strongly supported (such as the Indian Congress Party). Note that previous models of equilibrium in three-party spatial competition typically preclude such diverse outcomes in that they imply that only certain kinds of election results are possible. These include: studies that conclude that at equilibrium the center party must receive the largest vote share (Hug 1985), models that imply that the center party will receive the fewest

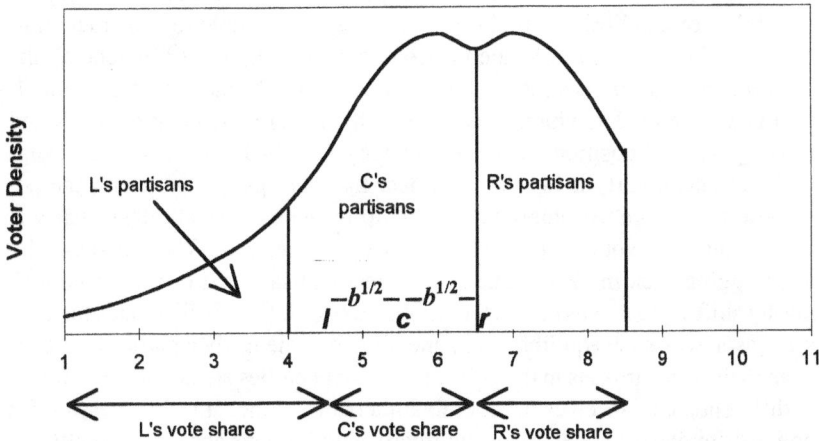

Fig. 2.6. Equilibrium configuration in which parties C and R receive equal vote shares ($b = 1$)

votes at equilibrium (Palfrey 1984; Austen-Smith and Banks 1988), and models that imply that all parties receive equal vote shares at equilibrium (Feddersen et al. 1990; Adams 1999a; Lin et al. 1999).[14]

In summary, I have shown how a spatial model that incorporates the behavioralists' empirical findings that partisanship influences voting, and that voters' partisan identifications correlate with their political ideologies, can illuminate policy divergence and policy stability on the part of political parties. Parties differentiate their policies because this is the only way to attract support from voters who identify with rival parties. Parties maintain stable positions, rather than leapfrogging their competitors, because voter partisanship forces leapfrogging parties to present policies significantly more extreme than those of their rivals and such extreme policies are electorally unattractive. As a result, the partisan vote model can motivate dispersed policy equilibria and, moreover, these equilibria are compatible with the diversity of electoral outcomes that characterize real world elections.

The Pressure for Responsible Parties

The equilibria illustrated in figures 2.4 through 2.6 are interesting in that each configuration locates the parties near their own partisans in the policy space. The fact that this "responsible" party behavior creates an equilibrium is explained by the intuition summarized above: when each party locates near its own partisans, rival parties are typically forced to take relatively extreme (and therefore electorally unattractive) positions in order to attract support from the favored party's partisans.

While this intuition explains why responsible party behavior enhances the possibility of equilibrium, might it nonetheless be possible to construct equilibria in which the parties locate far from their own partisans? In general, the answer is no. To gain insights on this point, consider the party configuration illustrated in figure 2.7, which is identical to figure 2.4 *except* that parties R and L have switched positions (and have thereby switched vote shares). Because each peripheral party is now located near the other party's partisans, the peripheral parties are extremely vulnerable to invasion by rivals. Thus, party R can capture L's vote share—which consists entirely of R's partisans—by leapfrogging back in the direction of its own partisans and R can accomplish this by shifting to r', slightly to the right of L (fig. 2.7). This illustrates the central reason why such equilibria are generally precluded: when parties locate far from their own partisans in the policy space, rival parties are no longer required to differentiate themselves in order to attract votes. Since it is this pressure for policy differentiation that drives multiparty equilibria, its absence typically ensures policy disequilibrium. This suggests that *configurations in which parties present ideologies at odds with their partisans' beliefs are inherently unstable*

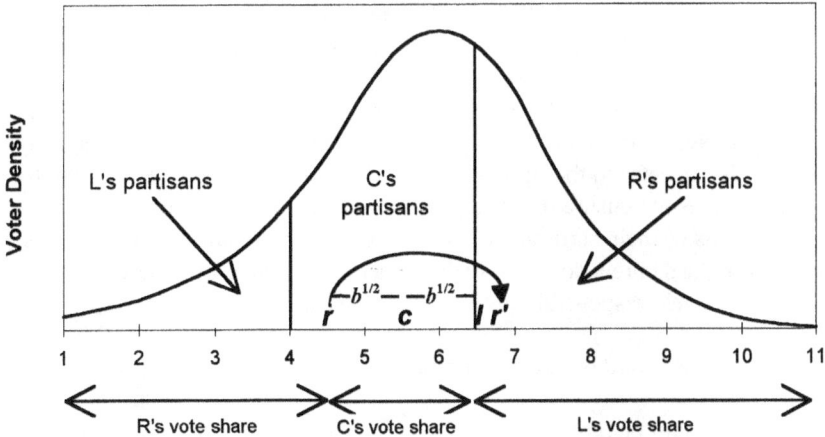

Fig. 2.7. Alternative party configuration in which party R is motivated to leapfrog party L ($b = 1$)

and typically motivate the parties to readjust their ideologies in the direction of their partisans.

An exception to this generalization arises when partisans are extremely attached to their parties, in which case "irresponsible" party behavior carries little electoral penalty. The most obvious condition is one in which every voter's partisan attachment is so strong that he or she supports the party no matter where it locates itself in the policy space. In this case, it is clear that any party configuration is an equilibrium; however, such a situation is both unrealistic and uninteresting. The strength in the present approach comes from demonstrating that equilibria can arise from more modest degrees of partisan attachment and furthermore that at equilibrium parties behave responsibly. In Adams 1998, I prove theorem 2.1, which obtains providing that the strength, b, of voters' partisan attachments is sufficiently weak that the following conditions hold:

1. The policy intervals that contain the partisans of parties L, C, and R all exceed $b^{1/2}$ in length.
2. There is no interval of length $b^{1/2}$ in the policy space that contains more than 25 percent of the electorate.[15]

THEOREM 2.1: *If an equilibrium exists, then at equilibrium L is the left-most party, C the center party, and R the right-most party. Furthermore, at equilibrium C presents an ideology preferred by one of its partisans.*

The theorem shows that when an equilibrium exists the parties will appeal on ideological grounds to voters who display partisan biases in their direction.

Hence, parties are motivated to provide their supporters with faithful policy representations, despite the fact that these voters are disposed to support them for nonpolicy reasons.

Figures 2.4 through 2.6 provide examples of equilibria consistent with theorem 2.1. Note that at equilibrium party L, while it is indeed the left-most party, nonetheless locates to the right of its partisans. This illustrates the fact that the theorem does not ensure that at equilibrium the parties provide "perfect" representations of their partisans, nor does it ensure that equilibria always exist. However, the theorem does ensure than when equilibria do exist parties will behave reasonably responsibly toward their partisans.

The Strategic Disadvantage of the Center Party

The equilibrium pictured in figure 2.5 carries additional interest from the fact that party C fails to win a plurality of the vote, despite having a plurality of the partisans in the electorate. This occurs because at equilibrium C loses the support of its left-most partisans, who defect to party L, which thereby permits party R to capture a plurality of the vote. If we define a party's proportion of partisans in the electorate as its "normal vote," then C's failure to obtain its normal vote costs it the election. Adams 1998 proves the following result, which holds providing that the two conditions given for theorem 2.1 are still in force:

THEOREM 2.2.   *For every possible policy equilibrium, C fails to obtain its normal vote.*

The intuition underlying theorem 2.2 revolves around the fact that, by theorem 2.1, C is the center party for all possible equilibria. Party C therefore faces the strategic dilemma that typically confronts centrist parties in spatial voting games: that they tend to be "squeezed" by surrounding opponents. While this squeezing effect is partially mitigated in my model because rival parties are motivated to differentiate themselves from the center party, this party will still lose some of its partisans, as in the equilibrium configurations given in figures 2.4 through 2.6, where C's left-most partisans defect to party L. Furthermore, unlike centrist parties in the standard Downsian model, party C cannot easily escape its dilemma by leapfrogging L or R since we have seen that C will be forced to take a relatively extreme position on the left or right in order to capture the support of L or R partisans.[16] Thus, when voters display partisan loyalties that correlate with their policy preferences, often the center party's only viable option is to locate at the most advantageous position *between* its two rivals. Unfortunately, the center party can converge toward one of its rivals only by diverging from the other, so these policy adjustments may have limited value.

While the results presented in sections 2.3 through 2.4 are suggestive, they rest upon several stylized assumptions, including the postulates that the spatial distributions of rival parties' partisans do not overlap and that the electorate is entirely partisan, that is, there are no independent voters. These assumptions help to illuminate the strategic logic that drives policy divergence, stability, and representation in three-party systems. However, they apparently limit the model's empirical implications. In the next section, I examine party equilibria for a historical election that allows us to relax these assumptions.

2.5. Partisan Bias and Party Equilibrium in Britain: An Empirical Example

Beginning with the formation of the Social Democratic–Liberal Alliance in 1981, British politics has been essentially a three-party system in which the left-wing Labour Party and the right-wing Conservatives compete with the relatively centrist Alliance.[17] This fact, combined with the operation of Britain's plurality voting system, which typically awards the largest party a parliamentary majority and hence motivates parties to maximize votes, suggest that British elections represent a promising testing ground for my arguments concerning parties' vote-seeking strategies in three-party elections.

In the 1987 British National Election Study (BNES), respondents were asked their opinions about government nationalization of industry, an issue that has been central to British politics during the postwar period, at least prior to the 1990s.[18] Respondents were asked to indicate their opinions on an 11-point Likert scale ranging from strongly supporting further nationalization (1) to strongly opposing further nationalization (11). Respondents were also asked to report their party identifications. The distribution of voters' positions by partisanship are shown in figure 2.8A, for partisans of Labour, the Alliance, and the Conservatives as well as for independents (those who reported no partisan identification).[19] This partisan distribution violates the assumptions used in the previous section in that it includes independent voters *and* in that the positions of Labour, Alliance, and Conservative partisans overlap. However, note that the number of independents is small relative to the number of partisans. Furthermore, there is a strong correlation between voters' partisanship and their positions on nationalization, with Labour partisans distributed overwhelmingly on the left, and Conservatives on the right, of the continuum. The relative proportions of party partisans are 44 percent Conservative, 31 percent Labour, and 20 percent Alliance. As was illustrated in figure 2.2, the mean positions of these parties' constituencies are: Labour partisans, 4.42; Alliance partisans, 6.27; and Conservative partisans, 7.95. Can this empirical partisan distribution accommodate the same type of party equilibria obtained for the stylized distributions analyzed in the preceding section?

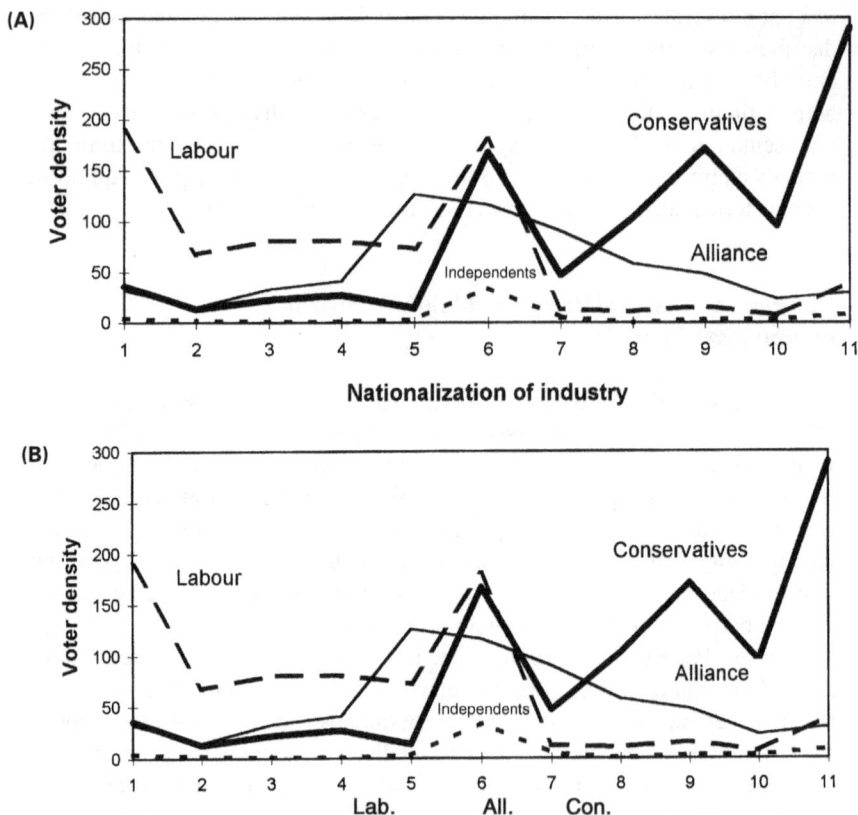

Fig. 2.8. Equilibrium analysis of party positioning on nationalization of industry, 1987 British general election. (A) Distributions of voters' policy preferences; (B) Equilibrium configuration, for $b^{1/2} = 2$. (Data from 1987 British General Election Study.)

The answer to this question is yes. Figure 2.8B shows an example of such an equilibrium for the situation in which the strength of voters' partisan attachments was set at $b^{1/2} = 2.0$. At equilibrium, the Conservative Party locates on the right at 7.40, the Alliance is positioned near the center at 6.15, and Labour locates on the left at 4.75.[20] Consistent with theorem 2.1, this equilibrium finds each party behaving responsibly toward its own partisans. Consistent with theorem 2.2, at equilibrium the centrist Alliance wins just 17 percent of the vote— 3 percent less than its normal vote (the Conservatives and Labour win 44 percent and 39 percent, respectively).

The strategic logic that drives this equilibrium is similar to that which obtained for the stylized partisan distributions discussed earlier. Both Labour and the Conservatives are motivated to locate on the same side of the issue as their partisans while at the same time differentiating themselves from the Alliance; this allows them to capture the more extreme Alliance partisans while retaining the support of the vast majority of their own partisans. The Alliance, meanwhile, faces the strategic dilemma outlined above: it cannot easily leapfrog its rivals since it would be forced to take an extreme left- or right-wing position in order to capture Labour or Conservative partisans.

One difference between this equilibrium configuration and those obtained for the earlier, stylized, partisan distributions, is that here the Labour and Conservative Parties squeeze the Alliance rather tightly. Thus, while the distance between adjoining parties in the stylized equilibria was $b^{1/2}$—which would imply a policy distance of $b^{1/2} = 2$ in the present case—in figure 2.8B this distance is only 1.40 policy units between Labour and the Alliance and 1.25 between the Alliance and the Conservatives. This occurs for two reasons. First, the presence of independent voters gives the peripheral parties, Labour and the Conservatives, added incentives to squeeze the Alliance. Second, the fact that the empirical partisan distributions overlap further enhances the peripheral parties' incentives to converge toward the Alliance. In the case of Labour, for instance, the fact that there exist a small number of center-right Labour partisans motivates Labour to move slightly closer to the Alliance than it otherwise would, since it can thereby retain the votes of some of these partisans, who would otherwise defect to the Alliance. A similar strategic logic drives the Conservatives leftward. However, while these incentives motivate a rather centralized equilibrium, the essential character of this "empirical" equilibrium mirrors the results obtained for the stylized analyses in the preceding section.

Equilibria for Varying Strengths of Partisan Attachment

Although it is encouraging that we have located an equilibrium in party strategies for the 1987 British general election, two questions that arise are, first, does this result generalize to elections for which voters display different levels of partisan attachment, b, and, second, what values of b are most realistic for historical elections? With respect to the second question, recall from section 2.3 that the electoral influence of partisanship is the subject of heated scholarly debate, so that no consensus exists concerning the "true" electoral impact of partisan attachments in historical British elections. However, to the extent that the results reported in recent empirical studies on British general elections provide rough estimates of the electoral impact of partisanship (relative to policy preferences) these suggest that the value of b lies at or below $b^{1/2} = 3.0$.[21]

For varying levels of $b^{1/2}$ between zero and 3, table 2.1 shows whether party equilibria exist and the parties' locations and vote shares at equilibrium.

TABLE 2.1. Equilibrium Configurations on Nationalization of Industry for Varying Degrees of Partisan Attachment, 1987 British General Election

Strength of Partisan Attachment	Parties' Equilibrium Locations			Parties' Vote Shares[a]		
	Labour	Alliance	Conservatives	Labour	Alliance	Conservatives
$b^{1/2} = 0$	—	—	—	—	—	—
$b^{1/2} = 0.5$	—	—	—	—	—	—
$b^{1/2} = 1.0$	—	—	—	—	—	—
$b^{1/2} = 1.5$	4.85	6.10	7.20	39%	17%	44%
$b^{1/2} = 2.0$	4.75	6.15	7.40	37	18	45
$b^{1/2} = 2.5$	4.50	6.35	8.10	38	18	44
$b^{1/2} = 3.0$	4.45	6.40	8.35	38	17	46
Partisans' mean positions	4.42	6.27	7.95	36[b]	19[c]	45[d]

[a]Parties' vote shares at equilibrium.
[b]Labour's share of the three-party vote, 1987 British general election.
[c]The Alliance's share of the three-party vote, 1987 British general election.
[d]The Conservatives' share of the three-party vote, 1987 British general election.

Also given are the mean positions of the Conservative, Alliance, and Labour partisans. The table indicates that when $b^{1/2}$ is less than 1.5 no equilibrium exists. This finding is consistent with the intuition developed for the stylized analysis (see fig. 2.3B) that when partisan bias is weak party competition resembles the pure Downsian model, in which multiparty equilibria are rare. For $b^{1/2} \geq 1.5$, equilibria exist in which Labour, the Alliance, and the Conservatives are arrayed from left to right.[22] Note that the greater the strength of voters' partisan attachments, the greater the policy distance that separates the parties at equilibrium; this is because (as outlined above) when party attachments are strong the Conservatives and Labour must substantially differentiate themselves from the Alliance in order to attract Alliance partisans. At equilibrium, the Alliance captures between 17 and 18 percent of the vote—less than its 20 percent normal vote. These results are consistent with theorems 2.1 and 2.2.

With respect to policy representation, note that each of the party equilibria reported in table 2.1 locates the party quite near the mean position of its partisan sympathizers. This correspondence is represented graphically in figures 2.9A–2.9D, which compare each party's equilibrium position against the mean position of its partisans for varying degrees of partisan voting. For every equilibrium configuration, each party locates within 0.75 units of its partisans' mean position along the 1–11 nationalization scale—a truly remarkable correspondence. While we shall see in subsequent chapters that applications to different historical elections do not always produce such a tight representational fit, these results strongly suggest that when voters choose according to the partisan vote

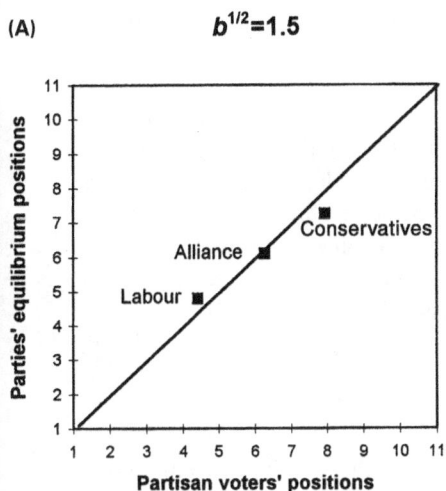

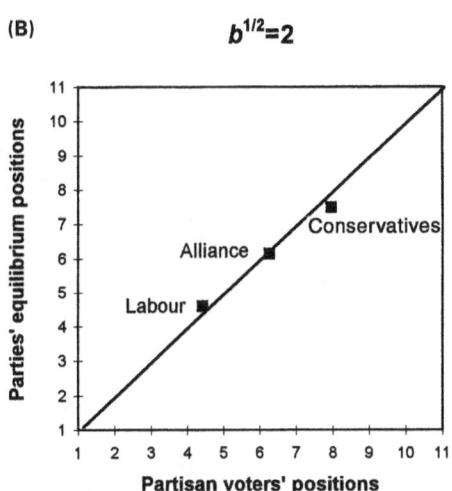

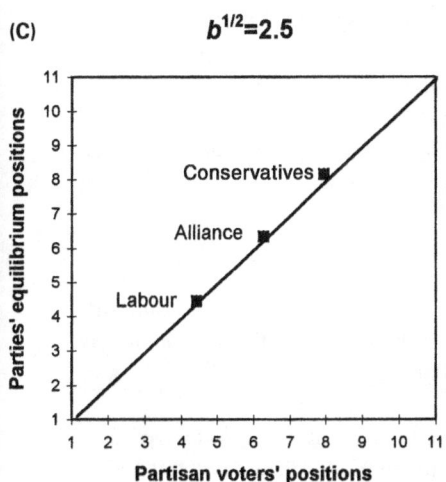

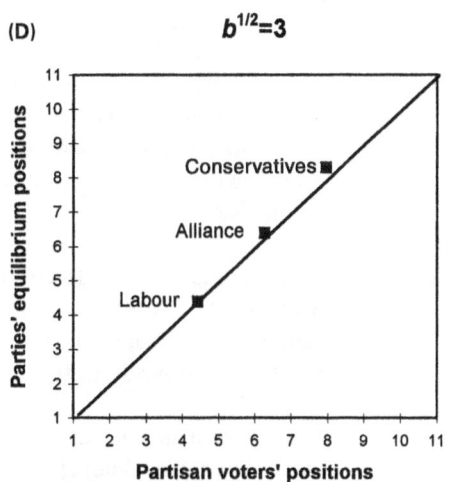

Fig. 2.9. Voter opinions and parties' equilibrium positions on nationalization of industry for varying degrees of partisan voting. (A) $b^{1/2} = 1.5$; (B) $b^{1/2} = 2$; (C) $b^{1/2} = 2.5$; (D) $b^{1/2} = 3$.

model parties have strong electoral motivations to behave responsibly toward their partisans.

In summary, this empirical application to the 1987 British general election suggests that for a wide range of assumptions concerning the strength of partisan bias the partisan voting model illuminates the empirical findings that political parties in contemporary democracies present stable, divergent policies that represent the beliefs of their supporters. The results of this initial application of the model therefore provide encouragement for further applications to historical elections in order to test whether the partisan voting model can provide a general explanation for the basis of responsible party government.

2.6. Connections to Previous Work

Although the central argument advanced here—that a partisan voting model can illuminate the empirical findings of policy divergence, stability, and representation in multiparty democracies—is new, to the best of my knowledge, I note that there are two strands of research that have anticipated aspects of my arguments. With respect to policy divergence, the argument advanced here, that voters' partisan attachments motivate parties to differentiate their policies from those of their rivals, has a basis similar to that of the argument developed by Feld and Grofman (1991) concerning the strategic effects of voters giving incumbent politicians the "benefit of the doubt"—that is, treating the policy distance between themselves and the incumbent as less than it actually is. The authors argue that a

> benefit of the doubt can force challengers to locate relatively far away from the incumbent in order to beat him. In this way, benefits of the doubt discourage tweedledum-tweedledee politics, because a challenger with nearly identical issue positions to the incumbent cannot win. (128)[23]

In Feld and Grofman's model all voters give the benefit of the doubt to the incumbent in a two-candidate election, while in my model different voters are attached to different parties in a multiparty contest; nonetheless, both partisanship and the benefit of the doubt provide the same strategic incentive, which motivates party policy differentiation.

From a theoretical perspective, the argument advanced above, that at equilibrium parties will target areas of natural strength, has been advanced in a related context: the study of resource allocation in multiparty systems. Snyder (1990), using a game-theoretic analysis of multiparty competition over seats in single-member districts, finds that parties maximize their expected seats by spending more in districts where they are "naturally strong" than in districts where they expect little support. While there are important differences between Snyder's approach and my own,[24] the fact that we reach substantively similar conclusions suggests that this motivation for parties to "play to their strengths" represents a generalized phenomenon.

2.7. Discussion

Partisan attachments have long been the subject of intensive empirical research, yet their implications for spatial competition and the possibility of party equilibria have received little scholarly attention. Thinking about political competition in terms of partisans giving their preferred parties a non-policy-related advantage enables us to account for features of multiparty competition that the standard Downsian model does not adequately represent. In particular, I have shown how partisan loyalty can illuminate the empirical findings of policy divergence, stability, and representation that characterize party behavior in contemporary democracies. The model also illuminates the strategic disadvantage faced by parties whose partisans are concentrated in the center of the policy space, such as the British Liberal–Social Democratic Alliance.

Although we have seen that the strategic logic of spatial competition under the partisan vote model is complex, the two central forces that drive my results are straightforward. These are: (1) the empirical fact that voters' party identifications correlate with their political ideologies and (2) the theoretical result that under the partisan vote model parties have electoral incentives to appeal on policy grounds to voters who display partisan biases in their direction. Because the partisans of different parties cluster in different regions of the policy space, parties have electoral motivations to present divergent policies, with each party appealing to its own partisans. Because parties can incur severe electoral penalties if they shift their positions away from their partisans' beliefs, parties are motivated to present stable policies. Finally, when parties present policies that appeal to their partisans, by definition they provide faithful policy representations.

Partisanship does not ensure voter support when parties locate far away from their partisans, even when these partisan attachments are relatively strong. Furthermore, when partisan attachments are weak, parties cannot ensure partisan loyalty even by locating near their partisans. This latter case is unlikely to support a multiparty equilibrium because as the degree of partisan attachment declines center parties are subject to being "squeezed" and in turn have an incentive to leapfrog their competitors. However, the empirical applications presented here located policy equilibria over a wide range of partisan voting parameters, and each of these equilibria located the parties near their partisans.

Although the empirical application to the 1987 British general election provides encouraging results, I note in closing that to this point we have yet to incorporate several empirical complications into our model. These include spatial competition over multiple policy dimensions, elections contested by more than three parties, and elections in which voter decisions are probabilistic from the parties' perspectives. I explore these subjects in chapters 4–6. We shall see that, while these complicating factors will lead us to modify our conclusions in certain respects, the central results developed here on policy stability, divergence, and representation in the 1987 British general election generalize to elections in other postwar party systems.

Before considering the complicating factors, however, in chapter 3 I consider another question raised by my simulation results of British voting data: what are the likely patterns of party policy behavior in situations for which policy equilibria do *not* exist?

Party Policy Trajectories in the Absence of Long-Term Equilibrium: Temporal Aspects of Policy Competition in Three-Party Elections

3.1. Introduction

This chapter extends the arguments developed in chapter 2, which concerned the existence of a policy equilibrium during a single election period, in two new directions. The first involves an analysis of the cross-time patterns of party policy competition in three-party elections for situations in which policy equilibria do not exist. I consider several questions. When voters display partisan loyalties, what is the strategic logic that drives disequilibrium results and how are parties' policies likely to evolve over a series of elections in the absence of a long-run policy equilibrium? Will parties present relatively stable policies or will they shift their positions dramatically between elections? Will the policies of competing parties diverge, and will they reflect the positions of the parties' supporters?

The second new direction involves comparing the predictions on party policies I generate from empirical applications to British voting data to British parties' actual policy trajectories during the postwar period. For these comparisons, I rely on a unique data source, the spatial "maps" of parties' policy positions in postwar elections that have been published by the Manifesto Research Group. These maps, which chart the policy positions of all major parties in some 20 democracies during the entire postwar period, are based upon detailed codings of the parties' election programmes. By comparing the temporal predictions generated from the partisan voting model against the spatial mappings published by the MRG, I hope to answer the question: can a spatial model based upon partisan voting account for British parties' actual policy trajectories during the postwar period?

With respect to temporal patterns of three-party competition, I present heuristic arguments that the central strategic motivation that can disrupt equilibrium involves the center party, which in certain cases has incentives to blur the distinctions between its policies and those of one of its rivals. This strategic motivation clashes with the peripheral parties' desire to present divergent policies (a motivation explained in chapter 2), and this tension between rival parties' conflicting objectives disrupts policy equilibrium. However, I then present reasons why, even in situations in which policy equilibria do not exist, parties' positions will typically be reasonably stable and divergent over time. That is, parties will alter their policies between elections, but each party typically varies its positions only within "ideologically delimited" areas of the policy space so that these policies are *stable* but not *static*. Each party's "ideologically delimited" area, moreover, consists of a range of policies that are acceptable to the party's partisans. These heuristic arguments illuminate how policy disequilibrium, as it is conventionally defined by spatial modelers, is nonetheless compatible with policy stability, divergence, and representation by political parties in three-party elections.

With respect to empirical applications to Britain, I find that when policy equilibria do not exist for spatial competition in a partisan electorate vote-seeking parties will nonetheless present reasonably stable, divergent policies that reflect their partisans' beliefs. These results are important, first, because they suggest that the heuristic arguments summarized above, which depend on restrictive assumptions about the distributions of voter preferences, generalize to real world settings in which these assumptions are relaxed. Second, these findings illuminate how the conditions for responsible party government can be satisfied even in the absence of a long-term policy equilibrium. In addition, I find that the temporal predictions I generate on British parties' policy trajectories strongly resemble the empirical patterns identified by the Manifesto Research Group. Thus, the spatial analysis of party competition in a partisan electorate accounts well for British parties' actual behavior during the postwar period.

While the specifics of my heuristic arguments and empirical applications are at times complex, I emphasize that the logic that drives my results is straightforward and revolves around the strategic motivation developed in chapter 2: that in multiparty elections *parties are motivated to appeal on policy grounds to their own partisans, that is, to those voters who are biased toward them for nonpolicy reasons.* We shall see that even in situations for which this motivation does not support a policy equilibrium it typically ensures policy divergence, policy representation, and considerable policy stability on the part of political parties.

I begin in section 3.2 by reviewing the MRG's empirical findings on temporal patterns of party policy competition. Section 3.3 argues heuristically that when long-term policy equilibria do not exist for three-party elections involving a partisan voter distribution the likely outcome is that over time parties will reasonably present stable, divergent policies that represent the views of their partisans. Section 3.4 presents empirical applications to British politics, which demonstrate a surprising degree of fit between the model's theoretical predictions and the MRG's empirical findings. Section 3.5 concludes.

3.2. Temporal Patterns of Policy Competition in Postwar Democracies: Empirical Results from the Manifesto Research Group

The analysis of parties' election programmes carried out by the Manifesto Research Group of the European Consortium for Political Research represents the most ambitious attempt to date to measure parties' policies in postwar democracies.[1] Through an empirical analysis of these programmes, which have been collected from all significant parties in some 20 democracies during the entire postwar period, the MRG has traced the policy evolution of over 80 parties.[2]

The coding procedures used to map the parties' policies from their election programmes are described in several of the MRG's publications, and I review them only briefly here.[3] The logic underlying the coding rules is that parties take positions by emphasizing the importance of certain policy areas compared to others. The coding procedure used to assess a party's policy positions therefore involves sorting the sentences—actually quasi sentences since they include the phrases between colons and semicolons—in the party's election programme into varying categories (e.g., welfare, defense, and law and order) and then taking the percentages in each category as a measure of the party's priorities. By comparing the relative policy emphases in different parties' programmes, one can compare the priorities of different parties; by comparing the emphases in the same party's programmes during different election periods, one can chart changes in this party's policy priorities across time. Hence, the MRG's empirical analyses can be used to analyze parties' policy priorities both *temporally* and *comparatively*.

Budge has undertaken such an analysis of parties' left-right positioning in 20 democracies during the postwar period. In programmatic terms,

> The right end [of the continuum] was constructed by adding together percentaged references to "Capitalist Economics," "Social Conservation," "Freedom and Domestic Human Rights," and "Military: positive." The left end was constructed by adding together percentages for "State intervention," "Peace and cooperation," "Democracy," "Social Services: positive," "Education: positive," and "Labour groups: positive." The final left-right [position] was computed as the total proportion of the [programme] devoted to right-wing references minus the total proportion devoted to left-wing references.[4]

Figure 3.1, which is reproduced from Budge et al. 1998, shows how this procedure works when it is applied to British parties during the postwar period. The parties' positions, as estimated from the MRG's coding procedures, accord well with historical impressions: these policies converge during the "Social Democratic consensus" of the 1950s and 1960s but diverge during the 1970s

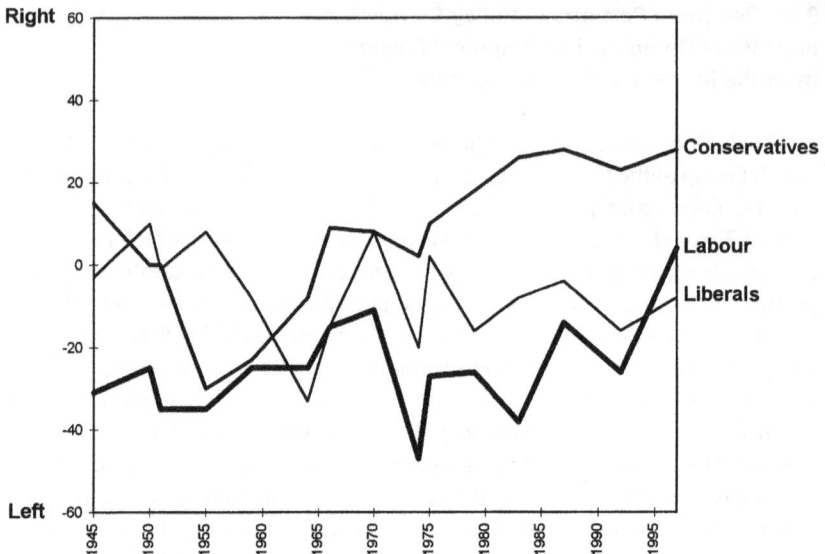

Fig. 3.1.   Left-Right trajectories of the three major British postwar parties as coded by the Manifesto Research Group. (Data from Manifesto Research Group Party Programme Dataset.)

and 1980s, when the Conservatives shifted sharply to the right. The MRG's methodology also registers Labour's shift toward the center between 1992 and 1997.

In addition to according with historical scholarship, figure 3.1 reveals three comparative and temporal patterns of party policies:

1. *The parties differentiate their policy priorities from each other.* This is clearly the case during the period 1945–50 and again after 1959. Only during the period of the Social Democratic consensus is there a move toward policy convergence, and even during this period the Liberals are coded as providing distinct alternatives to the two major parties.

2. *The parties rarely leapfrog, and when leapfrogging does occur it typically involves contiguous parties.* During the entire postwar period, there are only five occasions (1950, 1951, 1955, 1964, and 1997) when the parties leapfrog.[5] Given that there are 14 measured policy shifts for each party (one for each election after 1945) and that at each new election there are three possible instances of leapfrogging (the Liberals can leapfrog Labour, the Liberals can leapfrog the Conservatives, and Labour can leapfrog the Conservatives), the frequency of leapfrogging behavior is only five times out of 3 × 14 = 42 pos-

sible leapfrogging instances or about 12 percent. Furthermore, each of these occasions involves the Liberals, whose centrally located position is contiguous with both Labour and the Conservatives.

3. The parties' policies are not static but change over time. However, the parties' positions typically vary only within ideologically delimited areas of the policy space. Thus, the Labour Party's priorities changed substantially between 1964 and 1969, and again between 1983 and 1987, yet only its 1997 programme was coded as being (barely) to the right of center. Likewise, the Conservatives converged toward the center during the 1950s and veered right during the period of Margaret Thatcher's leadership, yet with the exception of the election programmes of 1954, 1959, and 1964 they are coded as taking right of center positions.

As reported in chapter 1 (see table 1.2), the MRG's empirical findings suggest that each of these patterns of British party competition generalize to other postwar democracies. Thus, in a study of 20 postwar party systems Budge (1994, table 1) found that in every country the proportion of parties' policy shifts that involved leapfrogging fell below 20 percent, as did the frequencies with which parties located outside of their traditional "ideological areas," defined as left of center for such traditionally left-wing groups as the Socialist, Labor, and Communist Parties and as right of center for such traditionally right-wing parties as the Conservatives and Christian Democrats.[6] The equilibrium analysis based upon partisan voting presented in chapter 2 provides one possible explanation for the empirical findings summarized above, namely, that parties plausibly converge to long-term policy equilibria for which parties present stable and divergent policies. However, equilibrium analysis by itself cannot provide a *general* explanation for the MRG's empirical findings, since results of the empirical applications to British politics also disclosed that for certain plausible assumptions about voting behavior policy equilibria did not exist (or at least could not be located in a reasonable number of iterations of party policy shifts in the simulations). For this reason, in seeking to make sense of the MRG's empirical findings I analyze the trajectories of party platforms over a series of elections for situations in which long-run policy equilibria do not exist.

3.3. Explaining Why Party Policies Are Stable but Not Static: Parties' Policy Trajectories in the Absence of a Long-Term Policy Equilibrium

As I noted in section 1.5, I will base my analysis of parties' cross-time policy trajectories primarily upon illustrative examples supported by computer simulations rather than deductive theorems, as in chapter 2. This is because the study of parties' policy trajectories presents severe analytical difficulties, which is why prior spatial analyses on this topic have typically relied on computer simulations (see, e.g., Jackson 1990; Kollman et al. 1992; and Lomborg 1996). The illustrative arguments I present below are designed to highlight the strategic logic of three-party competition in a partisan electorate for situations in which policy equilibria do not exist. My goal is to provide the reader with an intuitive understanding of the reasons why policy equilibria sometimes break down and the likely consequences for parties' cross-time policy trajectories. In the absence of general theorems, these examples obviously cannot provide insights into all possible electoral environments; however, they are intended to isolate strategic factors that recur in several contemporary three-party systems, including that of Britain. In the concluding section, I discuss the general relevance of these arguments for party competition.

Policy Instability without Leapfrogging: Partisanship and Pressures for Policy Change

To gain insights into the trajectories of party platforms when long-run policy equilibria do not exist, the first step is to identify the strategic motivations that are likely to disrupt equilibrium. As we shall see, the primary motivation in three-party contests belongs to the center party, which in some circumstances will seek to converge toward one of its competitors so as to blur the distinction between its own policies and those of this rival. The tension between the center party's incentive to converge and the peripheral parties' incentive to maintain policy divergence may preclude the existence of a long-run policy equilibrium.

To grasp this point, first recall from chapter 2 that in three-party spatial competition under the partisan vote model the two peripheral parties—which were labeled parties L and R and whose partisans were assumed to be concentrated on the left and the right ends of the policy spectrum, respectively—were motivated to diverge from the center party, C, in order to capture some of C's left- and right-most partisans. For the resulting policy equilibria, illustrated in chapter 2 (see figs. 2.4 through 2.6), party C captured no votes from its rivals' partisans but instead lost the support of some of its own partisans. As discussed in section 2.4, this occurs because C suffers a strategic disadvantage in three-party elections: that given its centrist positioning it can converge toward one peripheral party—and thereby recapture the votes of its partisans on the left (or right)—only by diverging from the other peripheral party, thereby forfeiting support from its partisans on the right (or left). Thus, in certain situations this strategic calculation motivates party C to maintain a centrist location that supports a policy equilibrium, albeit one in which C fails to obtain its "normal vote."

The question therefore arises: what is the likely outcome in situations in which party C has a clear electoral motivation to converge toward one of the peripheral parties? Such a scenario is illustrated in figure 3.2A, which shows a stylized voter distribution along with the left-right positions of parties L, C, and R, given as $l = 5.0$, $c = 6.0$, and $r = 7.0$, respectively. As in chapter 2, I assume that voters choose according to the partisan vote model given by equation 2.2. and that the strength, b, of voters' party identifications is set at $b^{1/2} = 1.0$. Thus, in figure 3.2A parties L and R are located at their vote-maximizing positions at a distance $b^{1/2} = 1.0$ to the left and right of party C, respectively. Note that in figure 3.2A the distribution of voters' policy preferences is also identical to those analyzed throughout chapter 2. But there is an important difference with respect to voter partisanship: here I assume that the distributions of the peripheral parties' partisans are more nearly equal in size, with voters in the policy interval [1.0,4.5] identifying with party L and those in the interval [7.5,11.0] identifying with party R. Given the peripheral parties' optimal positioning, party L captures the support of all voters located to the left of $l = 5.0$ (including C's left-most partisans), while R is supported by all the voters (including C's right-wing partisans) located to the right of $r = 7.0$.

Now, consider how changing our assumptions on the partisan distribution alters party C's strategic motivations—and hence the logic of party competition—compared to the results reported in chapter 2. In that chapter, we saw that party C could not enhance its vote share by converging toward one of its rivals. However, this is *not* the case here because the number of C's partisans located to the left of L's policy position ($l = 5.0$) significantly exceeds the number of partisans located to the right of R's position ($r = 7.0$). *In this case, party C is motivated to converge toward party L because it gains more votes on the left (by blurring the distinction between its policies and those of L) than it loses on the right (by increasing its policy distance from R).* To see this, consider the electoral consequences if C shifts left to about 5.6, as shown in figure 3.2B.[7] Note that this figure shows an enlarged view of the portion of the voter distribution between 3.0 and 9.0. This leftward shift motivates party C's left-wing partisans located in the policy interval [4.5,5.0] to switch their votes back to C because these voters' partisan attachments now outweigh their (slight) preference for L's policies.[8] While C's leftward shift sacrifices support from the narrow band of C's partisans located in the policy interval [6.7,7.0], who defect to party R,[9] it is easily seen that C's electoral gains on the left outweigh its losses on the right.

Note that in this example C gains additional votes by shifting its position *but without leapfrogging its competitors*. Party C is motivated to shift its position in order to blur the distinction between its policies and those of L. It is motivated to avoid leapfrogging, first, because this is not necessary in order to blur policy differences and, second, because, as outlined in chapter 2, leapfrogging

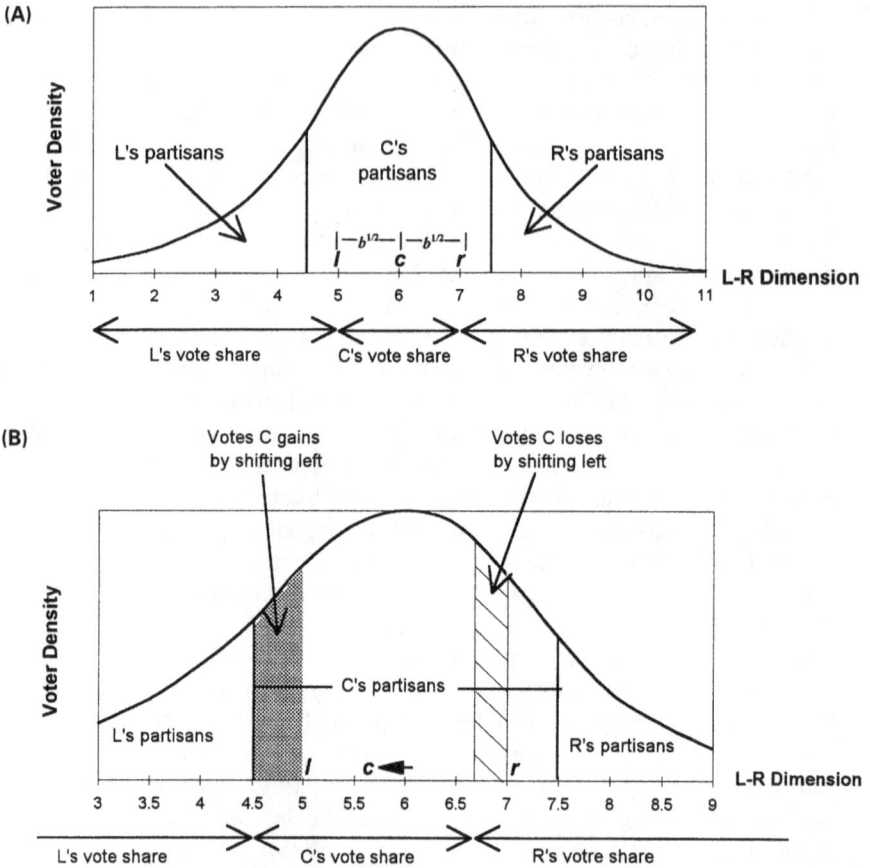

Fig. 3.2. An illustration of strategic incentives that can lead to oscillating policies under the biased voter model, with strength, b, of voter partisanship set at $b = 1.0$. (A) Initial voter and party configuration; (B) C's vote-maximizing position given $l = 4$ and $r = 6$ (magnified view); (C) Optimal policy responses by L and R given that C shifts to 5.6; (D) Optimal policy response by C given $l = 4.6$ and $c = 6.6$.

parties are typically motivated to present extreme policy positions, which are electorally unattractive.

To gain insights into the temporal pattern of party policies for the situation pictured in figure 3.2, consider how parties L and R will respond to C's policy shift from $c = 6.0$ to $c = 5.6$. Because L can obtain votes from C's partisans only by differentiating its policies from those of C, L is motivated to shift to the left, thereby thwarting C's effort to blur the policy differences between the two

(C)

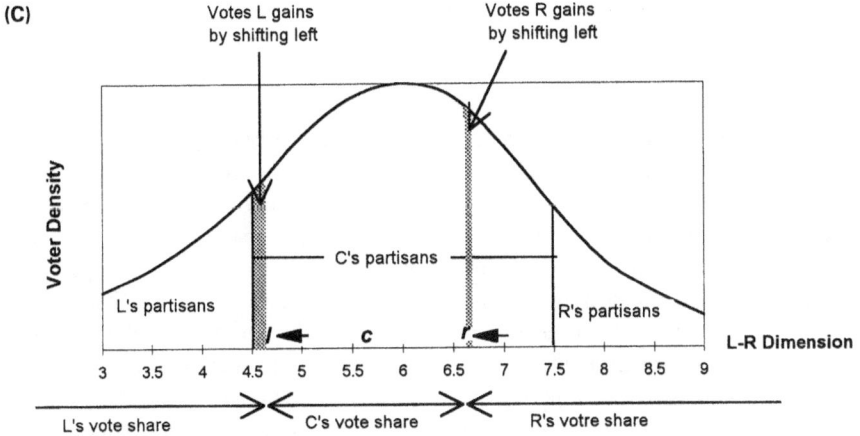

(D)

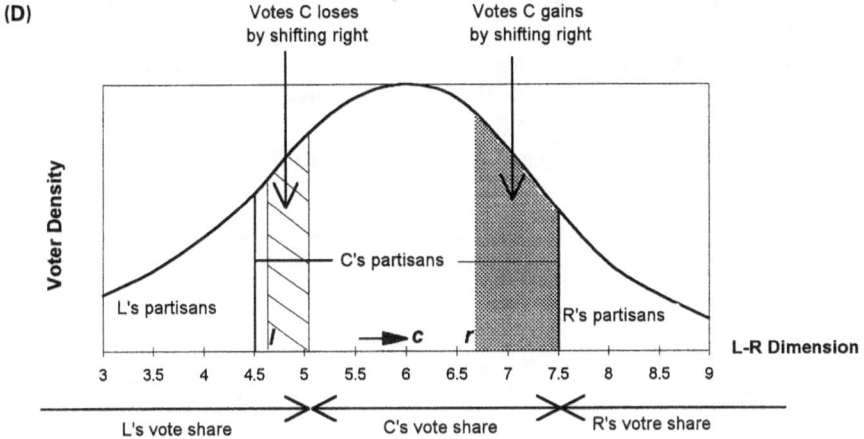

Fig. 3.2. (*continued*)

parties. Specifically, L maximizes support by diverging to a position to the left of C by the distance $b^{1/2} = 1$, at about $l = 4.6$, where it attracts all voters located to its left (fig. 3.2C).[10] Meanwhile, party R gains additional votes by shifting left from 7.0 to 6.6 because the latter position maintains a significant policy differential, compared to C, but also attracts additional C partisans located on the center right.

Note that the resulting party configuration pictured in figure 3.2C is identical to that of 3.2A, except that each party has shifted left by 0.4 units. Due to this leftward shift, the number of C's partisans who defect to R (i.e., all those in the policy interval [6.6,7.5]) now greatly exceeds the number who defect to L. Hence, for this party configuration C's strategic motivation is reversed, in that it has electoral incentives to shift toward party R (fig. 3.1D), because such a policy shift gains more votes on the right than it loses on the left. Specifically, C's new optimal strategy is to co-opt R's position by shifting right to about 6.15; with this rightward shift, C captures the votes of its right-wing partisans located in the policy interval [6.6,7.5], while losing support only from those voters located in the narrow policy interval [4.60,5.05]—a net vote gain.[11]

Party C's rightward shift will trigger further policy adjustments by parties L and R, which will provoke C to again adjust its policies, and so on. Figure 3.3 maps the sequence of parties' policy shifts, that is, the figure shows the parties' successive vote-maximizing positions, with each party successively updating its position in response to policy shifts by its rivals. This shows that the parties continually vary their positions without reaching a policy equilibrium. The logic that drives disequilibrium in this hypothetical case revolves around the strategic incentives created by voter partisanship. Voters' partisan loyalties motivate the peripheral parties L and R to differentiate their policies from those of party C, while C is motivated to blur its policy differences with its rivals. Since rival parties' policies cannot be simultaneously divergent and convergent, no long-term policy equilibrium exists.

Note that in figure 3.3 the trajectory of party platforms is such that parties'

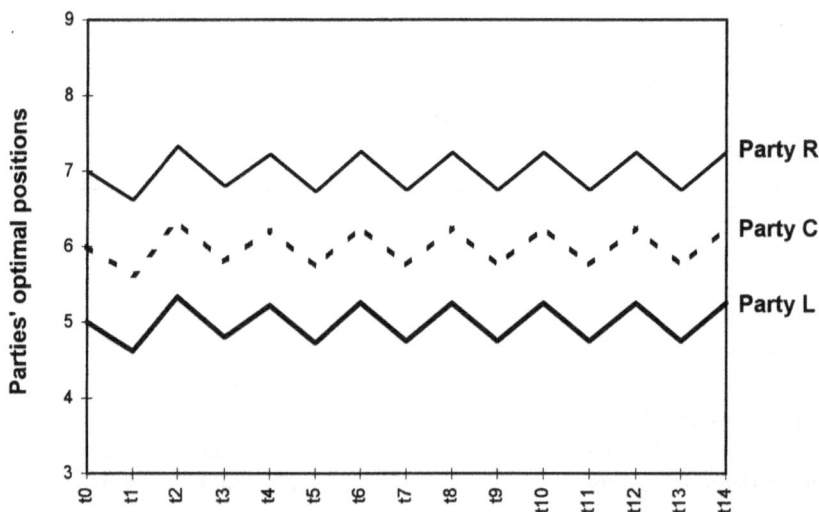

Fig. 3.3. Parties' policy trajectories for the voter distribution given in figure 3.2A

policies are *stable* but not *static,* in that parties vary their policies over time but always locate within circumscribed intervals of the policy space. Furthermore, the parties do not leapfrog. *These are precisely the empirical patterns identified by the MRG.* Thus, in this hypothetical example the logic of party spatial competition with partisan voters appears to be consistent with actual party behavior in postwar democracies.

Why Instances of Leapfrogging Typically Involve Contiguous Parties

An additional pattern that emerges from the MRG's empirical findings is that, while leapfrogging is uncommon, when instances of leapfrogging do occur they typically involve contiguous parties. In the context of three-party systems such as those of Britain and (until recently) Germany, this implies that cases of leapfrogging usually involve such parties as the centrist Liberal Democrats or the German FDP. Can a spatial model build on partisan voting account for this empirical finding?

The answer to this question is yes. This is because when voter partisanship correlates with ideology—again assuming that partisanship influences the vote independently of ideology—the center party can typically retain the votes of some of its partisans when it leapfrogs, while a peripheral party that leapfrogs over both of its rivals typically forfeits the support of a large proportion of its partisan constituency. Hence, leapfrogging is typically more electorally attractive for the center than for the peripheral parties (although we have seen that it is rarely advisable for *any* party). To grasp this point, consider the situation illustrated in figure 3.4, in which parties L, C, and R are again initially located at $l = 5.0$, $c = 6.0$, and $r = 7.0$, respectively, and the strength of voters' partisan attachments is again set at $b^{1/2} = 1$. Now compare the electoral consequences when party C leapfrogs L and locates at $c' = 4.0$ (fig. 3.4A) to the consequences when party R leapfrogs to the position $r' = 4.0$ (fig. 3.4B). When either C or R locates at 4.0, it captures the support of all of L's partisans located to the left of 4.0 because these voters' policy preferences for the leapfrogging party outweigh their partisan attachments to L. However, note that by locating at $c' = 4.0$ party C can additionally capture the votes of its own leftist partisans located in the policy interval [4,0,4.5], whose partisan attachments outweigh their slight policy preference for L. Party R cannot attract these voters' support by locating at $r' = 4.0$ since these voters are indifferent between L and R on partisan grounds and hence will support L based upon policy comparisons. Thus, party C wins more votes by leapfrogging than does party R because C can leapfrog a peripheral party and retain the support of part of its own partisan constituency.

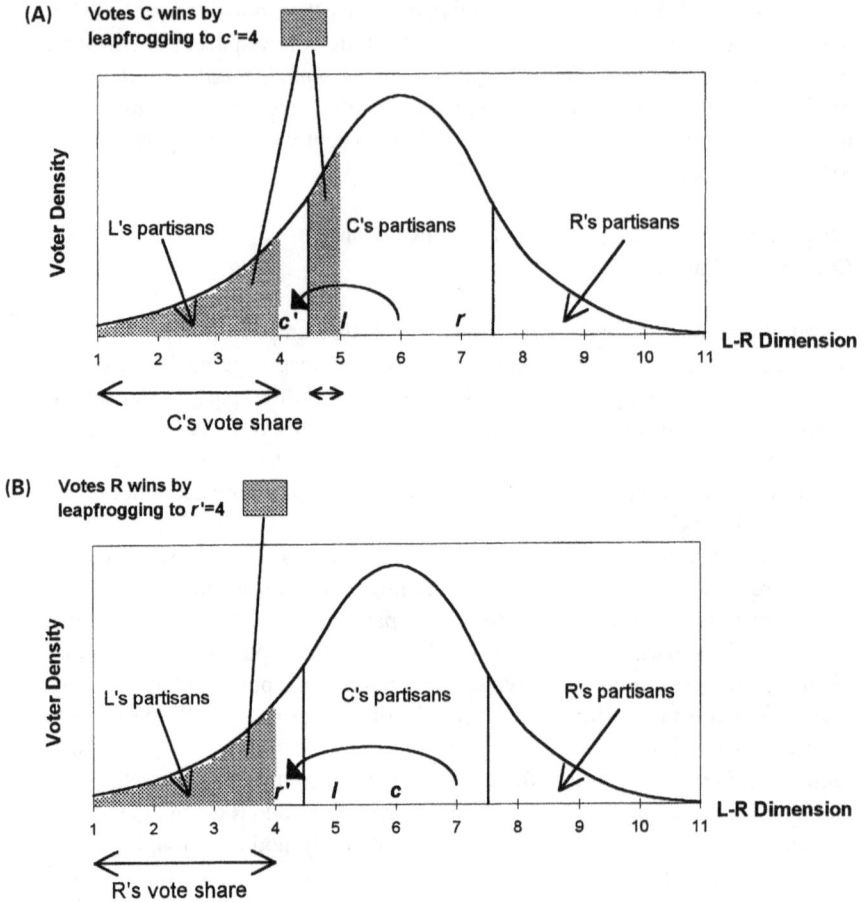

Fig. 3.4.   Illustration of why leapfrogging typically involves contiguous parties, with strength, *b*, of voters' partisan attachment set at $b = 1.0$. (*A*) Electoral consequences when C leapfrogs L; (*B*) Electoral consequences when R leapfrogs L.

Why Dynamic Party Trajectories are Compatible with Faithful Policy Representations

The examples presented above take as their starting point the premise that parties, at least initially, take positions that reflect their partisans' policy preferences. While this assumption illuminates the logic of why vote-seeking parties may pursue policy trajectories similar to those reported by the MRG, might it nonetheless be possible to develop alternative explanations for these policy trajectories that do not invoke the assumption of responsible parties?

In general, the answer to this question is no in the sense that even if parties occasionally propose policies inconsistent with their partisans' beliefs the fact of voters' partisan loyalties exerts strategic pressures on parties to rebound in the direction of their partisans' preferences, following a single "unrepresentative" policy proposal. The reason for this is the same one given in section 2.4: that policy configurations in which parties present policies at odds with their partisans' beliefs are inherently unstable. The scenario pictured in figure 3.5A illustrates this point. This shows a situation identical to the one pictured in figure 3.2A, except that the positions of parties L and R have been reversed so that L is located near R's partisans, while R is located near L's partisans. With each peripheral party located near the other's partisans, party L can improve its vote share by leapfrogging to the position l', slightly to the left of r, which in turn

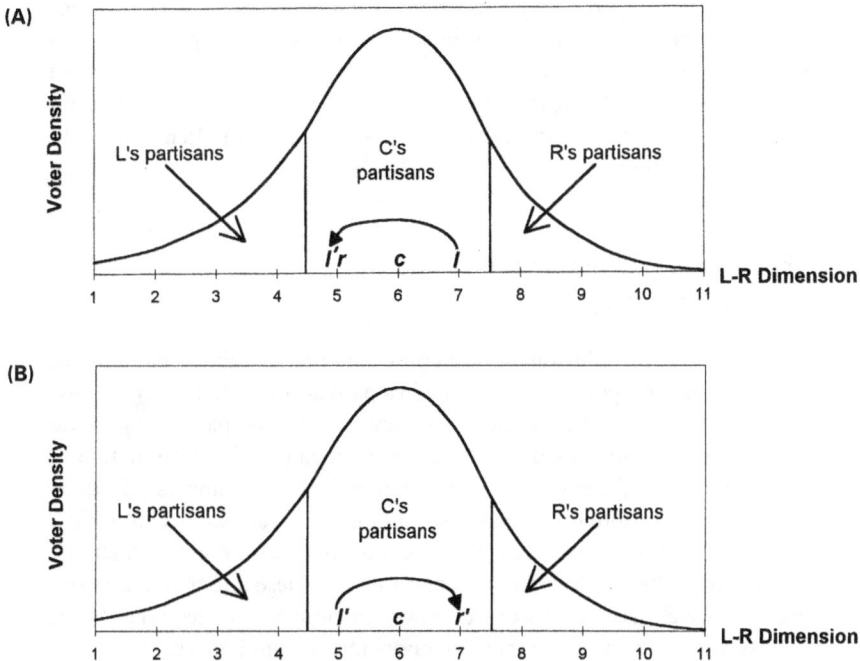

(A)

(B)

Fig. 3.5. Illustration of the instability of policy configurations in which parties locate far from their partisans, with strength, b, of partisan attachment set at $b = 1.0$. (A) Party L's optimal position given $c = 6$ and $r = 5$; (B) Party R's optimal position given $l' = 5$ and $c = 6$.

motivates R to leapfrog to $r' = l$, L's initial position (fig. 3.5B). At this point, the party and voter configuration is indeed identical to that of figure 3.2A, for which we saw that the trajectory of parties' policies was such that the parties presented stable but not static positions that reflected their supporters' beliefs. Hence, even when we deliberately "start" the parties at extremely unrepresentative policy positions, the long-term party trajectories that ensue find the parties immediately reverting to much more representative locations.

In summary, the examples presented in this section suggest reasons why, when three parties compete for votes from a partisan electorate and no equilibrium exists, the long-term trajectories of party policies will follow the empirical patterns identified by the Manifesto Research Group. Long-run policy equilibria may not exist in situations in which the center party is motivated to converge toward one of its rivals because this strategy conflicts with the peripheral parties' motivations to present divergent policy positions. However, in such situations the center party typically refrains from leapfrogging because, as outlined in chapter 2, the fact of voter partisanship forces leapfrogging parties to present extreme policies, which are likely to prove electorally unattractive. Furthermore, when leapfrogging does occur it usually involves contiguous parties because the center party typically gains more votes from leapfrogging than the peripheral parties do. Finally, parties typically present policies that reflect their supporters' beliefs because "unrepresentative" party policy configurations are extremely unstable and motivate parties to readjust their policies in the direction of their supporters.

3.4. Parties' Policy Trajectories in Britain: Empirical Applications

To the extent that the illustrative examples summarized above capture the strategic logic of party policy competition in a partisan electorate, they provide insights into why, even in the absence of policy equilibrium, parties in postwar democracies present policies that are stable, divergent, and representative of their supporters' beliefs. However, as in chapter 2, these examples rely upon stylized assumptions about the voter distribution, which apparently limit their generalizibility. Below I present simulation results based on election survey data from Britain that model party trajectories when these strong assumptions are relaxed. As we shall see, this exercise raises a number of conceptual issues, particularly with respect to how best to model the evolution of voter attitudes over time; however, I find that alternative assumptions about voter attitudes yield similar results on party policy trajectories so that my conclusions do not depend on a particular model of how voters evolve. These conclusions bear on the question: can the illustrative arguments developed above furnish a *general* explanation for responsible party government in three-party systems?

On Using Survey Data to Analyze Temporal Patterns of Party Policies: Two Approaches to Modeling the Evolution of Voter Attitudes

In analyzing dynamic aspects of party strategies using voter distributions derived from election survey data, it is desirable to incorporate the changes in voters' policy preferences (and partisanship) that occur over a series of elections. The most straightforward method to accomplish this would be to analyze voter distributions derived from a series of national election studies. However, as I discuss in appendix B, there are several reasons why this approach is unfeasible, especially for developing explanations for the MRG's findings that generalize across party systems. These problems include the lack of available longitudinal survey data in many Western democracies and changes in survey question wordings over time so that voter responses from different election surveys are often not comparable. Given that this preferred approach is unfeasible, I instead analyze party policy trajectories using two alternative sets of assumptions about the evolution of voter attitudes. The first assumption is that the voter distribution is stable over time. Specifically, I ask the question: if a voting distribution derived from a *single* election survey were stable—that is, if this distribution was unchanging over a series of elections—what would the trajectory of party policies look like over a series of elections? While this assumption of complete stability on the part of the electorate is obviously a simplification, this approach has previously been employed in a number of spatial modeling studies on the evolution of party policies (e.g., Kollman et al. 1992; Lomborg 1996; Merrill and Grofman 1999, chap. 9), in addition to which there is strong evidence that the Left-Right orientations of mass publics in Western democracies—including Britain—have been quite stable, at least over the past two decades (see, e.g., Dalton 1996, 137, fig. 6.4; and Rose and McCallister 1990, 23). For the second approach, which I describe in detail below, I instead asked the question: if a voter distribution derived from a single election study is *randomly varied* over time, what is the likely trajectory of party policies? This alternative approach allows me to investigate the effects of temporal changes in voter attitudes.

As I discuss below, it is probable that neither approach by itself perfectly captures the evolution of the British electorate over the postwar period; however, given the limitations of the available data, both approaches provide reasonable starting points for investigating trajectories of party policies. Furthermore, to the extent that these alternative methodologies yield similar conclusions we will have increased confidence that our results capture the underlying logic of party competition in a biased electorate. In this spirit, I proceed.

Party Policy Trajectories When the Voter Distribution is Stable

Because this chapter concerns party trajectories in the absence of the long-run equilibria that I located in simulations based on the 1987 British General Election Study, here I instead analyze policy trajectories using data from the 1992 BGES.[12] As in chapter 2, I generate the voter distribution based upon respondents' views on the nationalization of industry.[13] Figure 3.6A shows the distribution of respondents, ranging from 1 ("Nationalize more industries") to 11 ("Sell off nationalized industries"). Distributions are given for respondents who reported thinking of themselves as Labourites, Liberal Democrats,[14] or Conservatives as well as for independents, that is, those who reported no partisan identification.[15] Also shown are the parties' positions, as coded by a panel of experts who were asked to place the British parties in early 1993 (see Huber and Inglehart 1995); I will refer to these as the parties' *actual positions.* As was the case for the 1987 data analyzed in chapter 2, here we find a correlation between respondent partisanship and views on nationalization, with Labour sympathizers concentrated on the left and Conservatives on the right of the policy continuum. However, note that this correlation is weaker in 1992 than was the case in 1987 (see fig. 2.8A) in that in 1992 the Conservative Party's partisans are more centrist in orientation, with a significant minority of Conservatives (about 15 percent) actually located to the left of the midpoint 6.0. We shall see that this moderate Conservative distribution has an important effect on parties' policy trajectories.

The central questions are: do policy equilibria exist, and if not will the trajectories of party policy strategies for this empirical voter distribution follow the logic outlined in the heuristic arguments presented above? To answer these questions, I carried out calculations for varying values of the strength, b, of voter partisanship and used the results to generate spatial "maps" of the parties' successive vote-maximizing positions. (The methodology and assumptions I employed for this exercise are identical to the ones described in appendix A.) Here I present examples that illustrate this process given the assumption $b^{1/2} = 3$, about the value Endersby and Galatas (1997) estimate for voting in the 1992 British general election. Initially in the simulations, the parties were located at their actual positions along the nationalization scale, as shown in figure 3.6A. Next, with Labour and the Liberal Democrats fixed at these positions I varied the Conservatives' position from 1 to 11 in increments of 0.1 and computed their aggregate vote for each position. Figure 3.6B, which plots the Conservative vote (the vertical axis), shows that the Conservatives maximize votes by locating at 7.0, more than one unit to the right of the Liberal Democrats. This

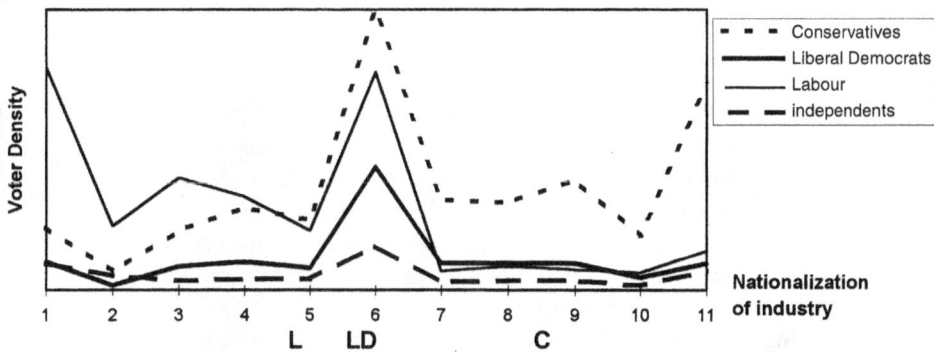

(A)

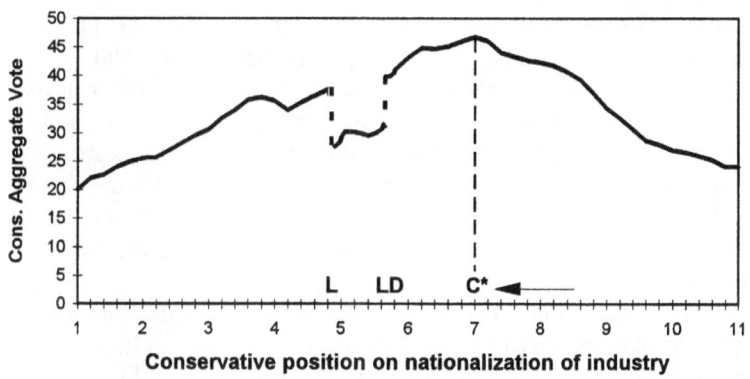

(B)

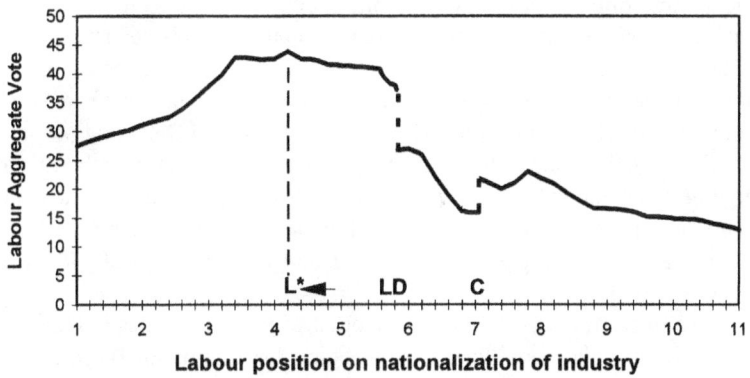

(C)

Fig. 3.6. Analysis of British parties' policy trajectories for the voter distribution derived from the 1992 British General Election Study. (*A*) Distribution of British voters' and parties' policy positions; (*B*) Conservative vote for varying positions given that $b^{1/2} = 3$; (*C*) Labour vote for varying policy positions given that $b^{1/2} = 3$.

right-wing positioning is optimal because it differentiates the Conservatives from their rivals and thereby attracts support from right-wing Liberal Democrats and Labour partisans. I then shifted the Conservatives to 7.0, their vote-maximizing position.

With the Conservative position shifted to 7.0 and the Liberal Democrats placed at their actual position, I next used an identical approach to locate Labour's optimal position (fig. 3.6C). This position is 4.2, which is 1.5 units to the left of the Liberal Democrats and nearly three units to the left of the Conservatives. Like the Conservatives on the right, Labour maximizes votes by locating on the left because this positioning captures support from leftist Conservative and Liberal Democratic partisans.

Using this approach, I next calculated the Liberal Democrats' vote-maximizing position, with Labour shifted to 4.2 and the Conservatives at 7.0. I then proceeded to calculate each party's vote-maximizing position in turn, with each calculation updated to reflect the rival parties' policy shifts. Unlike the results reported in chapter 2 for 1987, here I did not locate an equilibrium in vote-maximizing strategies. Instead, I found that over the course of 100 computed policy shifts for each party *the parties continually varied their positions but seldom leapfrogged and typically located within "ideologically delimited" areas of the policy space, with the Conservatives consistently locating on the right and Labour on the left. These are precisely the empirical patterns identified by the MRG.*

This result is illustrated in figure 3.7, which shows the trajectory of party positions over the first 14 of the 100 successive policy shifts I computed for each party (I illustrate the results for 14 "moves" because this corresponds to the number of postwar policy shifts measured by the MRG in Britain, one for each election held after 1945).[16] Over the course of this sequence, Labour's vote-maximizing position varies between 3.1 and 4.8, while the Conservatives shift between 5.9 and 8.4. Furthermore, these parties do not leapfrog. However, note that over the course of the 15 elections the Liberal Democrats *do* leapfrog the Conservatives and Labour. These results are consistent with the illustrative arguments developed earlier, which state that when policy equilibria do not exist in three-party systems the parties will present policies that are stable but not static, that leapfrogging will be infrequent, and that it will typically involve contiguous parties.

An interesting question to consider is: why do the parties fail to converge to long-term policy equilibria for the voter distribution analyzed here when such equilibria were consistently located for the distribution analyzed in chapter 2, which appears quite similar? The answer revolves around the fact, highlighted above, that one difference between the voter distributions of 1987 (fig. 2.8A) and 1992 (fig. 3.6A) is that the 1992 distribution locates a significant number of Conservative partisans to the left of center, which is of course in-

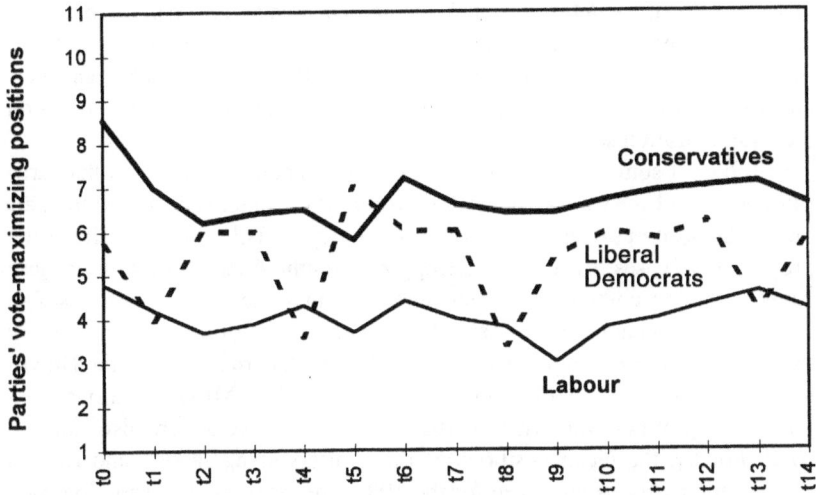

Fig. 3.7. Spatial mapping of British parties' policy trajectories for simulations based on a stable distribution of respondents from the 1992 British General Election Study, with strength, *b*, of partisan bias set at $b^{1/2} = 3.0$.

consistent with the stylized distributions used in the heuristic arguments. The presence of these "leftist Conservatives" creates strategic incentives for the Conservative Party to moderate its policies in an effort to secure these partisans' votes. As a result, the Liberal Democrats are more tightly squeezed in the simulations based on the 1992 voter data than was the case in the simulations based on the 1987 data. This squeezing effect in turn motivates the Liberal Democrats to periodically adjust their position, which disrupts convergence toward a policy equilibrium.

Temporal Patterns for Varying Degrees of Voter Bias

The essential features of a spatial mapping of party positions can be summarized by means of parameters that measure the degree to which parties differentiate their policies, the incidence of leapfrogging, and parties' tendencies to locate within circumscribed ideological areas. Thus, for figure 3.7, the mean Labour position (i.e., the average of Labour's 15 policy positions) is 4.1, that of the Liberal Democrats is 5.8, and that of the Conservatives is 6.95. The differences in these values capture the degree of policy differentiation. In addition, of the 42 party policy shifts (each party shifts 14 times over the course of 15 elections), approximately 24 percent (10 out of 42) involve leapfrogging and 100 percent (5 out of 5) of these leapfrogging incidents involve contiguous parties.[17] Finally, if we define Labour's ideological area as any position to the left of 6.0 (the center of the 1–11 scale) and the Conservatives' as any position to the right of 6.0, these parties take positions outside their ideological area 3 percent of the time (one out of 30; in fig. 3.7, the Conservatives locate at 5.9 on the nationalization scale at time $t5$).

Table 3.1 summarizes the results of temporal competition under the partisan vote model for varying degrees of voter bias. Columns 2–4 give the parties' mean positions over the course of 100 policy shifts.[18] Column 5 shows the proportion of cases involving leapfrogging, column 6 the proportion of these cases involving contiguous parties, and column 7 the incidence of cases in which parties locate outside their ideological areas. Results are reported for varying values of b, ranging from $b^{1/2} = 0$ (which corresponds to the Downsian model) to $b^{1/2} = 3$. For comparison, results of the MRG's historical spatial mapping of postwar British parties included in table 3.1 are also summarized. Finally, the mean positions of the Conservative, Labour, and Liberal Democratic partisans are given for the 1992 empirical voter distribution used in the simulations.

Table 3.1 shows that when b is low the parties take quite similar positions on average and the parties consistently leapfrog. This is consistent with stan-

TABLE 3.1.   Patterns of Party Policy Trajectories under the Partisan Vote Model for Simulations on a Stable Voter Distribution

Strength of Partisan Attachment (1)	Mean Party Positions			Leapfrogging		Positions Outside Ideological Area (7)
	Labour (2)	Liberal Democrats (3)	Conservatives (4)	Overall (5)	Contiguous (6)	
$b^{1/2} = 0$	5.4	5.7	5.6	50%	69%	45%
$b^{1/2} = 0.5$	5.2	5.7	5.9	47	79	40
$b^{1/2} = 1.0$	5.0	5.8	6.2	34	77	28
$b^{1/2} = 1.5$	4.9	5.7	6.3	22	88	24
$b^{1/2} = 2.0$	4.7	5.5	6.2	24	100	10
$b^{1/2} = 2.5$	4.6	5.9	6.5	14	100	8
$b^{1/2} = 3.0$	4.3	5.6	7.0	16	88	6
Partisans' mean positions	4.2	6.0	7.1			
MRG's empirical results				12	100	14

Note: Simulations are based on the respondent distribution on nationalization of industry from the 1992 British General Election Study.

Column 5 gives the percentages of parties' policy shifts that involve leapfrogging and column 6 the percentages of these cases that involve contiguous parties. Column 7 gives the percentages of parties' policy positions that fall outside the party's ideological area (Labour's ideological area is defined as the policy interval [1,6]; the Conservatives' ideological area is the interval [6,11]).

dard Downsian analysis (see section 1.3), which predicts that in three-party elections involving a nonpartisan electorate the parties are motivated to present extremely similar positions, which in turn encourages leapfrogging. For larger values of b, however, policy divergence increases, leapfrogging declines precipitously, and parties usually locate within their own ideological areas. When the degree of voter bias exceeds $b^{1/2} = 1.0$, the frequency with which parties leapfrog or locate outside their ideological areas is roughly similar to the parties' historical behavior, as measured by the MRG, although the frequency of leapfrogging is slightly higher in the simulations. Finally, note that for even moderate degrees of partisan attachment (e.g., $b^{1/2} \geq 1.0$) the parties' mean positions over the course of their policy trajectories are similar to the mean positions of their partisans.

Party Policy Trajectories for an Evolving Voter Distribution

The simulations based on the 1992 British voter distribution remove by assumption a potential source of instability in parties' policy trajectories: parties vary their policies over time in response to shifts in public opinion (see, e.g., Stimson et al. 1995 and McDonald et al. 1998). To investigate the effects of an evolving voter distribution, I reanalyzed the parties' policy trajectories using an alternative methodology, which varied the voter distribution over time. This approach proceeded as follows. First, a random sample of 200 respondents was drawn from the 1992 voter distribution pictured in figure 3.6A. Next, each party was initially located at its actual policy position for the 1992 election, and the parties were then successively relocated to their computed vote-maximizing positions, with each calculation updated to reflect the rival parties' policy shifts. (Note that to this point the approach is the same as that used for the simulations described earlier for the stable voter distribution, except that here the voter distribution is a random sample from the 1992 BGES). However, here this process continued for only four "moves" rather than 100, as in the earlier simulations. Next, with the parties located in the configuration they had reached after four moves, *a new random sample of 200 respondents was drawn from the 1992 voter distribution* and the parties then successively updated their positions four more times. This process was repeated over the course of 25 random voter distributions or 100 party policy moves in all.[19]

The point of these policy simulations was of course to investigate the likely trajectories of party policies when the voter distribution evolved over a series of elections. Because each voter sample was drawn from the same 1992 distribution, one might think that all distributions would be similar. However, because each sample involved a relatively small number of voters (200), there were significant variations in the distributions of voters' policy preferences as well as in the proportions (and distributions) of each party's partisans.[20] In this

way, this simulation strategy captured the moderate—but potentially important—changes in the electorate that occur over a series of elections.

Results for Simulations Based on the 1992 Voter Distribution
The question arises: will the trajectory of party policies based upon simulations
for this "evolving" voter distribution be similar to the trajectories computed for
the stable distribution analyzed above? The answer to this question is yes. Figure 3.8 shows the spatial mapping of the first 14 of the 100 successive policy
shifts computed for each party when the strength of voter partisanship was set
at $b^{1/2} = 3$. Compared to the earlier spatial mapping generated for the stable
voter distribution (fig. 3.7), the simulations on the evolving distribution show
comparable party trajectories, with the Labour Party consistently locating on
the left, and the Conservatives on the right, of the policy continuum. Leapfrogging is slightly more frequent for the simulations with the evolving distribution, and there is one occasion in which the Conservatives leapfrog Labour.
Still, both sets of simulations reveal the same temporal patterns on party policies: party policies are dispersed, parties rarely leapfrog, and leapfrogging usually involves contiguous parties.

Table 3.2 summarizes the results of party trajectories for the simulations
with an evolving voter distribution for varying strengths, b, of partisan attach-

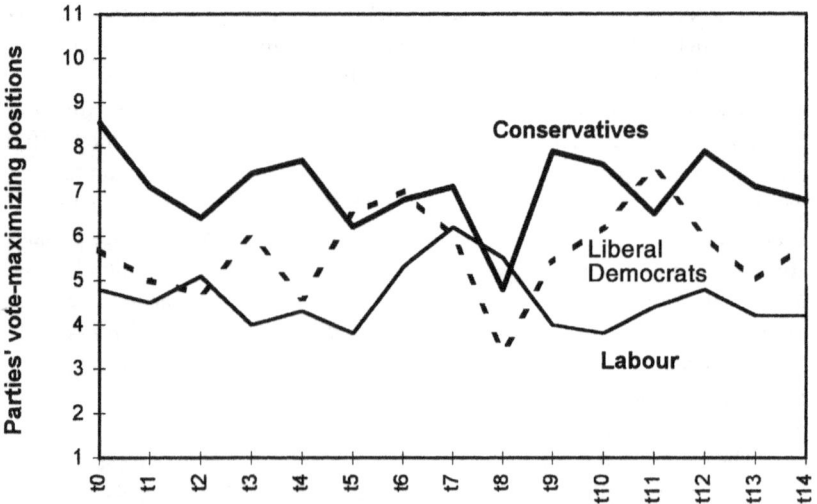

Fig. 3.8. Spatial mapping of British parties' policy trajectories for simulations based on evolving distributions of respondents from the 1992
British General Election Study, with strength, b, of partisan bias set at
$b^{1/2} = 3.0$.

TABLE 3.2.   Patterns of Party Policy Trajectories under the Partisan Vote Model for Simulations on a Variable Voter Distribution

Strength of Partisan Attachment (1)	Mean Party Positions			Leapfrogging		Positions Outside Ideological Area (7)
	Labour (2)	Liberal Democrats (3)	Conservatives (4)	Overall (5)	Contiguous (6)	
$b^{1/2} = 0$	5.6	5.7	5.8	50%	63%	49%
$b^{1/2} = 0.5$	5.2	5.8	6.0	36	75	37
$b^{1/2} = 1.0$	4.9	5.8	6.3	32	73	34
$b^{1/2} = 1.5$	4.9	6.0	6.4	28	88	20
$b^{1/2} = 2.0$	4.7	5.7	6.4	24	89	18
$b^{1/2} = 2.5$	4.4	5.6	6.3	18	77	11
$b^{1/2} = 3.0$	4.5	5.7	7.1	21	92	11
Partisans' mean positions	4.2	6.1	7.2			
MRG's empirical results				12	100	14

Note: Simulations are based on random samples drawn from the respondent distribution on nationalization of industry from the 1992 British General Election Study.
   Column 5 gives the percentages of parties' policy shifts that involve leapfrogging and column 6 the percentages of these cases that involve contiguous parties. Column 7 gives the percentages of parties' policy positions that fall outside the party's ideological area (Labour's ideological area is defined as the policy interval [1,6]; the Conservatives' ideological area is the interval [6,11]).

ment. The results are similar to those reported in table 3.1 for the simulations based on stable voter distributions. In particular, the mean party positions over the course of the simulation (columns 2–4) are virtually identical, regardless of whether the voter distribution is evolving or stable; this indicates that the degree of policy divergence by parties does not depend on our assumptions about the voter distribution. The incidence of leapfrogging reported in table 3.2 (columns 5–6) and the frequency with which parties located outside of their ideological areas (column 7) do increase slightly compared to the results reported in table 3.1. This indicates that when the voter distribution evolves over time parties' policies become slightly less stable and less representative of their partisans' beliefs; these differences undoubtedly stem from the argument, advanced earlier, that evolution of the voter distribution plausibly motivates parties to change their policies. However, note that these differences are very marginal. The essential conclusion that emerges from these simulations is that party policies will follow similar trajectories regardless of whether one assumes that voter attitudes are completely stable or that they undergo moderate change over time.

Results for Simulations Based on the 1987 Voter Distribution
To ensure that my conclusions about party policy trajectories with an evolving electorate did not depend on idiosyncrasies of the 1992 distribution, I performed an additional set of simulations based on the 1987 distribution, which was analyzed in chapter 2 (see fig. 2.8A). The assumptions and methodology I employed for these simulations were identical to those used for the simulations based on the 1992 data, that is, random samples of 200 respondents were successively drawn from the 1987 voter distribution and parties then shifted their policies four times for each voter sample. Table 3.3 reports complete simulation results for varying degrees of partisan attachment, while figure 3.9 shows the spatial mapping of the first 14 moves of the party policy trajectory computed for $b^{1/2} = 3$. Both the figure and the table reveal interesting patterns. The results summarized in table 3.3 show that the patterns of party policy trajectories obtained using the 1987 voter distribution mirror the results based on data from 1992 in that parties present stable, divergent policies that reflect their supporters' beliefs. These patterns are reflected in the spatial mapping in figure 3.9, which reveals a second interesting result: that over the course of the 14 party policy shifts there is only one instance in which a party presents the same policy during two consecutive time periods (the Conservatives locate at 7.9 at

TABLE 3.3. Further Simulations on Patterns of Party Policy Trajectories under the Partisan Vote Model for a Variable Voter Distribution

Strength of Partisan Attachment (1)	Mean Party Positions			Leapfrogging		Positions Outside Ideological Area (7)
	Labour (2)	Liberal Democrats (3)	Conservatives (4)	Overall (5)	Contiguous (6)	
$b^{1/2} = 0$	6.1	6.1	6.3	47%	68%	54%
$b^{1/2} = 0.5$	5.8	6.1	6.6	33	80	31
$b^{1/2} = 1.0$	5.4	6.2	6.7	25	85	27
$b^{1/2} = 1.5$	4.9	6.0	7.3	21	90	15
$b^{1/2} = 2.0$	4.6	6.1	7.4	22	87	8
$b^{1/2} = 2.5$	4.6	5.9	7.8	17	87	12
$b^{1/2} = 3.0$	4.5	6.2	8.0	18	100	5
Partisans' mean positions	4.4	6.3	8.0			
MRG's empirical results				12	100	14

Note: Simulations are based on random samples drawn from the respondent distribution on nationalization of industry from the 1987 British General Election Study.

Column 5 gives the percentages of parties' policy shifts that involve leapfrogging and column 6 the percentages of these cases that involve contiguous parties. Column 7 gives the percentages of parties' policy positions that fall outside the party's ideological area (Labour's ideological area is defined as the policy interval [1,6]; the Conservatives' ideological area is the interval [6,11]).

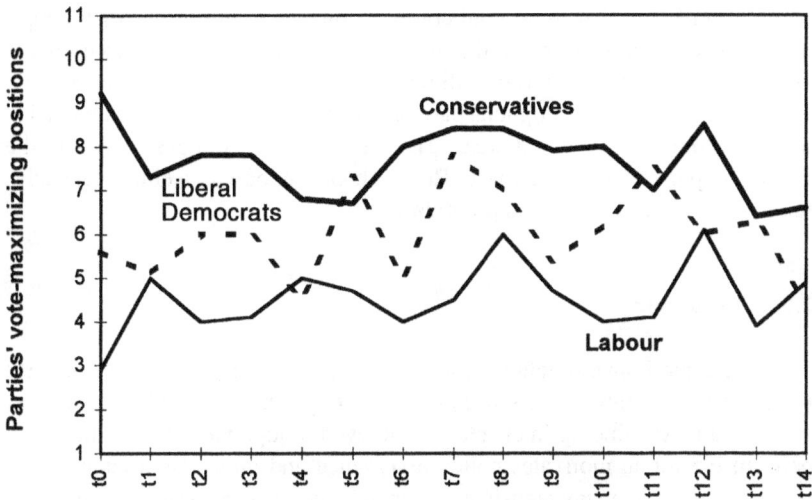

Fig. 3.9.   Spatial mapping of British parties' policy trajectories for simulations based on evolving distributions of respondents from the 1987 British General Election Study, with strength, *b*, of partisan bias set at $b^{1/2} = 3.0$.

times $t2$ and $t3$),[21] that is, there is only one instance in which even a single party reaches a temporary policy equilibrium, *despite the fact that in chapter 2 we found that a policy equilibrium exists for the full voter distribution of 1987 (for $b^{1/2} = 3$)*. These results suggest that even when successive voter distributions are generated from a larger distribution that admits a policy equilibrium the trajectory of party policies will be *stable but not static* in that parties will continually update their policies.[22]

Summary

The central finding that emerges from these situations is that, *regardless of the assumptions we make about how voter attitudes evolve, simulations based upon historical election data suggest that when voters have partisan motivations vote-seeking parties in Britain will present stable, divergent policies that reflect their supporters' beliefs.* This conclusion obtains for simulations based upon stable voter distributions and those that assume an evolving distribution, and it also extends to simulations based upon data from different historical elections. Given the limitations in available longitudinal data from British elections during the postwar period, it is not my place to say which simulation strategy (if any) incorporates the most "realistic" model of voter evolution. What is significant is that each model generates similar predictions about the trajectory of party policies and that these predictions accord well with the heuristic arguments presented in section 3.3: that when voters' party identifications correlate with their policy beliefs parties will rarely leapfrog, instances of leapfrogging will typically involve contiguous parties, and parties will rarely locate outside their ideologically delimited areas. These results are also consistent with the findings reported by the Manifesto Research Group, based on empirical analyses of British parties' election programmes.

3.5. Discussion

In this chapter, I have sought to relate the analysis of temporal aspects of party policies to the requirements of responsible party government. This analysis was motivated by the finding in chapter 2 that, even though party competition in a partisan electorate motivates policy divergence and policy representation by political parties, in many plausible scenarios no policy equilibrium exists. What we have seen here is how party policies are likely to evolve in the absence of such an equilibrium or in situations for which policy equilibria are short-lived due to changes in the voter distribution. I have shown how a spatial model with partisan voters can illuminate the policy trajectories of British political parties during the postwar period and in particular the reasons why these parties' behavior has been conducive to responsible party government.

Although the specifics of the heuristic arguments I have presented are at times complex, I emphasize that the central logic that drives my results on party trajectories is straightforward and revolves around the strategic party motivation discussed in chapter 2. This is that when voters display partisan attachments that correlate with their policy preferences then to the extent that these attachments incorporate an affective component that is independent of the voters' policy motivations vote-seeking parties are motivated to present divergent policies that reflect their partisans' beliefs. Parties are motivated to present divergent policies because this is the only way they can attract support from voters who identify with rival parties. Parties are motivated to appeal to their partisans on policy grounds because if they desert their partisans by leapfrogging an opponent the fact of voter partisanship typically forces them to present extreme policies (due to the pressure for policy divergence) that are electorally unattractive.

In this chapter, we have seen that an exception to above strategic logic arises in situations in which the center party is motivated to converge toward one of its rivals. In this case, the tension between the center party's incentive to converge and the rival party's desire for policy divergence typically disrupts equilibrium. However, even under this scenario each party is motivated to locate near its own partisans in the policy space, and furthermore the two peripheral parties are still motivated to pursue policy divergence. Given these strategic motivations, it is understandable—and virtually inevitable—that even when long-term policy equilibria do not exist parties will nonetheless present stable, divergent, and representative policies. What we have seen here is exactly how these policies are likely to evolve over time, given alternative sets of assumptions about the evolutions of voter attitudes.

Because my conclusions on parties' policy trajectories rest upon illustrative examples and simulation analyses carried out in a specific electoral context, that of British postwar politics, the question arises to what extent my results generalize to other party systems. In the absence of deductive theorems on cross-time patterns of party competition, there is no obvious answer to this question. However, I note that the logic of the illustrative examples was found to generalize to British politics in spite of the fact that the voter distribution in the examples differed from the empirical British voter distribution in one important way: in the examples the center party was assigned a large partisan constituency that exceeds the size of the centrist Liberal Democratic constituency in contemporary British politics. Thus, the fact that the logic outlined for the illustrative examples was found to generalize to the somewhat different British electoral context is encouraging. This also suggests that the logic of the heuristic arguments is likely to generalize to such contexts as Indian and Canadian politics, which feature large centrist parties. By contrast, the examples presented here are probably less applicable to the German three-party context that obtained prior to the 1990s, which featured the small, but pivotal, Free Democrat Party, which was bracketed by much larger parties on the left and the right. Of course in succeeding chapters we shall examine the extent to which these heuristic arguments apply to the French and the American party systems.

My results carry additional interest because of what they suggest about the uses of equilibrium analysis in spatial modeling. We have seen that a central feature of party competition with partisan voters is the absence of a long-term policy equilibrium. While disequilibrium would be viewed as a drawback by many spatial modelers, this result illuminates the MRG's empirical finding that parties vary their positions over time; furthermore, voter partisanship explains why parties rarely leapfrog. Thus, the biased voting model explains why parties' policies are *stable* but not *static*, a phenomenon that is not captured by spatial models that study policy equilibrium for a single election. While both perspectives are important, my results suggest that studying the temporal aspects of party competition can illuminate important features of party competition that are not considered in most spatial models.

In this regard, one striking implication of my simulation results on evolving voter distributions is that the question of whether a policy equilibrium exists *at any particular time* is almost irrelevant. This is because, first, even if a theoretical equilibrium exists for a particular voter distribution, parties may not converge to this configuration during the relatively short time period before this voter distribution "evolves." Second, the corollary to this argument is that, even if parties do converge to an equilibrium, this equilibrium is likely to be short-lived due to shifts in the voter distribution. Hence, in the context of an evolving electorate the trajectories of party policies may be quite similar regardless of whether or not policy equilibria exist for particular election periods.

CHAPTER 4

Party Competition in Postwar France under the Partisan Vote Model

4.1. Introduction

The results presented in chapters 2 and 3 demonstrated that a spatial model that posits partisan voters and vote-seeking parties accounts well for British parties' policy behavior during the postwar period. However, in some ways Britain represents an "easy" test of the partisan spatial model, first, because the logic of parties' vote-seeking strategies is fairly straightforward for British three-party elections compared to elections involving larger numbers of parties. Second, the assumption that parties single-mindedly seek votes appears particularly relevant to British politics since Britain's plurality voting system virtually always awards a parliamentary majority to a single party and therefore places a premium on electoral success.

In the next two chapters, I extend my analysis of party strategies under the partisan spatial model to the more "difficult" case of French postwar politics. Unlike the stable British political context, politics in postwar France has been characterized by considerable instability at the levels of both the party system and the behavior of the public. In addition, French elections feature more than three competitive parties, and the complex strategic environment of French parliamentary elections, described below, plausibly undercuts parties' motivations to maximize votes. These considerations suggest that party politics in postwar France represents a far more demanding test of the partisan spatial model.

I ask the question: does the strategic logic of policy competition in the three-party British system extend to party systems that feature four or more competitive parties? Furthermore, can a spatial analysis built on the assumption that parties maximize votes illuminate the policy strategies that French parties have pursued during the postwar period? Finally, what are the implications of the partisan vote model for the possibility of responsible party government in France, that is, when French parties compete for votes from a partisan electorate, should we expect them to present stable, divergent, and representative policies?

In this chapter, I argue that the answer to each of these questions is yes. With respect to policy strategies, I argue that the central strategic motivations that obtain for three-party competition in a partisan electorate—that parties have electoral incentives to appeal on policy grounds to voters biased toward them in part for nonpolicy reasons—extend to elections involving larger numbers of parties. Furthermore, although the French postwar political environment has been far more complex and unstable than that of Britain, the predictions on party policies I generate from empirical applications to French voting data well anticipate French parties' actual policy trajectories, as computed by the Manifesto Research Group. Specifically, my empirical applications suggest that vote-seeking parties in France will not converge to a long-term policy equilibrium but that they will present stable (but not static) policies that fall within circumscribed "ideological areas" of the policy space. With respect to responsible party government, I conclude that French parties are motivated to present divergent policies that reflect their partisans' beliefs. In summary, the central results I obtain suggest that *a spatial analysis based upon vote-seeking parties and partisan voters can illuminate party policy behavior, and responsible party government, in postwar France.*

Because the complex, unstable context of French postwar politics involves several complications that we did not encounter in our examination of British party competition, my analyses of French parties' policy trajectories extends over two chapters. This chapter focuses on party competition during the period from 1958—the first year of the French Fifth Republic—through the 1980s, a time span dominated by four political parties: the Communists, Socialists, RPR, and UDF.[1] The next chapter examines French electoral competition since the mid-1980s, a period that has seen the emergence of a fifth competitive party, the Far Right, anti-immigration National Front.

As was the case for my analysis of British parties' cross-time policy trajectories, presented in chapter 3, my approach here is almost entirely inductive and relies on illustrative examples and computer simulations rather than deductive equilibrium analysis. The reason is that, as discussed in section 1.5, I have been unable to deduce theorems on policy equilibrium in the basic partisan spatial model that generalize to elections involving four or more parties. However, while this shift to an inductive approach is not by choice, in defense of this strategy I note that it is especially well adapted to the study of French politics since, given the extremely unstable nature of party politics and mass voting behavior in France prior to the late 1980s (which I discuss below), it appears improbable that French political parties could ever have converged to a long-term policy equilibrium during this period. Hence, an equilibrium analysis of French parties' postwar policies appears inappropriate, even were I able to deduce the relevant theorems. In the absence of policy equilibrium, I therefore rely primarily on simulations of French parties' policy trajectories, the same approach I employed in chapter 3 with respect to British parties' trajectories.

In section 4.2, I present some simple examples designed to show why the central strategic motivation developed for partisan spatial competition in three-party elections, that vote-seeking parties should present policies that appeal to their partisans, extends to elections involving four or more parties. Section 4.3 reviews French party politics during the postwar period, with particular emphasis on the evolving natures of the party system and the mass electorate as well as the complex strategic context of parliamentary elections. I then present applications of the partisan spatial model to French election data, which suggest that, for a wide range of assumptions concerning the electoral impact of partisanship, the four major French postwar parties during the period 1958–88 were motivated to present divergent, stable, and representative policies. These results account well for French parties' actual policy behavior during this time period, as reflected in the analyses of parties' programmes carried out by the Manifesto Research Group. Section 4.4 discusses the connections between these results and previous research. Section 4.5 is a summary.

4.2. Extending the Logic of Party Policy Competition in a Partisan Electorate to Elections Involving at Least Four Parties

As outlined in chapters 2 and 3, the central strategic motivation that drives parties' policy strategies in three-party elections is straightforward: when voters display party loyalties that correlate with their policy preferences, vote-seeking parties are motivated to present policies that reflect their partisans' beliefs. This motivation for parties to behave "responsibly" toward their partisans arises because such positioning ensures that rival parties cannot capture the votes of the responsible party's partisans by co-opting this party's policies; instead, rival parties are motivated to present divergent policies so that the responsible party is assured of ideological "breathing space," which typically guarantees it a respectable vote share. As a result, three-party configurations in which the parties behave responsibly toward their partisans are usually stable in that they discourage parties from leapfrogging because a leapfrogging party is typically forced to present a relatively extreme policy that is electorally unattractive.

I emphasize that, although the analyses presented in chapters 2–3 develop this argument in the context of three-party elections, the underlying logic of why parties should behave responsibly toward their partisans extends to elections involving larger numbers of parties. The reason is that the argument that responsible behavior assures the responsible party of an ideological breathing space obtains for any multiparty election, and so does the argument that responsible party positioning discourages leapfrogging by forcing leapfrogging parties to present extreme policies. To see this, consider the situation illustrated in figure 4.1, which presents a stylized distribution of French voters' policy positions for partisans of the RPR, the UDF, the Socialists, and the Communists, the four parties that dominated French politics during most of the 1970s and 1980s. As was the case for the voter distributions analyzed in chapters 2 and 3, voter positioning in figure 4.1 correlates with party identification: all voters in the far left policy interval [1,4] identify with the relatively small French Com-

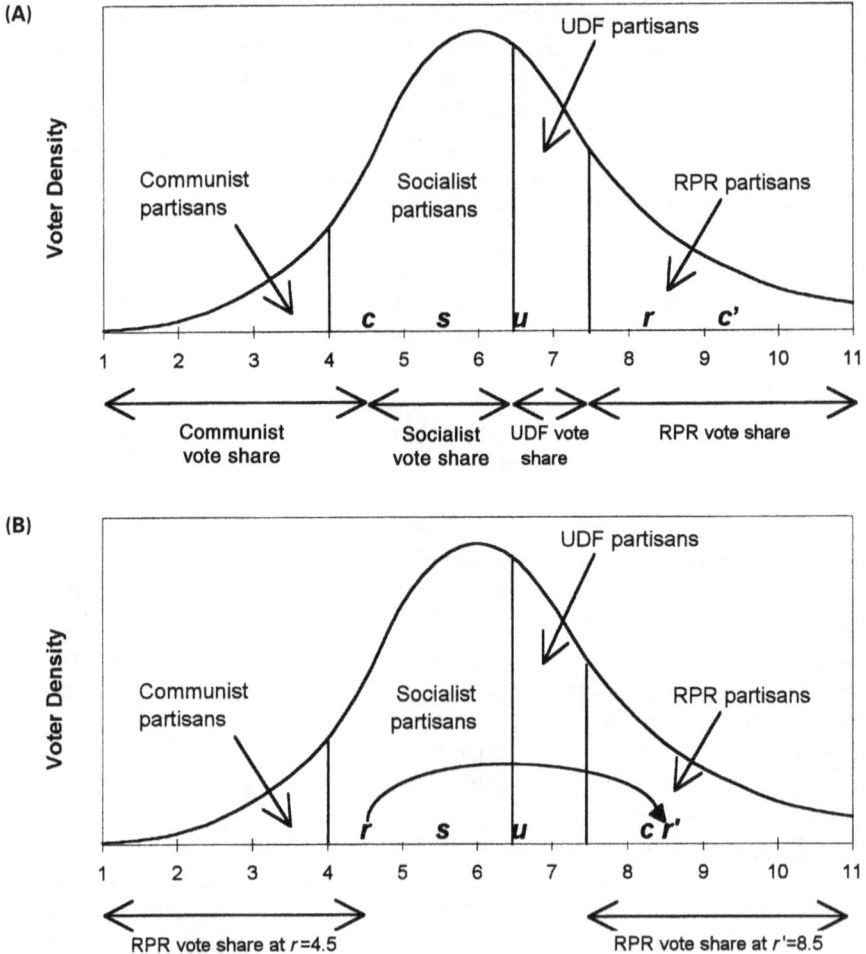

Fig. 4.1. Examples of policy equilibrium and the pressures for policy representation for four-party spatial competition in France. (*A*) Equilibrium configuration for $b = 1.0$; (*B*) Alternative party configuration, which does not admit a policy equilibrium.

munist Party. Center-left and centrist voters located in the policy interval [4,6.5] are Socialists; center-right voters in the policy interval [6.5,7.5] identify with the UDF, and right-wing voters to the left of 7.5 are partisans of the RPR. I assume that voters evaluate parties according to the partisan vote model given in equation 2.2 and that the strength of voter partisanship is set at $b^{1/2} = 1$. This partisan distribution reflects the empirical findings on France summarized in chapter 2 (see especially fig. 2.2) that partisanship correlates with policy preferences and that, at least since 1981, the Socialists have typically had the largest partisan following.

Now consider the party configuration illustrated in figure 4.1A, for which the parties are assumed to behave responsibly toward their partisans in that the Communists locate on the left at $c = 4.5$, the Socialists take the center-left position $s = 5.5$, the UDF is positioned on the center-right at $u = 6.5$, and the RPR proposes the right-wing position $r = 8.2$ (the policy position $c' = 9.2$ is discussed below). Note that by locating at 4.5, at a policy distance of $b^{1/2} = 1$, to the left of the Socialists, the Communists capture the support of all voters—including Socialist partisans—located to the left of 4.5. Nonetheless, of the four parties the Communists receive the smallest vote. This result notwithstanding, in this four-party example the Communists cannot increase their electoral support by leapfrogging for the reason that was outlined in chapters 2–3 with respect to three-party elections; namely, that, because all rival parties behave responsibly toward their own partisans, if the Communists leapfrog they are forced to present an extreme policy that is electorally unattractive. Thus, for the party configuration given in figure 4.1A, the Communists' optimal leapfrogging position is $c' = 9.2$ at a policy distance $b^{1/2} = 1$ to the right of the RPR. It is easily seen that this right-wing policy attracts less electoral support for the Communists than does the leftist position, $c = 4.5$.

In fact, the configuration pictured in figure 4.1A represents an equilibrium in vote-maximizing strategies. The reason for this is that, just as responsible behavior by rival parties motivates the Communists to maintain their left-wing position, this responsible behavior also dissuades the right-wing RPR from converging toward the UDF. This is because, given the UDF's center-right location, all of its partisans in the policy interval [6.5,7.5] will support the UDF even if the RPR is more attractive on policy grounds.[2] This example suggests that when voter partisanship correlates with policy preferences the central logic of policy stability and policy divergence for three-party competition generalizes to elections with larger numbers of parties.

A further example that supports this conclusion is given in figure 4.1B, which illustrates why, in four-party elections, policy configurations for which parties present positions at odds with their partisans' beliefs tend to be unstable. The party configuration pictured in figure 4.1B is identical to that of 4.1A except that the Communists and the RPR have switched positions. In this scenario, the parties present divergent policies, but this configuration is unstable since the RPR can improve its vote share by leapfrogging to the right-wing position r', thereby co-opting the Communist party's position. With such a rightward shift, the RPR recaptures the votes of all its partisans since these voters are then nearly indifferent between the Communists and the RPR on policy grounds and therefore vote RPR out of partisan loyalty. This example of four-party elections is similar to the earlier arguments developed with respect to three-party competition (see, e.g., fig. 3.5) that when parties behave irresponsibly by locating far from their own partisans in the policy space they are vulnerable to "invasion" by rival parties since rival parties can capture the irresponsible party's supporters by co-opting its policies.

These examples provide intuitions as to why, in elections involving more than three parties, vote-seeking parties are motivated to behave responsibly toward their partisans. Of course, it would be preferable to develop deductive results for elections involving at least four parties, comparable to the three-party theorems presented in chapter 2. In the absence of such theorems, I turn to simulations based on survey data from historical elections in France. As I suggest below, there are several reasons why these empirical applications represent particularly demanding "tests" of the partisan spatial model. To the extent that these applications illuminate French parties' actual policy behavior, we will have added confidence that the above heuristic arguments capture the underlying logic of party strategies in elections involving four or more parties.

4.3. Empirical Applications to French Politics

The Evolution of the French Party System and the Emergence of a Partisan Alignment under the Fifth Republic

Unlike the stable British party system, politics in postwar France has been marked by extreme instability—both at the level of the party system and in terms of the political preferences of the mass electorate—especially prior to the 1970s. Furthermore, French parties compete in a complex strategic environment that plausibly motivates them to pursue goals other than vote maximization. These factors complicate the analysis of French parties' policies compared to the relatively straightforward British electoral context analyzed in chapters 2 and 3. To demonstrate these points, I briefly review the evolution of the French postwar party system as well as the strategic context of French parliamentary elections.

Party politics in postwar France was initially marked by extreme instability, which was reflected in a low incidence of party identification at the level of the mass electorate. During the twelve-year duration of the Fourth Republic

(1946–58), which was a parliamentary democracy that featured a proportional representation electoral system, the "political supply" (Lancelot 1986) of competing parties was large, in that many parties contested parliamentary elections, and this supply was also variable in that new and sometimes short-lived parties frequently formed while existing parties sometimes changed their names as well as the basis of their appeal between elections.[3] This unstable political climate, in which voters were confronted with constantly changing sets of party choices over successive elections, disrupted development of the enduring mass-elite linkages that typically characterize electorates in mature, advanced, industrial societies. As a result, Pierce writes, "At the outset of the Fifth Republic . . . the incidence of party identification was so limited, and the party system so fluid that it hardly makes sense to speak of the existence at that time of some partisan alignment based on enduring party allegiances" (1995, 41).

The French Fifth Republic (1958–) differs from the Fourth in that a strong presidency was grafted onto the Fourth Republic's parliamentary system. Under this premier-presidential system, both the president and representatives to the National Assembly are selected via two-stage plurality elections.[4] While the party system remained fluid during the early years of the Fifth Republic, political conflict was simplified beginning in the mid-1960s, when two competing electoral coalitions regularly opposed each other in parliamentary and presidential elections: a left-wing coalition composed of the Communist and Socialist Parties and a center-right coalition whose composition has changed over time but that has been dominated since the late 1970s by two parties, the right-wing Rassemblement pour la Republique, a neo-Gaullist party established in 1976, and the Union pour la Democracie Francaise, a center-right party grouping founded in 1978.[5] These party coalitions were motivated in part by the strategic logic of the two-stage plurality method used to elect representatives to the National Assembly, which motivates parties promoting similar ideologies to form electoral alliances that enhance their ability to win seats.[6] These electoral alliances have allowed the Communists and Socialists on the Left, and the UDF and RPR on the Right, to emerge as the four preeminent parties since the late 1970s, at least in terms of electing candidates to the National Assembly. Primarily as a result of this greater clarity and stability of party competition, the incidence of party identification in France has increased sharply, from around 50 percent of the electorate in the late 1950s (Converse and Depeux 1966) to approximately 70 percent by the late 1980s (Pierce 1995, chap. 3). I also note that, given the presence of four competitive parties, French National Assembly elections typically do not award a single party a parliamentary majority, so that French governments typically require the legislative support of a coalition of parties. Finally, the 1980s saw the emergence of another significant party, the extremely right-wing, anti-immigration National Front, which has consistently captured between 9 and 15 percent of the vote in the first round

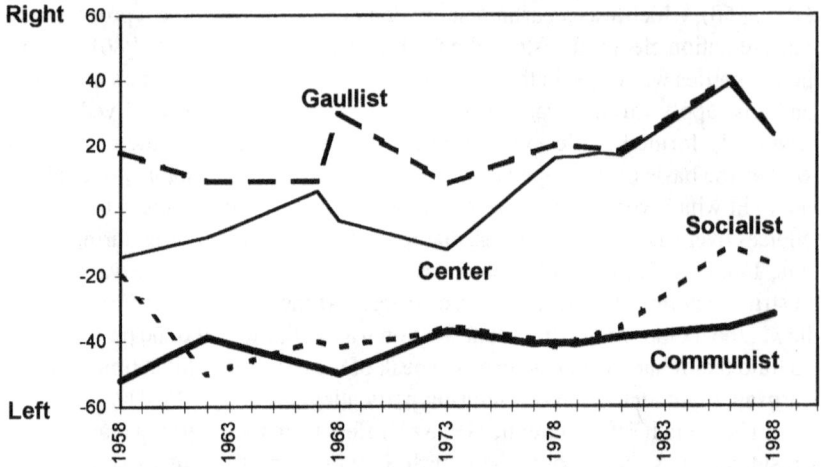

Fig. 4.2. Left-Right trajectories of the major parties during the French Fifth Republic as coded by the Manifesto Research Group. Joint programs are Communists-Socialists, 1973; and Gaullists-Center, 1981. (Data from Manifesto Research Group Party Programme Dataset.)

of parliamentary elections, although it has elected few candidates to the National Assembly.

Figure 4.2 displays the policy trajectories of the Socialists, the Communists, the RPR and the UDF based on the Manifesto Research Group's codings of parties' election programmes from 1958, the first year of the Fifth Republic, through 1988 (I consider the policy trajectory of the National Front below). As expected, the Communists and Socialists consistently present leftist policies, with the Communists typically locating to the left of the Socialists, although not as far to the left as one might expect (note that in 1973 the two parties issued a common election programme). The same pattern can be seen in the center-right coalition, which finds the UDF and its predecessors (see note 5) consistently presenting centrist policies—which shade to the right beginning in 1978—while the RPR and its predecessors consistently locate on the right (note that the UDF and RPR presented a common programme in 1981 and that no data are available for the UDF following the 1981 programme, which is treated as being in force through 1985; see Klingemann et al. 1994, chap. 7). The MRG's results on the French parties' policy trajectories reveal similar patterns to those that obtained in Britain: the parties present divergent policies that are stable but not static, leapfrogging is uncommon, and leapfrogging always involves contiguous parties.

Empirical Applications of the Partisan Vote Model
to French Politics: Simulations on the Four Major
Parties for a Stable Voter Distribution

In seeking to illuminate French parties' policy trajectories via a spatial analysis based on partisan voters, we confront two complications beyond those encountered in our applications to British politics. First, as discussed above, both the French party system and the French electorate have evolved significantly over time, something we must account for in empirical applications to French parties' policy trajectories. Second, the French system of electoral alliances, combined with the fact that most parties cannot realistically aspire to win a single-party parliamentary majority, creates a complex strategic environment that plausibly weakens French parties' incentives to maximize votes.[7] This raises the question: can a spatial model of party competition that assumes partisan voters and vote-seeking parties illuminate French parties' policy trajectories given the complex and unstable political environment of postwar France? To answer these questions, I carried out simulations on French voting data using a variety of alternative assumptions about voters and parties that were intended to capture different aspects of the French electoral environment.

All of these simulations were based on distributions of French voters' Left-Right self-placements and party identifications derived from Pierce's 1988 French Presidential Election Survey.[8] Figure 4.3A shows this distribution for respondents who classified themselves as feeling close to one of the four major postwar parties—the Communists, Socialists, UDF, and RPR—as well as for voters who classified themselves as independents.[9] The parties' Left-Right positions, as perceived by the respondents, are also shown. Note that, as in the cases of the British voter distributions analyzed in chapters 2–3, the distributions of the competing French parties' partisans overlap, but there is a strong correlation between party bias and Left-Right self-placement: virtually all Socialist and Communist sympathizers place themselves on the Left, while partisans of the UDF and the RPR place themselves overwhelmingly on the Right.

The first set of simulations on party policy trajectories I carried out involved the simplest possible assumptions about voters and parties: that over the period 1958–88 the four major French parties competed to maximize votes, while the distribution of voters' policy preferences and partisanship remained completely stable. This simulation approach omits strategic complications arising from the presence of numerous smaller French parties (as well as the National Front, a major party since the mid-1980s), and it also fails to account for the progressive increase in voter partisanship over the 1958–88 period. Nevertheless, these simulations provide a baseline against which to compare subsequent simulation results that are based on more realistic assumptions.

For these simulations, I employed the same approach used for the appli-

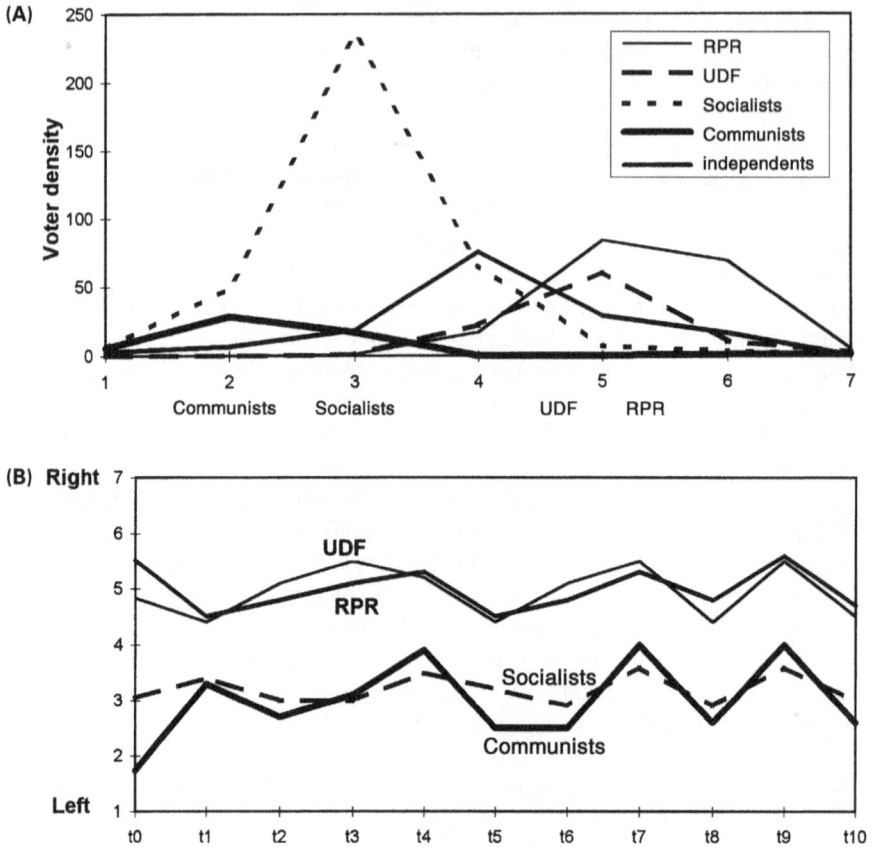

Fig. 4.3. Spatial mapping of French parties' policy trajectories for simulations on a stable voter distribution. The voter distribution is based on Pierce's 1988 French Presidential Election Study. (A) Distribution of voters' Left-Right self-placements and mean party placements; (B) Evolution of French parties' policy strategies for $b^{1/2} = 1.0$.

cations to British voting data (see section 3.4), that is, the parties were initially located at their actual (perceived) positions and I then calculated the parties' successive vote-maximizing positions for varying assumptions on the strength, b, of voter partisanship, with each calculation updated to reflect the rival parties' policy shifts.[10] Each simulation involved 120 successive party policy shifts.[11] As was the case for the simulations on British politics reported in chapter 3, here the parties did not converge to equilibria in vote-maximizing locations. Instead, *the parties presented policies that were stable but not static, and each party was located within ideologically delimited intervals of the policy space. These simulation results match the MRG's empirical findings.*

This result is illustrated in figure 4.3B, which shows the French parties' policy trajectories over the first 10 of these 120 policy shifts, computed when the strength of voter partisanship was set at $b^{1/2} = 1.0$. Note that the parties invariably remain within their ideological areas, with the Communists and Socialists locating to the left and the RPR to the right of the center point 4.0; the UDF, which is actually a Center-Right party, also takes consistently right-wing positions.

Table 4.1 summarizes simulation results on parties' policy trajectories for varying levels of the strength of partisan attachment, ranging from $b^{1/2} = 0$ (the standard Downsian model) to $b^{1/2} = 2.0$. Columns 2–5 give the parties' mean positions over the course of 120 policy shifts. Column 6 shows the proportion of cases involving leapfrogging,[12] column 7 the percentage of these cases that involve contiguous parties, and column 8 the incidence of cases in which parties locate outside their ideological areas. For comparison, the results of the MRG's historical mapping of postwar French parties (pictured in figure 4.2) are summarized. The mean positions of the partisans of the Communists, Socialists, UDF, and RPR for the 1988 voter distribution given in figure 4.3A are also shown.

TABLE 4.1. Patterns of French Parties' Policy Trajectories for Simulations on a Stable Voter Distribution

Partisan Attachment (1)	Mean Party Positions				Leapfrogging		Positions Outside Ideological Area (8)
	Communists (2)	Socialists (3)	UDF (4)	RPR (5)	Overall (6)	Contiguous (7)	
$b^{1/2} = 0$	4.0	4.2	4.2	3.9	80%	53%	55%
$b^{1/2} = 0.5$	3.6	3.5	4.3	4.5	29	85	16
$b^{1/2} = 1.0$	3.0	3.1	4.6	4.9	15	100	6
$b^{1/2} = 1.5$	2.7	3.2	5.1	5.1	15	100	0
$b^{1/2} = 2.0$	2.5	3.0	4.7	5.1	12	100	7
Partisans' mean positions	2.4	3.1	4.9	5.4			
MRG's empirical results					12%	100%	0%

Note: Simulations are based on the respondent Left-Right distribution from Pierce's 1988 French Presidential Election Study.

Column 6 gives the percentages of parties' policy shifts that involve leapfrogging and column 7 the percentages of these cases that involve contiguous parties. Column 8 gives the percentages of parties' policy positions that fall outside the party's ideological area; the Communists' and Socialists' ideological area is defined as the policy interval [1,4]; the ideological areas for the RPR is defined as the policy interval [4,7]; the UDF is not assigned an ideological area.

Table 4.1 shows that for all positive values of b, including weak degrees of partisan attachment such as $b^{1/2} = 0.5$, the simulations yield results on parties' policy trajectories that are largely consistent with the MRG's empirical findings. The parties' mean policy positions are divergent, with the Communists and Socialists locating on the left and the UDF and the RPR on the right, while leapfrogging is uncommon and nearly always involves contiguous parties. Furthermore, the parties' policy positions reflect their partisans' beliefs. Thus, in these simulations the parties present stable, divergent, and representative policies—precisely the behavior that enhances the functioning of responsible party government.

Policy Trajectories for an Evolving Distribution: Party Competition in an Era of an Emerging Partisan Alignment

While the simulation results presented above demonstrate a surprising degree of fit with the MRG's empirical findings, these simulations omit two real world factors that potentially destabilized party competition in postwar France. The first is the fact that the distribution of French voters' policy preferences has undoubtedly changed over time, an influence that I incorporated into the simulations on British politics by randomly varying the voter distribution. However, in the case of French postwar politics we encounter an additional complicating factor; namely, a partisan alignment, which emerged in the French electorate during 1958–88, that saw a sharp increase in the incidence of party identification. Thus, the above simulations on a stable voter distribution do not capture the relatively low levels of French partisanship that obtained during the early years of the Fifth Republic. Therefore, to the extent that voter partisanship motivates vote-seeking parties to present stable policy trajectories, these simulation results may exaggerate the degree of policy stability to be expected from vote-seeking parties in postwar France, especially during the 1960s and 1970s.

To simulate French parties' policy trajectories over the period 1958–88 for an evolving *and increasingly partisan* voter distribution, I employed the following methodology. First, a random sample of 200 respondents was drawn from the 1988 voter distribution pictured in figure 4.3A, for which approximately 82 percent of the respondents reported a party identification. Next, to incorporate the fact that the French electorate was less partisan in the late 1950s than it was in 1988, the voting weight given to each randomly selected nonpartisan respondent was multiplied by a scale factor of four, that is, each independent respondent was assumed to represent four voters. Given this specification, the expected proportion of partisans in the randomly generated electorate dropped from 82 to 53 percent, about the same frequency of party identification reported by Converse and Dupeux (1966) based on voter surveys of the 1958 election.[13]

Next, each party was initially located at its actual policy position for the 1988 election, as given by the respondents' mean party placements, and then the parties were successively relocated to their computed vote-maximizing positions, with each calculation updated to reflect rival parties' policy shifts. This process continued for only four policy shifts per party rather than 120, as in the earlier simulations on a stable electorate.[14] Next, with the parties located in the policy configuration they had reached after four moves, a new random sample of 200 respondents was drawn from the 1988 voter distribution. *However, for this fresh voter distribution each independent voter's voting weight was multiplied by a scale factor of 3.9 rather than 4.0.* Given this specification, the expected proportion of partisans in the randomly generated electorate increased from 53 to 54 percent, which is consistent with the empirical finding that the French electorate became increasingly partisan during the period 1958–88. The parties' positions were then successively updated four more times. This process was repeated for 28 additional random voter distributions, with the independent voters' voting weights in the distributions successively reduced to 3.8, 3.7, 3.6, and so on. For the thirtieth and final voter distribution, for which independent voters' weights were set at 1.0 (i.e., independent voters were weighed no more heavily than partisans) the expected partisan frequency was 82 percent, exactly the frequency of the 1988 voter distribution given in figure 4.3A.

The point of these simulations was to investigate French parties' policy trajectories given the assumption of an evolving and increasingly partisan electorate. By randomly drawing fresh voter samples, I ensured that the voter policy distribution varied over the course of the simulations. By reducing the voting weight assigned to independent voters for each successive random sample, I ensured that the incidence of voter partisanship in the electorate increased over the course of the simulations, from an expected value of 53 percent for the initial voter distribution to 82 percent for the final distribution. These partisan frequencies are consistent with the results of French survey research over the period 1958–88.[15]

The question arises: does the trajectory of French parties' policies based on simulations for this evolving distribution resemble the trajectories computed for the stable distribution analyzed above? The answer is a provisional yes, although some interesting differences emerge with respect to party policy stability, particularly in the simulations based on the "earlier," less partisan, voter distributions. The entire spatial mapping of 120 party policy shifts is given in figure 4.4A for simulations in which the strength of voter partisanship was set at $b^{1/2} = 1.0$; in addition, figures 4.4B and 4.4C show enlarged mappings of the first and last 10 of these policy shifts, respectively. Compared to the earlier spatial mapping generated for the stable voter distribution (fig. 4.3B), the parties' policy trajectories for the evolving distribution are somewhat erratic, particularly during the "early" stages of the simulations when the simulated elec-

(A)

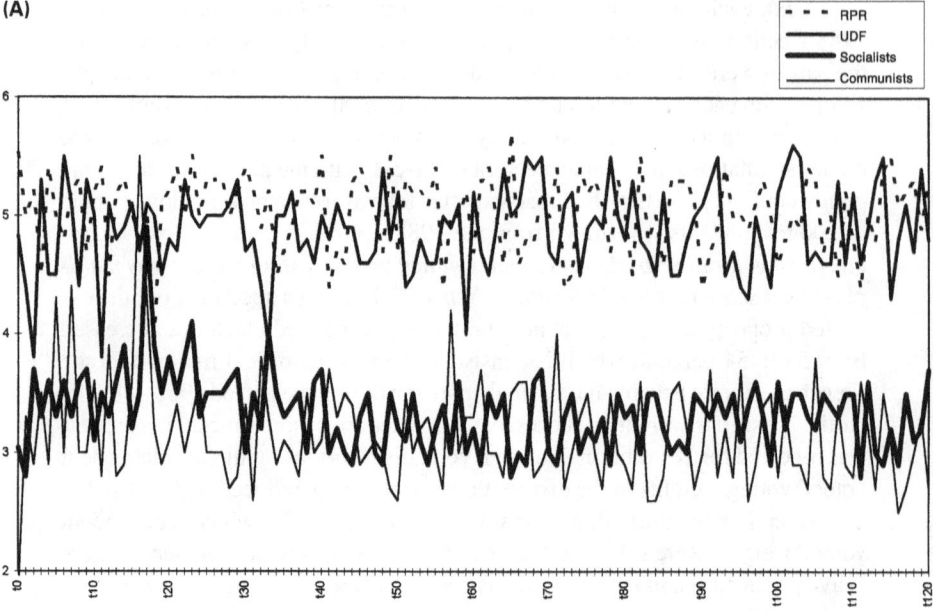

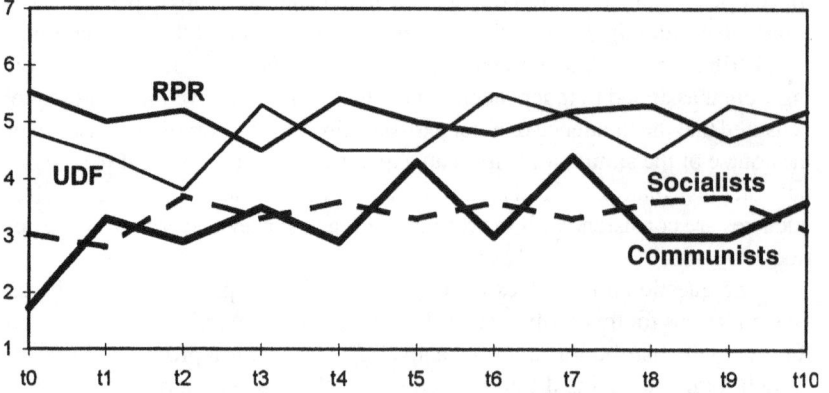

Fig. 4.4. Spatial mapping of French parties' policy trajectories for simulations based on an evolving, increasingly partisan, voter distribution. (A) Parties' policy trajectories for $b^{1/2} = 1.0$; (B) Parties' policy trajectories from $t0$ to $t10$; (C) Parties' policy trajectories from $t110$ to $t120$.

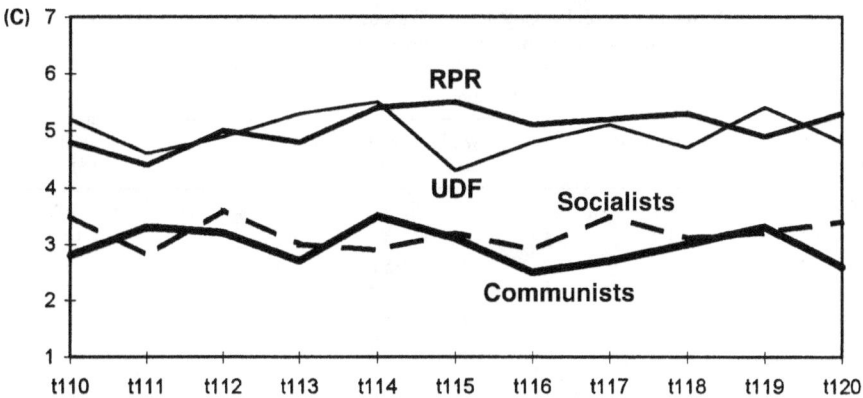

Fig. 4.4. (*continued*)

torate is less partisan. For instance, figure 4.4B shows that over the course of
the first 10 policy shifts there are two occasions when the traditionally leftist
Communist Party leapfrogs to a center-right position, while on another occasion the traditionally right-wing RPR shifts slightly to the left of center; thus,
while the parties' policies in the early stages of the simulations are relatively
stable and representative, vote-seeking parties are occasionally motivated to
sharply shift their policies, thereby "deserting" their partisans. By contrast, the
parties' trajectories in the "later" stages of the simulation (fig. 4.4C), for which
the electorate is more partisan, find the parties presenting quite stable, divergent policies that reflect their partisans' beliefs, patterns similar to the trajectories generated for the earlier simulations on a stable voter distribution, as shown
in figure 4.4C.

Table 4.2 summarizes the results on parties' policy trajectories for simulations in which the voting distribution is evolving and increasingly partisan.
These results are similar to those reported for the stable voter distribution (table
4.1), except that party policies are slightly less stable when the voter distribution evolves, as reflected in small increases in the frequency of leapfrogging
(column 6), and in the incidence of parties shifting outside their ideological areas increases (column 8). This increased policy instability is caused by the factor discussed above, that in these simulations the electorate is less partisan, and
hence vote-seeking parties' motivations to appeal to their partisans—thereby
presenting stable policies—is reduced. Nonetheless, these results confirm that,
even in simulations involving an evolving, relatively independent electorate,
vote-seeking French parties are motivated to present divergent policies, to
avoid leapfrogging noncontiguous parties, and to consistently locate within ideologically delimited areas of the policy space. These results thereby throw light

TABLE 4.2.   Patterns of French Parties' Policy Trajectories for Simulations Based on an Evolving, Increasingly Partisan, Voter Distribution

Strength of Partisan Attachment (1)	Mean Party Positions				Leapfrogging		Positions Outside Ideological Area (8)
	Communists (2)	Socialists (3)	UDF (4)	RPR (5)	Overall (6)	Contiguous (7)	
$b^{1/2} = 0$	3.7	4.2	4.0	4.0	76%	53%	51%
$b^{1/2} = 0.5$	3.7	3.5	4.2	4.5	36	81	19
$b^{1/2} = 1.0$	3.1	3.2	4.9	5.0	20	100	2
$b^{1/2} = 1.5$	2.9	3.2	5.0	5.1	21	100	0
$b^{1/2} = 2.0$	3.3	3.0	4.6	5.0	17	95	7
Partisans' mean positions	2.4	3.1	4.9	5.4			
MRG's empirical results					12%	100%	0%

Note: Simulations are based on the respondent Left-Right distribution from Pierce's 1988 French Presidential Election Study.

Column 6 gives the percentages of parties' policy shifts that involve leapfrogging and column 7 the percentages of these cases that involve contiguous parties. Column 8 gives the percentages of parties' policy positions that fall outside the party's ideological area. The Communists' and Socialists' ideological area is defined as the policy interval [1,4]; the ideological area for the RPR is defined as the policy interval [4,7]. The UDF is not assigned an ideological area.

on the major French parties' actual policy behavior during the postwar era, as measured by the Manifesto Research Group's codings of parties' election programmes.

As concerns policy representation, the results reported in table 4.2 show that as long as the strength of voter partisanship is at least moderately strong (i.e., for $b^{1/2} \geq 1.0$) parties present representative policies in that their mean positions over the course of their policy trajectories closely match their partisans' beliefs. This is represented graphically in figure 4.5, which compares the parties' mean positions against the mean positions of their partisans for varying values of b. This shows that for $b^{1/2} \geq 1.0$ each party invariably locates within 0.9 units of its partisans' mean position; furthermore, with the exception of the Communist Party, which is consistently less extreme than its partisans, each party locates within 0.4 units of the partisan mean.[16] These results support the heuristic arguments presented in section 4.2, that in elections involving more than three competitors vote-seeking parties are motivated to behave responsibly toward their partisans.

Finally, one other interesting aspect of the simulation results is that, even though French voters are predominantly centrist (see fig. 4.3A), the parties' policy trajectories are consistently noncentrist (see figs. 4.3B and 4.4A). This occurs because, even though the overall voter distribution is shaded toward the center, the central tendency of each party's partisans is noncentrist. Because all

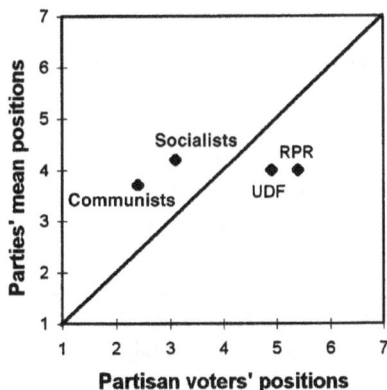

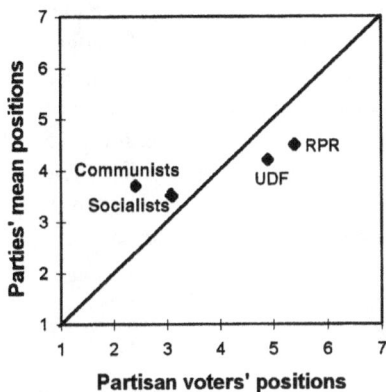

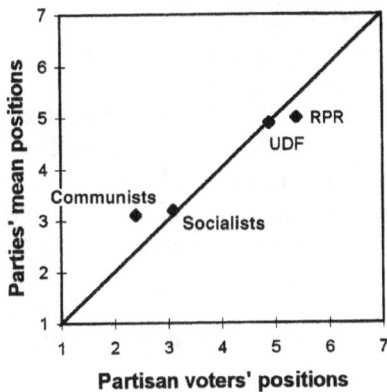

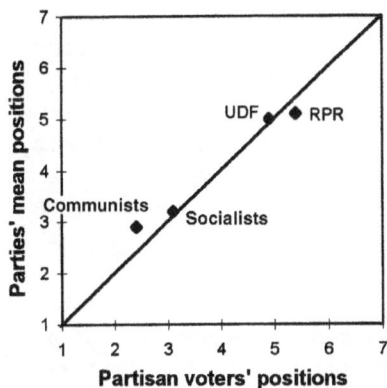

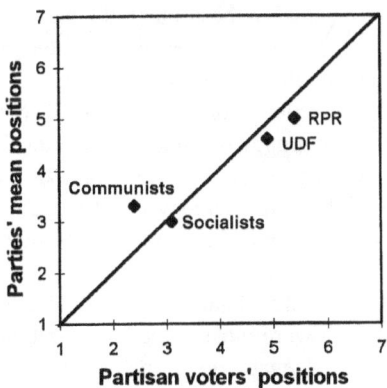

Fig. 4.5. Voters' Left-Right positions and mean party positions over the course of simulated policy trajectories.

parties have electoral motivations to present policies that appeal to their partisans, these parties consistently present noncentrist policies.

Summary

Two important conclusions emerge from the simulations reported here on the major postwar French parties' policy trajectories. The first is that when French parties seek votes from an electorate whose policy preferences and partisan attachments are derived from historical election data we find that they are motivated to present stable, divergent policies that reflect their partisans' beliefs. Thus, the partisan spatial model can explain parties' actual policy behavior in postwar France, as measured by the MRG, and the model also sheds light on why responsible party government is workable in France. These simulation results are important because, in contrast to the relatively "simple" and stable British postwar political context, French parties have competed in a complex, evolving political environment that is not easily captured via formal analysis. The simulations on an evolving distribution suggest a second interesting conclusion, that parties' policies become increasingly stable as the electorate becomes increasingly partisan. This conclusion makes intuitive sense, for, given that voter partisanship motivates vote-seeking parties to present stable policies (and this is after all a major theme of this book), it is understandable that the more partisan the electorate the more stable parties' policies should be.

4.4. Connections to Previous Work

One of the most interesting findings from the preceding section is the one summarized above, that as the electorate becomes more partisan vote-seeking parties are motivated to present increasingly stable policies. While this result was obtained in the context of simulations on a stable constellation of four competitive French parties, the argument that a partisan electorate would stabilize party competition in France has been advanced in a related context: that of the analysis of party formation. Both Pierce (1995) and Converse and Dupeux (1966) have argued that a major impetus for the formation of "flash" parties in France during the early postwar period was the underdeveloped nature of partisan attachments. Pierce writes that during the late 1950s, when about half the French electorate had no partisan attachment,

> The remaining half [of the electorate] was accessible to whichever parties were most attractive to individual voters at any given electoral moment. New parties, which were rarely in short supply, could count on a large pool of potential supporters, while the existing parties . . . were constantly un-

der threat. The reserve army of new voters, combined with unattached older ones, produced a continuing supply of recruits for France's political entrepreneurs. (1995, 41)

The simulation results presented here, combined with the Pierce-Converse-Dupeux argument, thereby suggest that the development of a partisan alignment in postwar France and the increased stability of the French party system were self-reinforcing. As the French electorate became more partisan, new parties were discouraged from forming (the Pierce-Converse-Dupeux argument) *and* the existing parties had electoral motivations to present increasingly stable policies (the conclusion suggested by my simulations).

From a theoretical perspective, the simulation results on French parties, coupled with the earlier results on Britain, have interesting implications for the long-standing debate over competing models of party leaders' motivations. In an influential article, Strøm (1990; see also Muller and Strøm 1999) summarizes two of these alternative models of party behavior, that of the *vote-seeking party,* which maximizes votes, and that of the *policy-seeking party,* which seeks to implement desired policies.[17] As Strøm notes, political scientists typically assume that these alternative motivations conflict, that is, that party leaders cannot simultaneously advocate their preferred policies and maximize electoral support. However, my simulation results on Britain and France, which find that right-wing parties such as the RPR and British Conservatives maximize votes by locating on the Right, while the traditionally left-wing Socialist, Communist, and British Labour Parties maximize votes by positioning themselves on the Left, suggest a different conclusion. Specifically, my results imply that *when voters are moved by a combination of policy motivations and partisan loyalties parties maximize votes by advocating policies that largely reflect their sincere policy preferences.*[18] This result follows from the strategic logic of the partisan spatial model, which motivates vote-seeking parties to reflect their partisans' beliefs. If this conclusion is correct, then the fundamental "tension" between party elites' wish to attract votes and their desire to advocate their sincere policy beliefs disappears when parties compete for votes from a partisan electorate.

On a related point, the simulation results on French parties are relevant to the current debate over the nature of policy voting, which concerns the empirical status of the traditional proximity model of voting compared to that of the directional model proposed by Rabinowitz and Macdonald (1989). Rabinowitz and Macdonald argue that the directional model, which posits that voters evaluate parties' policies based upon their direction and intensity, is supported by the empirical finding that in many real world party systems the center of the policy space is dense with voters but "empty" of political parties (see Rabinowitz, Macdonald, and Listhaug 1991, 157–66). The authors argue that non-centrist party positioning is inconsistent with proximity voting, reasoning that if voters evaluate parties based on policy proximity then vote-seeking parties would move to the Center, where most voters are located. However, my simulation results show that vote-seeking French parties consistently avoid centrist policies when voters are motivated by proximity voting *and* partisanship because, even though the French electorate as a whole is relatively centrist, the distribution of each party's partisans is noncentrist and "pulls" the vote-seeking parties away from the Center. Hence, contrary to Rabinowitz and Macdonald's argument, given a partisan electorate, proximity voting is indeed compatible with noncentrist party positioning.[19]

4.5. Conclusion

The simulation results presented in this chapter suggest that a model based upon vote-seeking parties and partisan voters can provide *general* insights into party behavior, and responsible party government, in real world political contexts. Here we have seen the operation of the partisan spatial model applied to postwar French politics. Compared to the political context of postwar Britain, the strategic environment of French postwar elections is both complex, in that parties have plausible motives besides maximizing votes, and unstable, in that both the French party system and the electorate have evolved significantly over time. Nevertheless, simulations based upon historical election data show that the partisan spatial model can illuminate the policy trajectories of the four major French postwar parties over the history of the Fifth Republic. These results hold under the unrealistic assumption of a stable electorate, but, more importantly and more generally, they also obtain for more realistic simulations that incorporate a crucial aspect of the French postwar electoral environment, namely, that the electorate has grown increasingly partisan over time.

In closing, I note that, although this analysis of French postwar politics has involved greater complexity than my earlier applications to Britain, in focusing on the period 1958–88 I have largely ignored recent developments in French politics that complicate matters still more. These relate to the emergence of the National Front, a fifth major French party whose anti-immigrant emphasis is not easily assimilated onto the traditional Left-Right economic dimension of French political competition. This is the subject of the next chapter.

PART II
Extensions of the
Basic Partisan
Vote Model

CHAPTER 5

Party Competition in Postwar France, Part II: Party Policies since the Mid-1980s

5.1. Introduction

To this point, I have analyzed the strategic logic of party competition in Britain and France using a simple voting model in which partisan voters are viewed as biased toward their own party but indifferent between all rival parties on non-policy grounds. I have also assumed the most basic model of policy voting, in which voters evaluate parties along a unidimensional policy continuum. This simple approach has enhanced our understanding of parties' strategic motivations since this basic partisan spatial model has so few "working parts" that we can easily grasp the dynamics of party competition in a partisan electorate. Furthermore, while this simple partisan voting model abstracts from many complexities of real world voters' decision processes, it is arguably defensible in the context of British and French postwar politics, in which party competition has largely revolved around issues related to Left-Right ideology, while partisan voters plausibly feel allegiance to a single party.

However, in certain situations the basic partisan voting model not only simplifies but significantly distorts the voting decision, and in these cases use of this model may obscure the strategic logic of parties' policy strategies. In part II of this book, I introduce more complex models of partisan voting and explore their implications for party competition. These models include: (1) one in which voters display varying degrees of partisan attachment to different parties, (2) voting over multiple policy dimensions, and (3) probabilistic voting. In addition, in chapter 7 I sketch a voting model that incorporates the possibility of voter abstention and I explore the model's implications for spatial competition in the United States, which has a two-party system in which voter turnout is quite low.

A natural point of departure in developing the implications of these more complex voting models is party competition in postwar France. The first reason for this is that the system of party electoral alliances in French parliamentary and presidential elections, involving the Communists and Socialists on the Left and the UDF and RPR on the Right, has plausibly altered the nature of partisanship in France, so that partisan voters feel some degree of loyalty toward their party's coalition partner in addition to their feelings of partisan attachment (In chapter 6, I present empirical evidence that supports this hypothesis). Second, the rise of the Far Right, anti-immigration National Front during the 1980s has introduced a number of policy debates in France that do not fit along the traditional Left-Right economic dimension. Given these developments, the simple model of partisan voting explored in chapters 2–4, which posits that voters feel loyalty toward a single party and evaluate parties' policies along a single dimension, may significantly distort the nature of voters' decision processes in contemporary France.

In this chapter, I report the results of simulations on spatial party competition in France, both when partisan voters display loyalties toward their parties' coalition partners and when voters evaluate parties along multiple policy dimensions. (I defer analysis of probabilistic voting to chapter 6). For these latter simulations, I include, in addition to the four French parties analyzed in chapter 4, the National Front, the party that has emphasized immigration policy and does not fit easily along the traditional Left-Right dimension. I ask the question: does the strategic logic of party competition under these more complex voting models parallel the logic of the basic partisan model?

5.2.   A Partisan Vote Model with Coalition Bias

In the basic partisan vote model introduced in chapter 2 (see eq. 2.2), all partisan voters are assumed to be biased toward the party with which they identify and indifferent to all other parties on nonpolicy grounds. This "dichotomous" model of partisan voting is a reasonable starting point for analyzing the strategic effects of partisanship; however, some scholars have suggested a "graduated" partisan model in which voters possess varying degrees of nonpolicy attachment to different parties. Thus, Converse and Pierce (1992b) present empirical evidence to the effect that when French, West German, Dutch, and Norwegian partisans desert their parties they are more likely to defect to rival parties than to others. Dow (1997b, table 2) reports results consistent with this "graduated partisanship" hypothesis in his analysis of voting in the 1995 French presidential election, in which he calculates that the RPR's partisans were not only biased toward the RPR candidate, Jacques Chirac, but were also biased in favor of the UDF candidate, Eduard Balladur, compared to the Socialist Lionel Jospin. This conclusion is also supported by Adams and Merrill's (2000, table 3) empirical results on voting behavior in the 1988 French presidential election.

Given the empirical results summarized above, it seems worthwhile to explore whether the phenomenon of graduated partisanship alters parties' strategic calculus compared to their strategies for the dichotomous partisan model.

Such an approach seems especially relevant to French politics given the long-standing Communist-Socialist electoral alliance on the Left and the RPR-UDF alliance on the right (see section 4.3). From the perspective of partisan voters, the fact of their party's electoral alliance plausibly enhances their evaluation of the alliance partner. In addition, French partisans frequently cast votes for the candidate of their party's alliance partner in the second round of parliamentary and presidential elections when their preferred party's candidate is eliminated or withdraws after the first round.[1] This action may further raise the alliance partner in partisan voters' estimations.

Formally, I incorporate a partisan voter's "coalition bias" toward his or her preferred party's coalition partner by modifying equation 2.2 to include the term c_{iK},

$$U_k(K) = b_{iK} + c_{iK} - (x_i - k)^2 \tag{5.1}$$

where c_{iK} is a dummy variable, which equals c if voter i identifies with party K's coalition partner, and equals zero otherwise; and c is defined as the *strength of coalition bias*. (Recall from chapter 2 that b_{iK} is also a dummy variable that equals b if voter i identifies with K and equals zero otherwise). Given this specification, voter's i's non-policy-related utility for party K equals b if i identifies with K, equals c if i identifies with party K's coalition partner, and equals zero otherwise. I further assume that $0 \leq c \leq b$, that is, partisans are at least as strongly biased toward their party as they are biased toward their party's coalition partner. I label the model so specified the *coalition partisan vote model*— although I will sometimes employ the abbreviated label the coalition vote model—as opposed to the basic partisan vote model analyzed in chapters 2–4. (Note that in eq. 5.1 the basic partisan vote model is a special case of the coalition vote model, for which $c = 0$.)

Before performing simulations on French parties' policy trajectories when voters choose according to the coalition vote model, let us clarify our theoretical expectations. How is the introduction of coalition bias likely to affect parties' policy strategies? We may draw inferences from our earlier conclusion concerning the strategic implications of partisan bias, that vote-seeking parties are motivated to appeal on policy grounds to voters biased toward them for non-policy reasons. This suggests a first hypothesis.

HYPOTHESIS 1:   *Under the coalition vote model vote-seeking parties are motivated to present policies that appeal to both their own partisans and voters who identify with their party's coalition partner.*

If this hypothesis is correct, it implies that partisan voters' coalition bias gives the Communist Party added incentives to present policies that appeal to Socialist voters, while the Socialists have additional incentives to target Communist voters. A similar argument applies with respect to the UDF's and RPR's strategic motivations vis-à-vis their partisans.

A further question to consider is: how is coalition bias likely to alter French parties' policy trajectories, compared to the trajectories computed in chapter 4, for spatial competition under the basic partisan model? For this basic model, we found that vote-seeking French parties were typically drawn to regions of the policy space dense with their own partisans but would occasionally leapfrog to regions populated primarily by rival parties' partisans (see, e.g., fig. 4.4B). If hypothesis 1 is correct, it implies that on those occasions when parties "desert" their own partisans they are likely to shift toward regions of the policy space dense with their coalition partner's partisans. Thus, when voters choose according to the coalition vote model,

HYPOTHESIS 2:   *Over time parties will shift their policies between regions of the policy space dense with their own partisans and regions dense with their coalition partner's partisans.*

An additional inference arises from the empirical observation that in France Communist and Socialist partisans display similar policy preferences, as do the partisans of the UDF and RPR (see fig. 4.3A).[2] Given hypothesis 2, this implies when parties seek votes from an electorate that displays coalition biases,

HYPOTHESIS 3:   *Parties will typically vary their policies within narrow policy intervals, comprising the region of the policy space dense with their own partisans and the partisans of their coalition partner.*

Hypothesis 3 thereby suggests an additional explanation for the MRG's empirical finding that French parties rarely take positions outside of their ideological areas. If the only times French parties desert their own partisans are when they target their coalition partner's partisans, then, since both types of partisans are clustered in similar regions of the policy space, parties will rarely shift outside of their own ideological area. Hence, in toto hypotheses 1–3 imply that voters' coalition biases enhance parties' policy stability.

5.3. Empirical Applications of the Coalition Vote Model: Testing Hypotheses 1–3

To investigate the likely outcomes when French parties seek votes from an electorate that displays coalition bias, I performed simulations on parties' policy trajectories, using the same distribution of respondents given in figure 4.3A, which was derived from Pierce's 1988 French Presidential Election Study. For the simulations, I assumed that the strength, c, of voters' coalition bias was equal to one-fourth the strength, b, of their partisan bias, that is, $c = b/4$. Given the lack of empirical research on coalition bias, this assumption is necessarily speculative; however, this ratio reflects the empirical estimates reported by Dow (1997b, table 2) and Adams and Merrill (2000, table 3) based upon maximum likelihood analysis of French voting data.

I performed simulations using both the assumption of a stable voter distribution and the assumption of an evolving distribution, using the same methodology and assumptions described in chapter 4. Because both distributional specifications yielded similar conclusions, here I report results for the stable voter distribution.[3] These simulations support hypotheses 1–3, which state that when voters display coalition biases in addition to their partisan biases vote-seeking parties will present stable policy trajectories that reflect both their own partisans' beliefs and the beliefs of their coalition partner's partisans. This result is illustrated in figure 5.1, which compares parties' computed policy trajectories for the basic partisan vote model versus their trajectories under the coalition vote model, with the strength of partisan attachment set at $b^{1/2} = 0.5$. For the basic partisan model, parties' simulated policy trajectories over 10 policy shifts are quite unstable in that parties constantly leapfrog and frequently shift outside of their ideological area (fig. 5.1A).[4] This is especially true of the Communist Party, which leapfrogs to a right-wing position on three occasions. By contrast, when voters choose according to the coalition vote model (with b set at $b^{1/2} = 0.5$ and c set at $c^{1/2} = 0.25$), parties' policy trajectories are extremely stable and we find each party presenting policies that reflect its own partisans' beliefs as well as the beliefs of its coalition partner's partisans (fig. 5.1B).[5]

Why, in this example, is party policy behavior more stable when voters display coalition biases compared to when voters display only the standard partisan biases? To grasp the underlying intuition, consider the strategic motivations of the Communists, whose party behaves most erratically under the basic partisan spatial model. Under this basic model, as long as the Socialists propose a center-left policy the Communists cannot capture the votes of the vast majority of the Socialists' partisans because most of them are themselves located on the center-left (see fig. 4.3A) and their partisan attachments therefore ensure their support for the Socialist Party. As a result, whenever the Socialists present a center-left position *and* the UDF and the RPR shift toward the center, the Communists are motivated to leapfrog to a right-wing position in order to capture the support of right-wing partisans. By contrast, under the coalition vote model the Communists can capture a significant number of Socialist partisans regardless of the Socialist Party's location because these partisans are somewhat biased toward the Communist Party. Hence, the Communists are motivated to take positions that reflect the beliefs of their own partisans as well as those of Socialist partisans, and as a result the Communists present stable policy trajectories.

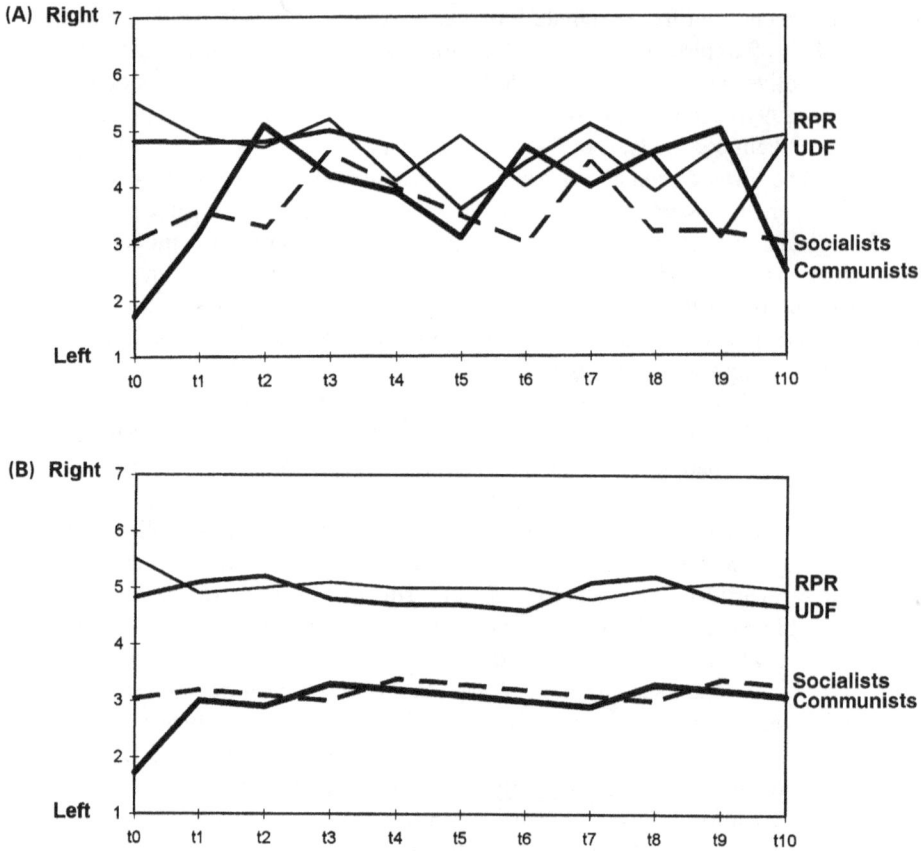

Fig. 5.1.   French parties' policy trajectories for alternative models of partisan voting. Trajectories for the basic partisan vote model are calculated for $b^{1/2} = 0.5$. Those for the coalition partisan vote model are calculated for $b^{1/2} = 0.5$ and $c^{1/2} = 0.25$. (A) Parties' policy trajectories for the basic partisan vote model; (B) Parties' policy trajectories for the coalition partisan vote model.

One other aspect of figure 5.1B deserves comment. Note that over the course of the parties' policy trajectories the Socialist and Communist Parties continually present extremely similar policy positions, as do the UDF and RPR. This occurs because, with each party motivated to appeal to its coalition partner's partisans (as well as to its own), both left-wing parties target the same group of voters, as do the two right-wing parties. As a result, although the policies proposed by the Socialist-Communist coalition diverge sharply from those proposed by the UDF-RPR coalition, the partners' policies do not diverge. This prediction accords well with the Manifesto Research Group's spatial mapping of the French parties' policy trajectories, pictured earlier in figure 4.2. In terms of political representation, this outcome is probably not ideal in that voters have only two distinct policy options from which to choose. Thus, while the coalition vote model motivates French parties to present stable policies, it also promotes a "polarized" party system that effectively reduces French voters' policy alternatives.

Table 5.1 summarizes results on parties' policy trajectories when voters choose according to the coalition vote model for varying degrees of partisan and coalition bias. (Note that these results may be compared to those reported in table 4.1, on French party competition under the basic partisan model.) Columns 1–2 give the strength of partisan attachment, b, and coalition bias, c, respectively, with c set at $b/4$ (which implies that $c^{1/2} = b^{1/2}/2$). Columns 3–6 give the mean positions of the Communists, the Socialists, the UDF, and the RPR, respectively, over the course of 120 policy shifts. Columns 7–8 report results on the incidence of leapfrogging, and column 9 reports the frequency with which parties shift outside of their ideological area. Also given are the mean positions of each party's partisans as well as summaries of the MRG's empirical findings.

For moderate to strong degrees of partisan attachment and coalition bias (i.e., $b^{1/2} \geq 1.0$ and $c^{1/2} \geq 0.5$), the simulation results are similar to those obtained under the basic partisan model (see table 4.1) in that parties rarely leapfrog, leapfrogging virtually always involves contiguous parties, and parties seldom locate outside of their ideological area. Each of these results is also consistent with the MRG's empirical findings. However, as discussed above, important differences emerge for simulations with b and c set at $b^{1/2} = 0.5$ and $c^{1/2} = 0.25$. For this weak degree of partisan and coalition attachment, we have seen that parties' policies are stable and divergent under the coalition vote model but unstable and similar under the basic partisan model. In addition, note that under the coalition vote model the coalition partners' mean policy positions are quite similar. Thus, these simulations suggest that *when French parties compete for votes from an electorate that displays coalition biases parties will propose stable and representative policies, regardless of the strength of voters' partisan attachments. Furthermore, each party will typically present policies that are similar to those of its coalition partner but diverge from the policies presented by members of the rival coalition.*

Summary

The results presented here suggest that when we expand the partisan vote model to include voter bias arising from electoral coalitions, parties are motivated to present policies that are quite stable over time. This is because the coalition

TABLE 5.1. French Parties' Policy Trajectories for Simulations Based on the Coalition Partisan Voting Model

Strength of Partisan Attachment (1)	Strength Coalition Bias (2)	Mean Party Positions				Leapfrogging		Positions Outside Ideological Area (9)
		Communists (3)	Socialists (4)	UDF (5)	RPR (6)	Overall (7)	Contiguous (8)	
$b^{1/2} = 0$	$c^{1/2} = 0$	4.1	4.0	4.0	3.8	80%	45%	44%
$b^{1/2} = 0.5$	$c^{1/2} = 0.25$	2.9	3.0	4.8	4.9	14	100	0
$b^{1/2} = 1.0$	$c^{1/2} = 0.5$	3.0	3.3	5.0	5.1	10	97	2
$b^{1/2} = 1.5$	$c^{1/2} = 0.75$	2.9	3.2	4.9	5.0	13	96	0
$b^{1/2} = 2.0$	$c^{1/2} = 1.0$	3.0	3.3	4.9	4.9	17	91	4
Partisans' mean positions	2.4	3.1	4.9	5.4				
MRG's empirical results						12%	92%	0%

Note: Simulations are based on a stable distribution of respondents' Left-Right self-placements derived from Pierce's 1988 French Presidential Election Study.

Column 7 gives the percentages of parties' policy shifts that involve leapfrogging and column 8 the percentages of these cases that involve contiguous parties. Column 9 gives the percentages of parties' policy positions that fall outside the party's ideological area. The Communists' and Socialists' ideological area is defined as the policy interval [1,4]; the ideological area for the RPR is defined as the policy interval [4,7]. The UDF is not assigned an ideological area.

vote model gives parties added electoral incentives to appeal to their coalition partners' supporters and, since these supporters typically hold policy beliefs similar to those of their own partisans, parties "home in" on relatively narrow regions of the policy space dense with these two types of voters. Parties thereby maintain stable ideological orientations and present policies that reflect their partisans' beliefs. The notion of coalition bias also illuminates an aspect of French party behavior that the basic vote model cannot explain: that the members of the two French electoral coalitions present policies that are quite similar.

I emphasize, however, that the contrasts between parties' policy trajectories under the basic partisan vote model and their behavior under the coalition model are differences in degree, not in kind. Over a wide range of assumptions about voting behavior, both models encourage parties to present stable policies that appeal to voters who approve of the parties for nonpolicy reasons. Given that the coalition vote model expands the voting constituency that approves of each party, it makes sense that when these two models do generate contrasting predictions about parties' policy trajectories—as occurs in French politics when the strength of voters' partisan and coalition attachments is low—we should expect greater party stability for the coalition vote model than for the basic partisan model.

5.4. The Rise of the National Front and Multidimensional Spatial Competition

To this point, I have assumed that spatial competition in postwar France can be described in terms of a unidimensional, Left-Right continuum. This assumption is useful for generating comparisons with British spatial competition because comparative analyses of elections conclude that Left-Right ideology is the only dimension that generalizes across countries (see, e.g., Budge 1994). Furthermore, empirical voting studies suggest that in many contemporary democracies voters are more strongly swayed by Left-Right ideology than they are by other policy dimensions (see, e.g., Adams and Merrill 2000, table 3; Alvarez and Nagler 1995; and Whitten and Palmer 1995, tables 1 and 2).[6]

These results notwithstanding, there exists strong evidence that policy dimensions that are at best weakly related to Left-Right ideology significantly influence voters. This has unquestionably been the case in postwar France, where foreign policy disputes have at times dominated political debate, particularly during the early postwar period.[7] In addition, during the past 15 years the issue of immigration policy has been persistently raised by the Far Right, anti-immigration National Front, a party that gained a significant following beginning in the mid-1980s.[8] While empirical studies on French voting suggest that vot-

ers' views on immigration have less electoral impact than does Left-Right ideology (see, e.g., Adams and Merrill 2000, table 3), the immigration issue plausibly crosscuts ideology, creating a second dimension to policy competition in
France. This is illustrated in table 5.2, which shows respondents' Left-Right
self-placements cross-tabulated with their views on immigration, as reported in
Pierce's 1988 French Presidential Election Study. The results show that although right-wing ideology is associated with opposition to immigration this
association is far from perfect. I also draw the reader's attention to a second interesting aspect of this distribution, which will assume considerable importance
in our subsequent analysis of party policy strategies: that respondents are quite
polarized on the immigration issue, with almost 35 percent of them located at
the extremes of the 1–7 immigration scale. Also given in table 5.2 are the parties' mean perceived positions as well as the mean positions of each party's partisans. The Socialists and Communists, as well as their partisans, are perceived

**TABLE 5.2. Distributions of Respondents' Positions on Left-Right Ideology
and Immigration, 1988 French Presidential Election Study**

Immigration Policy		Left-Right Ideology							Total
		1	2	3	4	5	6	7	
Immigrants should be integrated into	1	6	29	67	25	15	4	0	**146**
French society	2	1	15	26	18	14	6	0	**80**
	3	1	7	36	21	16	6	2	**89**
	4	2	14	42	42	40	11	2	**153**
	5	0	2	14	18	26	19	1	**80**
	6	0	0	12	17	18	18	6	**71**
Immigrants should go home	7	1	10	16	21	14	26	8	**96**
Total		**11**	**77**	**213**	**162**	**143**	**90**	**19**	**695**

	Respondents' Mean Party Placements		Respondents' Mean Self-Placements	
	Left-Right	Immigration	Left-Right	Immigration
Communists	1.7	2.3	2.4	2.7
Socialists	3.1	2.4	3.1	3.0
UDF	4.9	4.1	4.9	3.8
RPR	5.6	4.5	5.4	4.3
National Front	6.6	6.8	6.0	6.1

as taking pro-immigration positions; the UDF, the RPR, and these parties' partisans are moderate on this issue; and the National Front is viewed as extremely anti-immigration, which reflects the beliefs of its partisans.

It is well known that under the standard Downsian spatial model parties typically present less stable positions when they compete over multiple policy dimensions than when they compete along a unidimensional continuum (see McKelvey 1976). Thus, the fact that the National Front has gained a significant following by emphasizing immigration policy raises the question: do my simulation results on French parties' Left-Right policy trajectories generalize to spatial competition over multiple dimensions in elections involving the National Front?

As we shall see, the answer to this question is yes. To investigate this issue, I respecified equation 5.1 to incorporate voter utilities over multiple policy dimensions:

$$U_i(K) = b_{iK} + c_{iK} - \sum_{j=1}^{n}(x_{ij} - k_j)^2 \qquad (5.2)$$

where $j \in \{1, \ldots, n\}$ is the set of policy dimensions over which the parties compete for votes.[9]

Using this voting specification, I performed simulations on spatial competition involving the *five* major parties that have contested French elections since the mid-1980s: the Communists, Socialists, UDF, RPR, and National Front. These simulations employed the same methodology described in chapter 4 but were based upon the two-dimensional voter distribution given in table 5.2 so that parties were allowed to vary their positions on both Left-Right ideology and immigration policy.[10] As was the case for the simulations on coalition voting reported in the previous section, I found that two-dimensional simulations based on a stable voter distribution and simulations for an evolving distribution yielded similar results. Below I report the results for the stable distribution.

Simulations Based on the Basic Partisan Vote Model
For the first set of simulations, I assumed that voters chose according to the basic partisan vote model given in equation 2.2. In the simulations, the parties were initially located at their actual perceived positions along each dimension, as reported in table 5.2, and I then calculated the parties' successive vote-maximizing positions, with each calculation updated to reflect the rival parties' policy shifts. This process continued over the course of 120 policy shifts, with the parties moving in the sequence Communists, Socialists, UDF, RPR, and National Front.[11]

Figures 5.2A through 5.2F show the parties' trajectories over the first six

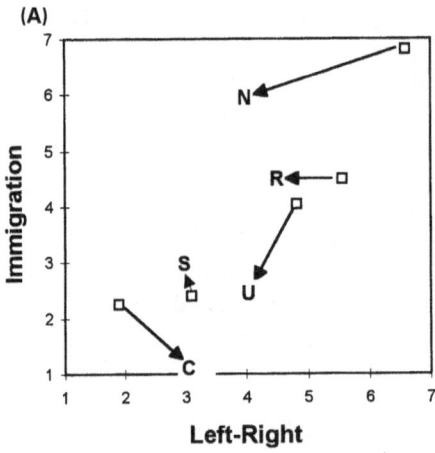

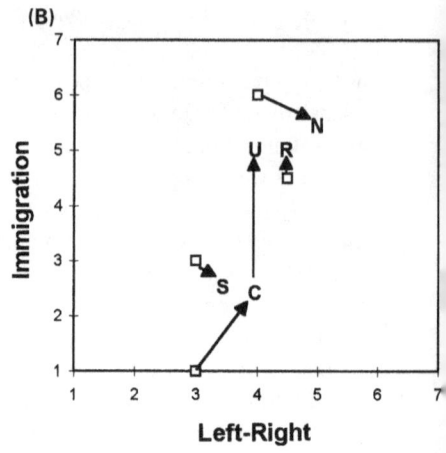

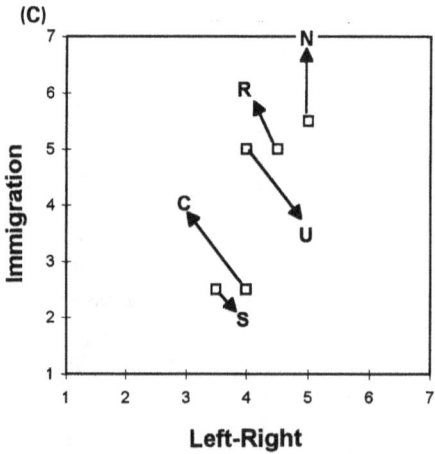

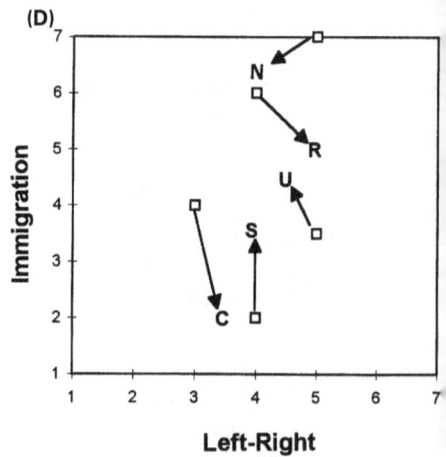

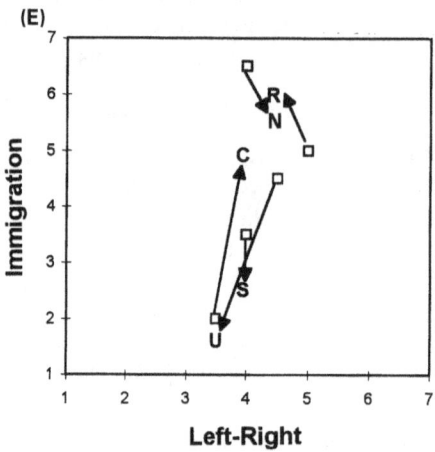

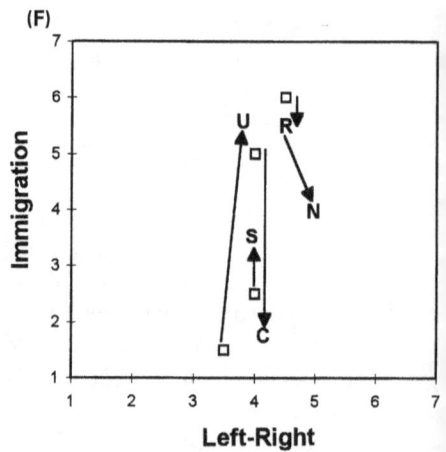

Fig. 5.2. Parties' policy trajectories for two-dimensional spatial competition under the basic partisan vote model for $b^{1/2} = 2.0$. (A) $t0 - t1$; (B) $t1 - t2$; (C) $t2 - t3$; (D) $t3 - t4$; (E) $t4 - t5$; (F) $t5 - t6$.

of the 120 computed party policy shifts, with the strength of voters' partisan attachments set at $b^{1/2} = 2.0$. At the beginning of this sequence (time $t0$), the parties locate at their actual (perceived) positions, and then at time $t1$ they shift to their updated vote-maximizing positions, as shown in figure 5.2A; in this example, the parties converge toward the center on the Left-Right dimension but remain dispersed on immigration. Figures 5.2B through 5.2F show the parties' subsequent policy shifts at the time periods $t2, t3, \ldots, t6$.

Here I focus on three related features of this policy trajectory, which we shall see recur frequently in the simulations on two-dimensional spatial competition for France. The first and most important feature is that the parties display strong tendencies to differentiate their policies on immigration but to converge on Left-Right ideology. Indeed, this pattern is so pronounced that, although the parties compete in a two-dimensional policy space, *party competition is to some extent one-dimensional in that parties compete by varying their immigration policies while maintaining stable (and centrist) left-right positions.* Part of the explanation for this pattern is that, as noted above, respondents' views are much more polarized on immigration than they are with respect to ideology and hence there is a wide range of electorally viable immigration policies that parties can propose. Indeed, the distribution of voters' immigration positions is so polarized that the parties generally avoid centrist positions along this dimension. However, the voter distribution is only part of the story, for not only are the parties' Left-Right positions more similar to each than are their immigration positions, but their Left-Right positions are more alike in these simulations on two-dimensional competition than they were in the one-dimensional simulations reported earlier. To see this, note that for the two-dimensional policy trajectories pictured in Figures 5.2A through 5.2F the parties' vote-maximizing ideologies invariably lie between 3.0 and 5.0 on the 1–7 left-right scale. By contrast, in the trajectories pictured in figures 4.3B and 4.4, which were computed for unidimensional competition on Left-Right ideology, the parties varied their positions between about 2.5 and 5.5 on the 1–7 scale. Thus, in these examples *the introduction of a second dimension of spatial competition, immigration policy, motivates vote-seeking parties to moderate their Left-Right ideologies.* As I show below, this "moderating" effect of immigration policy upon parties' ideologies is a pattern that emerges repeatedly in simulations of two-dimensional competition in France.

What accounts for this result? My reconstruction of the strategic logic that motivates parties to moderate their Left-Right positions, when they compete on ideology *and* immigration, revolves around the fact that French voters are polarized on the immigration question. This polarity motivates vote-seeking French parties to frequently propose extreme pro- or anti-immigration policies that appeal strongly to the voting constituency that supports them but alienate the remainder of the electorate. In this situation, the party can realistically at-

tract votes *only* from the constituency that shares its extreme immigration position, and it is therefore motivated to present a moderate ideology so as to avoid
alienating any part of the constituency it attracts via its immigration policy.
Hence, parties that are extreme with regard to immigration have strategic incentives to be moderate with respect to ideology.[12]

A second interesting feature of the policy trajectories pictured in figures
5.2A through 5.2F is that the parties typically present Left-Right ideologies *similar to* but *less extreme than* their partisans' positions. Thus, the Socialists and
Communists shift their ideologies within the left-right interval [3,4], while their
partisans locate overwhelmingly in the interval [1,3] (see fig. 4.3A); meanwhile, the RPR and the National Front shift their ideologies within the left-right
interval [4,5], but their partisans are clustered predominantly in the interval
[5,6]. This pattern is explained by the strategic logic outlined above, that with
the introduction of the immigration dimension vote-seeking French parties are
motivated to moderate their ideologies. As a result, although the parties present
Left-Right positions that generally reflect their partisans' beliefs, here this "representational fit" is not as tight as in the case of unidimensional competition
along the Left-Right dimension.

The third, related point concerning figures 5.2A through 5.2F is that over
time the parties' immigration policies are less stable than their Left-Right ideologies, particularly in the case of the UDF, which switches erratically between
pro-immigration and anti-immigration positions.[13] This pattern is also related
to the fact that voters are polarized on the immigration issue, and as a result
there is a wide variety of electorally viable positions on immigration that parties can propose. It is therefore understandable that parties may successively
propose two positions on immigration that are quite different but both electorally attractive.

Table 5.3 summarizes the results for temporal patterns of policy competition when the five French parties compete on both Left-Right ideology and immigration policy and voters choose according to the basic partisan model. Results are given for varying degrees of partisan attachment, ranging from $b^{1/2} =$
0 (the standard Downsian model) to $b^{1/2} = 2.0$. Columns 2–6 report the parties' mean positions on Left-Right ideology (the first coordinate) and immigration (the second coordinate) over the course of 120 policy shifts. Column 7 reports the frequency with which parties locate outside of their ideological areas.
Also given are the mean positions of each party's partisans along each dimension. (I do not report the incidence of leapfrogging behavior for reasons explained in note 13).

The results presented in table 5.3 suggest that the patterns of parties' policy trajectories that I identified above, with respect to figures 5.2A through 5.2F,
recur frequently for simulations involving five parties and two policy dimensions. First, note that in all simulations for which voters display partisan at-

TABLE 5.3. French Parties' Policy Trajectories for Two-Dimensional Spatial Competition (Left-Right × immigration) and Voting under the Basic Partisan Model

Strength of Partisan Attachment (1)	Mean Party Positions					Positions Outside Ideological Area (7)
	Communists (2)	Socialists (3)	UDF (4)	RPR (5)	NF (6)	
$b^{1/2} = 0$	4.2,4.0	3.8,4.0	3.7,4.2	4.0,3.8	4.4,3.8	40%
$b^{1/2} = 0.5$	3.6,3.8	3.4,3.0	4.1,3.9	4.3,4.6	4.5,4.3	17
$b^{1/2} = 1.0$	3.7,3.4	3.3,3.0	4.0,3.7	4.6,4.6	4.7,4.9	14
$b^{1/2} = 1.5$	3.7,3.3	3.3,2.8	4.0,3.9	4.5,4.5	4.8,5.3	15
$b^{1/2} = 2.0$	3.4,3.0	3.8,3.1	4.2,3.6	4.2,4.8	4.5,5.2	4
Partisans' mean positions	2.4,2.7	3.1,3.0	4.9,3.8	5.4,4.3	6.0,6.1	

Note: In columns 2–6, the first coordinate represents the party's mean Left-Right position over the course of 120 policy shifts; the second coordinate represents the party's mean position on immigration. Column 7 gives the percentages of parties' Left-Right positions that fall outside the party's ideological area. The Communists' and Socialists' ideological area is defined as the policy interval [1,4]; the ideological area for the RPR and the National Front is defined as the policy interval [4,7]. The UDF is not assigned an ideological area.

tachments (i.e., for $b > 0$) the parties' ideologies tend to be more centrist than their immigration policies (with the location 4.0 along the 1–7 ideology and immigration scales defined as the most centrist positions). Furthermore, with respect to policy representation, the parties' mean Left-Right positions are consistently similar to but less extreme than the mean positions of their partisans. In addition, the parties faithfully represent their partisans' beliefs about immigration, with the Communist and Socialist Parties presenting consistently pro-immigrant policies that mirror their partisans' mean positions, while the UDF and the RPR take middle of the road positions that reflect their supporters' moderate tendencies. In the simulations, the National Front takes moderately anti-immigration positions that are similar to but less extreme than its partisans' opinions. Finally, note that even for weak degrees of partisan attachment (i.e., $b^{1/2} = 0.5$) the parties seldom locate outside of their ideological areas, although this result may overstate the degree of parties' policy stability since, as noted above, they tend to shift their immigration policies to a greater extent than they shift their ideologies.

In toto, these results suggest that the introduction of a second policy dimension, immigration, along with the entry into the party system of the National Front, motivates subtle but important changes in French parties' behavior. As was the case for unidimensional competition, parties competing on the basis of both ideology and immigration policy have electoral incentives to take positions that appeal to their partisans, and this strategic dynamic motivates parties to present stable, divergent, and representative policies. However, in the two-dimensional setting parties' ideologies are somewhat less representative than was the case for unidimensional ideological competition. This difference plausibly arises because French public opinion is polarized on the immigration issue, and this distribution gives parties strategic incentives to moderate their ideologies so that they present positions similar to but less extreme than the ideologies of their supporters.

Simulations for the Coalition Vote Model
I next performed alternative simulations on two-dimensional spatial competition in which the French parties were assumed to seek votes from an electorate that displayed coalition biases. These simulations produced conclusions on parties' policy trajectories that differed somewhat from the results obtained for the basic partisan model. These differences are illustrated in figures 5.3A through 5.3F, which show the first six of 120 party policy shifts computed given the specification $b^{1/2} = 2.0$ and $c^{1/2} = 1.0$. When compared to the computed party trajectories pictured for the basic partisan model (see figs. 5.2A through 5.2F), these results suggest that when voters display coalition biases vote-seeking parties competing on the basis of both ideology and immigration policy have added incentives to present stable, representative policies. Thus, in the policy trajectories pictured in figures 5.3A through 5.3F, the parties adjust their positions only gradually over time, even with respect to the polarized immigration dimension, and furthermore their positions generally reflect their partisans' beliefs. This supports the hypotheses, developed earlier, that when voters display coalition biases parties are motivated to "home in" on the narrow sectors of the policy space that are dense with their own partisans as well as the partisans of their coalition partner. In addition, note that, as was the case for simulations on unidimensional competition under the coalition vote model, here the parties display strong tendencies to converge toward their coalition partner while diverging from the members of rival coalition.[14]

Table 5.4 summarizes results for temporal patterns of policy competition when voters display coalition biases and the French parties compete on both Left-Right ideology and immigration policy. When partisan and coalition attachments are very weak (i.e., for $b^{1/2} = 0.5$ and $c^{1/2} = 0.25$), results are comparable to those reported in table 5.3, for the basic partisan model, in that parties frequently shift outside their ideological areas and present convergent, unrepresentative policies. However, for moderate to high degrees of partisan and coalition attachment (i.e., for $b^{1/2} \geq 1.0$ and $c^{1/2} \geq 0.5$), the parties rarely shift outside of their ideological areas and all parties except the National Front present policies that closely match their partisans' mean positions. In addition, note that, as was the case for simulations on unidimensional competition under the coalition vote model, here the parties take positions on both dimensions that are similar to those of their coalition partner but diverge from the positions

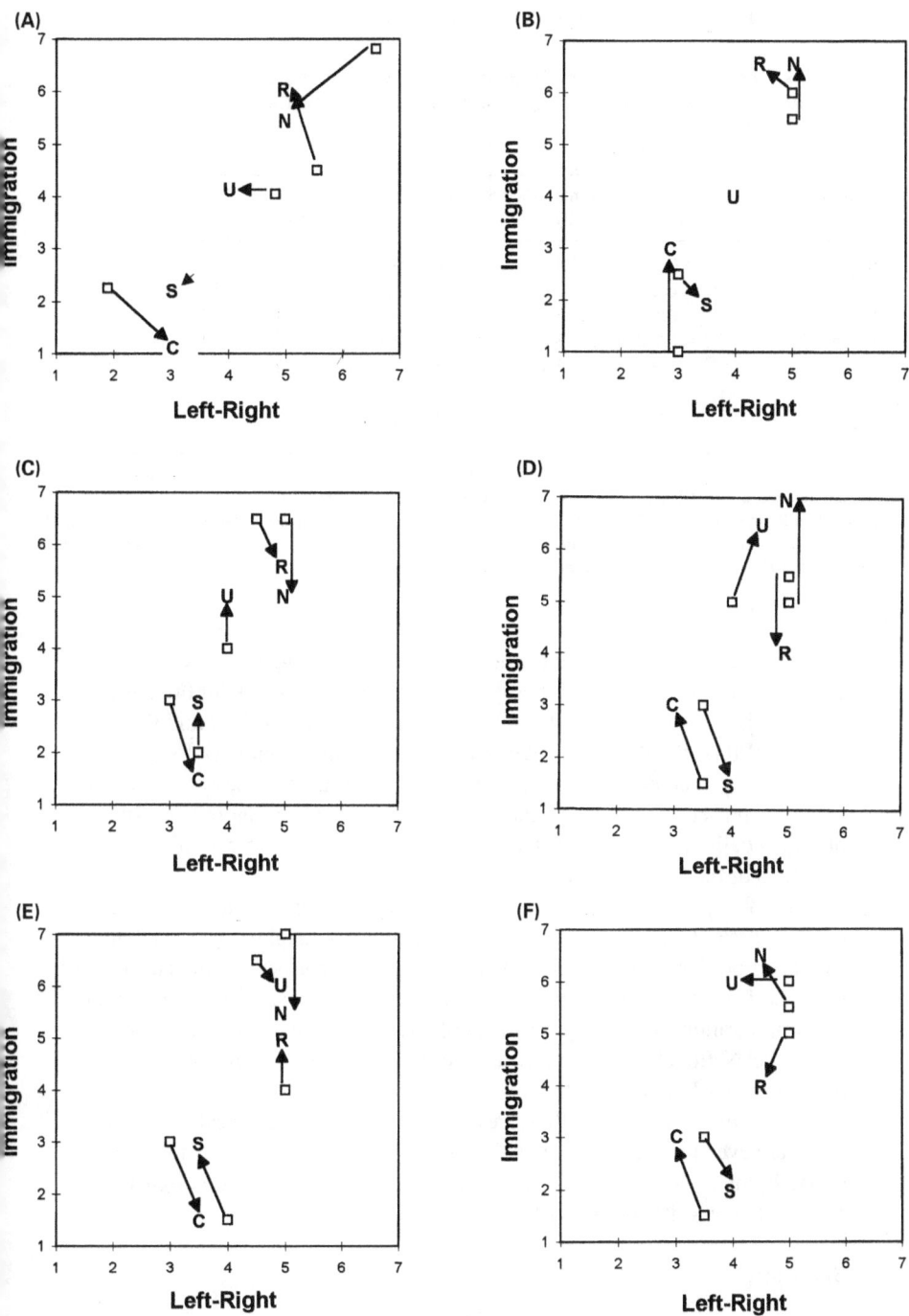

Fig. 5.3.   Parties' policy trajectories for two-dimensional spatial competition under the coalition partisan vote model for $b^{1/2} = 2.0$ and $c^{1/2} = 1.0$. (A) $t0 - t1$; (B) $t1 - t2$; (C) $t2 - t3$; (D) $t3 - t4$; (E) $t4 - t5$; (F) $t5 - t6$.

TABLE 5.4.   French Parties' Policy Trajectories for Two-Dimensional Spatial Competition (Left-Right × immigration) and Voting under the Coalition Model

Strength of Partisan Attachment (1)	Attachment to Coalition Partner (2)	Mean Party Positions					Positions Outside Ideological Area (8)
		Communists (3)	Socialists (4)	UDF (5)	RPR (6)	NF (7)	
$b^{1/2} = 0$	$c^{1/2} = 0$	4.2,4.0	3.8,4.0	3.7,4.2	4.0,3.8	4.4,3.8	40%
$b^{1/2} = 0.5$	$c^{1/2} = 0.25$	3.6,3.6	3.5,3.2	4.1,4.2	4.2,4.5	4.5,4.5	21
$b^{1/2} = 1.0$	$c^{1/2} = 0.5$	3.2,3.0	3.4,2.9	4.6,4.5	4.7,4.7	4.4,4.7	6
$b^{1/2} = 1.5$	$c^{1/2} = 0.75$	3.2,3.1	3.3,2.8	4.4,4.2	4.5,4.6	4.6,5.1	6
$b^{1/2} = 2.0$	$c^{1/2} = 1.0$	3.1,2.4	3.3,2.8	4.3,4.4	4.6,4.7	4.7,5.6	0
Partisans' mean positions		2.4,2.7	3.1,3.0	4.9,3.8	5.4,4.3	6.0,6.1	

Note: In columns 3–7, the first coordinate represents the party's mean Left-Right position over the course of 120 policy shifts; the second coordinate represents the party's mean position on immigration. Column 8 gives the percentages of parties' Left-Right positions that fall outside the party's ideological area. The Communists' and Socialists' ideological area is defined as the policy interval [1,4]; the ideological area for the RPR and the National Front is defined as the policy interval [4,7]. The UDF is not assigned an ideological area.

taken by members of the rival coalition. These results suggest that when voters display coalition biases the parties that participate in the two major French electoral coalitions—the Socialists and the Communists on the Left and the UDF and the RPR on the Right—behave similarly when they compete along two dimensions and a unidimensional continuum. In both cases, these parties are motivated to present stable, representative policies that are similar to the positions of their coalition partner but that diverge from the policies espoused by the members of the rival coalition.

With respect to the National Front, note that in the simulations this party rarely shifts outside of its ideological area and tends to take positions that are similar to but less extreme than the positions of its partisans. This is true despite the fact that, on average, the National Front proposes the most strongly anti-immigration, right-wing positions of any of the five parties. However, because the National Front's partisans hold such extreme views on both immigration and Left-Right ideology (their mean positions are 6.0 and 6.1, respectively, on the 1–7 left-right scale and the 1–7 immigration scale), these partisans are even more extreme than the party that represents them. Thus, the National Front is "reasonably" representative of its partisans, although not as representative as its four competitors.

Summary

Two important conclusions emerge from the simulations reported here on French parties' policy trajectories when spatial competition encompasses multiple dimensions and elections involve the National Front. The first is that when French parties seek votes from an electorate that cares about both Left-Right ideology *and* immigration policy the parties are motivated to present divergent, stable, and (reasonably) representative policies. Thus, the central results on French party competition reported in chapter 4 generalize to a two-dimensional context that plausibly characterizes French politics in the 1980s and 1990s.

The second conclusion is that, to the extent that results on two-dimensional spatial competition in France differ from results on Left-Right competition alone, the central difference is that in the two-dimensional context the parties' policies are somewhat less representative of their partisans' beliefs. A plausible explanation for this result is that the French electorate is quite polarized on immigration policy, the "new" dimension in French politics, and this voter dispersion motivates vote-seeking parties to moderate their ideologies. In addition, I note that partisans of the National Front, the "new" major French party, hold such extreme views that the National Front's vote-maximizing positions appear moderate compared to its supporters' beliefs. These considerations aside, I emphasize that the contrast between the results on two-dimensional, five-party elections and my earlier results on one-dimensional, four-party elections are differences in degree, not kind. For both types of elections, the behavior of vote-seeking French parties is characterized by policy stability, divergence, and reasonably faithful representation—patterns that enhance the prospects for responsible party government.

5.5. Conclusions

The central conclusion developed here is that results on voting with coalition bias and over multiple policy dimensions follow a similar logic, and produce similar outcomes, to spatial competition under the basic partisan vote model on a single policy dimension. For each model of voter choice, parties are motivated to present policies that reflect their partisans' beliefs, and hence over time parties rarely renege on their basic ideological orientations.

Of course, the more complex vote models studied here do motivate subtle innovations in party strategies. Thus, under the coalition vote model parties are motivated to present policies that are similar to those of their coalition partner but diverge from the policies proposed by the members of the rival coalition. This strategic incentive has conflicting implications for responsible party government. On the one hand, the fact that coalition partners' positions tend to be similar reduces the range of distinct policy alternatives available to French voters. On the other hand, voters' coalition biases motivate parties to present quite stable policy trajectories, which plausibly crystallize their policy images in the minds of voters, thereby enhancing the functioning of responsible party government. The other complication analyzed in this chapter, that voters' decisions are influenced by immigration policy, also affects party positioning in that it gives parties strategic incentives to moderate their ideologies. This effect slightly weakens mass-elite linkages in that it motivates French parties to present ideologies similar to but less extreme than their partisans' beliefs.

CHAPTER 6

Extensions to Probabilistic Voting

6.1. Introduction

The preceding four chapters explored the implications of a voting model that incorporates a finding supported by extensive behavioral research, that voters are moved by partisan loyalties in addition to policy motivations. When applied to multiparty spatial competition, the central findings for this partisan vote model are:

1. Parties have electoral incentives to appeal on policy grounds to voters who support them in part for nonpolicy reasons. Thus, party leaders are motivated to behave "responsibly" toward their party's partisans, which typically ensures a reasonable degree of policy representation.

2. The pressure for different political parties to appeal to different voting constituencies creates incentives for policy divergence and stability. In certain cases, this leads to a divergent equilibrium in parties' vote-maximizing policies—an outcome that is virtually precluded under the standard, multiparty, Downsian spatial model. However, the more common outcome is one in which parties shift their positions over time but rarely leapfrog and remain within ideologically delimited areas of the policy space. These outcomes correspond closely to the historical patterns identified by the Manifesto Research Group, based upon its analyses of party programmes in some 20 postwar democracies.

3. Applications of the basic partisan vote model to empirical data from historical elections in Britain and France suggest that the conclusions summarized above apply for a wide range of assumptions about the electoral impact of voter partisanship. These conclusions also extend to more complex voting models, which incorporate voters' loyalties to their party's coalition partner, and voting over multiple policy dimensions, features that plausibly characterize voters' decision processes in contemporary French elections.

In this chapter, I investigate the implications of a still more complex vote model, which incorporates, in addition to voter partisanship, an unmeasured random term that renders the vote choice indeterminate from partisanship and policy voting alone. This model captures an important strategic aspect of party competition, that party leaders (as well as voting researchers) cannot predict voter decisions with certainty but can at best assign probabilities to voters' choices. I ask the question: to what extent do the conclusions on deterministic partisan voting summarized above extend to situations in which partisan voters choose probabilistically?

In this chapter, I show that the central strategic imperative I have identified for party competition in a partisan electorate, that vote-seeking parties are motivated to appeal to their partisans on policy grounds, extends to situations in which voters choose probabilistically. For this reason, the probabilistic partisan vote model, like the deterministic model explored in chapters 2–5, motivates parties to present divergent policies that reflect their partisans' beliefs. At the same time, I show that the introduction of probabilistic voting entails two revisions of our earlier conclusions on party strategies. First, when voters' decisions are influenced by unmeasured motivations—and particularly when these motivations significantly influence voters' decisions—an equilibrium in parties' vote-maximizing positions is extremely likely to exist. This result stands in sharp contrast to the analyses reported in chapters 3–5, which suggest that when voters decide on the basis of partisanship and policies alone party equilibria are the exception not the rule. Second, when voters choose probabilistically, vote-seeking parties have additional motivations to shift toward the center of the policy space compared to their strategies under deterministic voting assumptions. As a result, when parties seek support from an electorate that is moved by policies, partisanship, *and* unmeasured motivations, they will typically present policies *similar to* but *less extreme than* their supporters' beliefs.

Thus, the introduction of probabilistic voting motivates parties to present policies that are *more centrist* than those we obtained for deterministic voting but also *more stable* in that probabilistic voting behavior enhances the prospects for party policy equilibrium. In summary, under probabilistic voting assumptions, vote-seeking parties can be expected to present stable, divergent, and (reasonably) representative policies. These outcomes illuminate the finding that responsible party government functions well in contemporary democracies, a conclusion I support with both deductive theorems and empirical applications to French and British politics.

I begin in section 6.2 by developing a model of partisan voting that incorporates a random component that represents unmeasured motivations that render the vote choice indeterminate from the parties' perspectives. In section 6.3, I explore the logic of party competition for this probabilistic model under the simplifying assumption that all voters are independent, that is, that they display no partisan attachments. Section 6.4 extends this perspective to elections involving partisan voters. I present examples designed to illuminate the logic of party competition for probabilistic partisan voting, which suggests that the introduction of probabilistic voting leaves unchanged the central motivation derived in chapters 2–5 for deterministic partisan voting; namely, that parties have electoral incentives to present policies that appeal to their partisans. However, these examples also suggest reasons why, when voting is probabilistic, vote-seeking parties have additional incentives to moderate their policies. In section 6.5, I present theoretical results concerning the existence of multiparty equilibrium for the probabilistic partisan vote model, and section 6.6 reports empirical applications to voting data from Britain and France. Section 6.7 briefly summarizes the results of further studies by Adams and Merrill (1999a, 2000) that bear on the question: do my conclusions on party policy strategies in a partisan electorate generalize to electorates that choose according to still more general voting models that incorporate group loyalties rooted in class, religion, and income? Section 6.8 presents a summary and conclusion.

While the main body of this chapter emphasizes an intuitive understanding of party competition with probabilistic voting, appendix C presents a more rigorous formal analysis of party strategies and equilibrium results.

6.2. A Model of Probabilistic Choice for Partisan Voters

A major justification for exploring the implications of the partisan vote model introduced in chapter 2 is that this model captures a central finding from behavioral research, that voter partisanship influences the vote. However, behavioralists also find that they cannot predict survey respondents' vote intentions with certainty from policy preferences and partisanship alone, nor can they perfectly anticipate the vote from any combination of voter attributes, including sociodemographic characteristics, retrospective evaluations of incumbent performance, and so on. To incorporate this uncertainty, I modify equation 2.2 to incorporate a random component, μ_i, which is conceptually equivalent to the random term that behavioralists employ for voting analyses based upon maximum likelihood estimation models such as logit and probit:

$$U_i(K) = b_{iK} - s(x_i - k)^2 + \mu_{iK} \tag{6.1}$$

where μ_{iK} represents unmeasured sources of voter i's utility for party K and is generated from an underlying distribution (specified below). Note that equation 6.1 also differs from equation 2.2 in that it includes a policy salience coefficient, s, that indicates the importance voters attach to policies relative to their unmeasured motivations.[1] As with deterministic policy voting, voters select the parties that maximize their utilities, but the random components render voters' choices indeterminate from partisanship and policy proximity alone. I label the model so specified the *probabilistic partisan vote model* (PPV). Note that this voting model is similar to those used in previous studies of spatial competition with probabilistic voting (e.g., Enelow and Hinich 1981, 1984; Hinich and Munger 1994; Coughlin 1992; Lin et al. 1999) *except* that it includes a measured nonpolicy component that these studies omit.

The probability that voter i votes for party K depends on the value of the measured partisan component b_{iK} and the policy component $s(x_i - k)^2$ in equation 6.1 as well as the distribution of the error term μ_{iK}. The assumption I employ here, which is characteristic of logit analysis, is that each μ_{iK} is generated independently from a type I extreme value (EV) distribution.[2]

The logit has been widely used in empirical analyses of voting in multi-candidate and multiparty elections (Adams and Merrill 1999a; Adams and Merrill 1999b, 2000; Alvarez and Nagler 1998; Iversen 1994a; Rivers 1988; Whitten and Palmer 1996) and is convenient in that it leads to a simple closed form for the probability, $P_i(K)$, that voter i will vote for party K:

$$P_i(K) = e^{b_{iK} - s(x_i - k)^2} / \left[\sum_{J \in \Re} e^{b_{iJ} - s(x_i - j)^2} \right] \tag{6.2}$$

where $\Re = \{A, B, \ldots, N\}$ represents the set of competing parties. In words, equation 6.2 states that the voter i's probability of voting for party K equals the exponential of i's evaluation of K, based upon measured partisan and policy motivations, divided by the sum of the exponentials of i's measured partisan and policy evaluations over each competing party. While the proof of this proposition is not particularly illuminating (see Train 1986, 53–54), a central aspect of equation 6.2 is that $P_i(K)$ increases with $[b_{iK} - s(x_i - k)^2]$ but decreases with $[b_{iJ} - s(x_i - j)^2]$, where $J \neq K$—that is, voter i is more likely to vote for K the more highly i evaluates K based upon measured policy and partisan motivations and the *less* highly i evaluates the rival parties based upon these measured motivations.

6.3. Party Policy Strategies for Probabilistic Voting with Independent Voters

Because the logic of party competition for the PPV model is complex, I first explore multiparty spatial competition in an *independent electorate,* for which $b_{iJ} = 0$ for all voters, i, with respect to all parties, $J \in \Re$. This exercise highlights a central feature of probabilistic voting models, that they present parties with added incentives to propose centrist policies that appeal to all segments of the electorate, a motivation that we shall see extends to party competition for the probabilistic partisan vote model.

For independent voters, equation 6.2 simplifies to

$$P_i(K) = e^{-s(x_i - k)^2} / \left[\sum_{J \in \Re} e^{-s(x_i - j)^2} \right] \tag{6.3}$$

Figure 6.1 provides insights into voters' choice probabilities and parties' policy strategies when they seek votes from an independent electorate. In these examples, I posit the distribution of voter preferences given in figure 6.1A, which is similar to the distribution used for the examples presented in chapters 2–5. In this example, the three parties L, C, and R locate at $l = 4.0$, $c = 5.0$, and $r = 6.0$, respectively. Note that the center party, C, is tightly "squeezed" between its two rivals, so that under the deterministic voting model employed in chapters 2–5 party C would receive few votes from an independent electorate.

Recall that the salience of voters' policy motivations relative to unmeasured factors is given by the policy salience coefficient s. When s is extremely high in equation 6.3, we approach the limiting case of deterministic policy voting, while when s approaches zero voters attach little importance to policies relative to their unmeasured motivations and independent voters' choices appear almost random from the analyst's (and the parties') perspective. Figure 6.1B illustrates this point by picturing the probability, $P_i(C)$, that an independent voter, i, votes for C (the vertical axis) as a function of i's left-right position, x_i, for three different values of s. For $s = 2.0$, voters place intense weight on party policies, so that if i holds centrist views then $P_i(C)$ is high but when i takes a right- or left-wing position $P_i(C)$ approaches zero. For $s = 0.15$, voters place less emphasis on policies and the probability that i votes for C varies only between about $P_i(C) = 0.20$, for extreme right- and left-wing positions, and $P_i(C) = 0.36$ for centrist positions. Finally, for $s = 0.05$, $P_i(C)$ is quite unresponsive to changes in i's position, x_i.

Figure 6.1C illustrates the same variability but from the perspective of changes in party C's position. Here the curves represent C's expected vote $EVC(c,s)$ (the vertical axis) over the voter distribution given in figure 6.1A as a function of C's left-right position, c, and the policy salience coefficient, s, with L and R fixed at $l = 4.0$ and $r = 6.0$, respectively.[3] Note that when voters are primarily policy driven (i.e., at $s = 2.0$) party C suffers a severe electoral penalty by locating near the center because it is then squeezed between its rivals on the left and right and attracts virtually no support from the wings. This is the same phenomenon that motivates leapfrogging behavior under deterministic policy voting.

For moderate ($s = 0.15$) and low ($s = 0.5$) degrees of policy voting, by contrast, the center becomes electorally attractive and C maximizes expected votes by locating at the voter mean, 5.0, despite the fact that only the narrow band of centrist voters in the policy interval [4.5,5.5] actually prefer C on policy grounds!

Why, in this hypothetical example, are centrist positions electorally attractive when voters attach little weight to policies given that centrist positions are disastrous when voters are primarily policy oriented? The central intuition is that as voters deemphasize policies the *manner* in which policy voting influences party support changes. For high levels of policy voting, party support re-

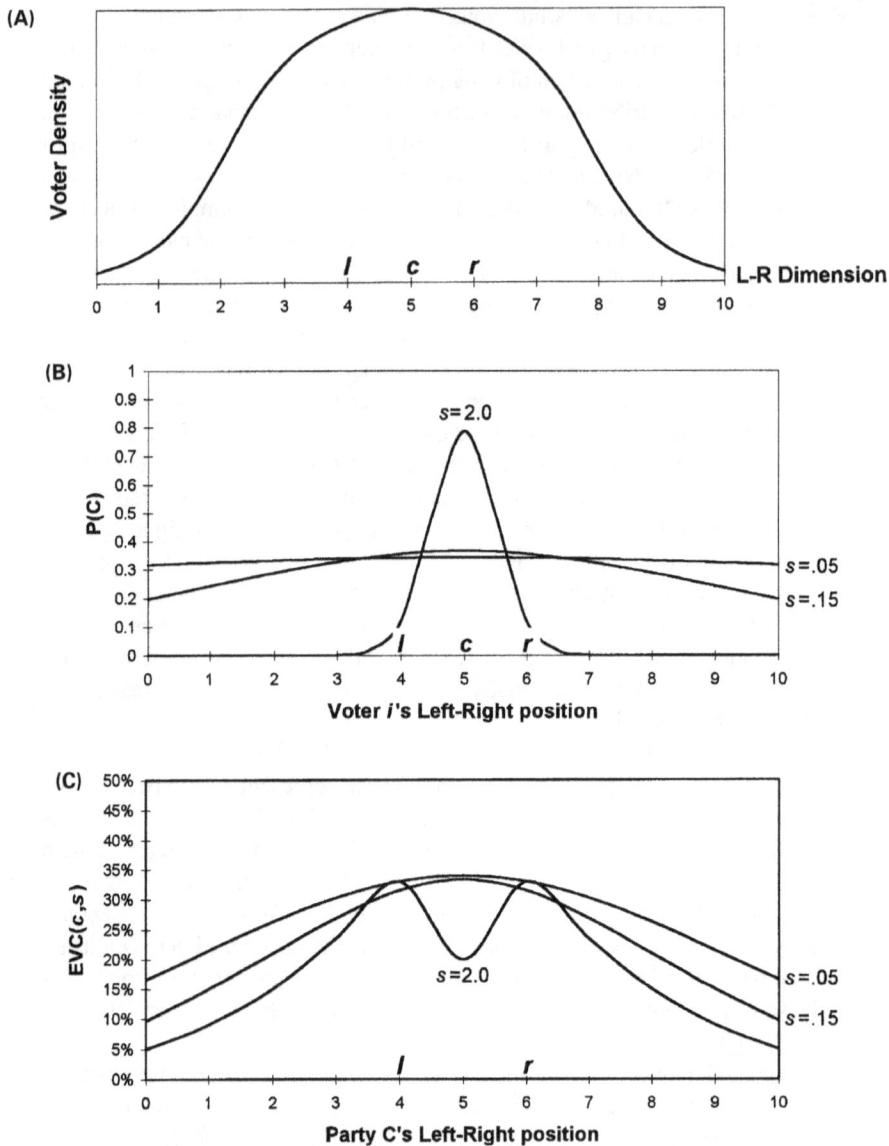

Fig. 6.1. Spatial competition involving independent voters who choose probabilistically. (*A*) Initial policy distribution of voters and parties L, C, and R; (*B*) $P_i(C)$ as a function of voter *i*'s Left-Right position; (*C*) EVC (*c,s*) as a function of party C's Left-Right position.

flects the proportion of voters who are nearest the party in the policy space, so that when centrist parties are squeezed they receive little electoral support. By contrast, when policy voting is low, that is, for s near zero, support for a party reflects the *general acceptability* of the party's platform as measured by the electorate's total policy losses. Because parties minimize these policy losses by locating near the center of the voter distribution, it follows that when voters deemphasize policies vote-maximizing parties have electoral incentives to propose centrist policies.[4]

This intuition is supported by the following theorem, which obtains providing that each party K selects its platform from a finite set of feasible platforms, which includes the mean voter position:

THEOREM 6.1:   *Assume the probability function for independent voters given by equation 6.3. Then there exists η such that for all $0 < s < \eta$ each party $K \in \Re$'s vote-maximizing platform is the mean voter position.*

PROOF: See appendix C.

In words, the theorem states that when the importance of voters' measured policy motivations is sufficiently small relative to their unmeasured motivations each party maximizes its expected vote by locating at the voter mean, regardless of rival parties' positions. An immediate corollary to theorem 6.1 is that *when s is sufficiently small an equilibrium exists for which all parties locate at the voter mean.*[5] I emphasize that this result contrasts sharply with the logic of party competition under the deterministic Downsian spatial model, for which we have seen that multiparty equilibria are extremely unlikely to exist (see section 1.2).[6]

Figure 6.2 illustrates how the existence of this convergent equilibrium depends on the value of s. In this example, I assume the voter distribution given in figure 6.1A, and I place parties L and R at the voter mean 5.0 while varying C's position across the policy dimension.[7] The vertical axis shows C's expected vote, $EVC(c,s)$, for varying values of the policy salience coefficient s. When s is high ($s = 2.0$), C maximizes votes by locating at the center-left or the center-right and there is no convergent equilibrium. When policy voting is moderate to low (i.e., $s = .05$ or $s = .15$), by contrast, C is drawn to the center and a convergent equilibrium exists.

This analysis suggests that when voters are independent the introduction of random, unmeasured voter motivations results in two changes in vote-seeking parties' policy strategies compared to their strategies under the deterministic vote model. First, when the strength of voters' policy motivations is low relative to their unmeasured motivations, parties should propose centrist policies that appeal broadly to the electorate, regardless of the policy strategies pursued by their competitors. Second, probabilistic choice by voters motivates policy

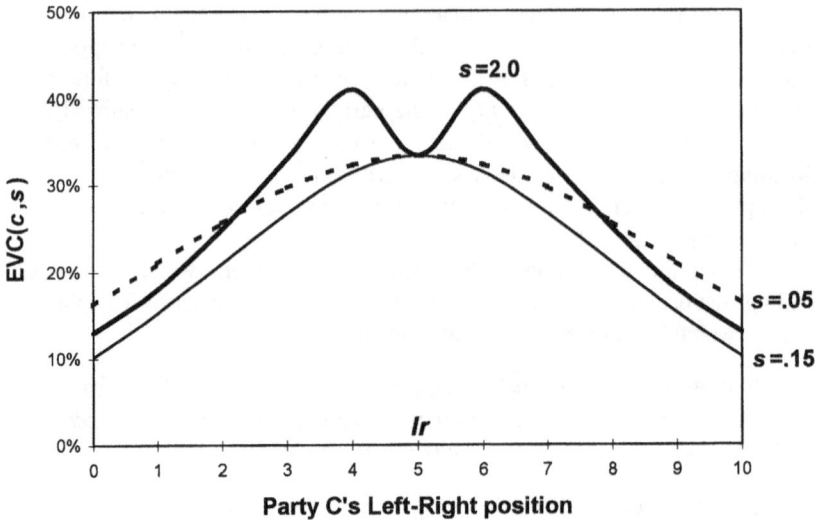

Fig. 6.2. Party C's expected vote as a function of Left-Right position, with parties L and R located at the voter mean 5.0. Calculations are based on the voter distribution given in figure 6.1A, for independent voters.

stability in parties in that policy equilibria are likely to exist. Below I show that aspects of these strategies carry over to party competition in a partisan electorate.

6.4. Party Policy Strategies for Probabilistic Voting in a Partisan Electorate: The Motivation to Present Centrist Yet Representative Policies

Theorem 6.1 established that when they seek support from independent voters who are moved in part by unmeasured motivations vote-seeking parties have incentives to present policies that minimize policy losses over all voters, that is, they should weigh the policy preferences of the entire electorate. This contrasts with the strategic logic that obtains under the deterministic partisan vote model analyzed in chapters 2–5, for which parties are motivated to reflect their partisans' beliefs, even when these partisans are significantly more left- or right-wing than the electorate as a whole. This raises the question: when voters are moved by both partisan loyalties *and* random, unmeasured motivations, should vote-seeking parties propose policies that appeal to the electorate as a whole or should they target their own partisans?

The answer is that when voters choose according to the PPV model vote-seeking parties have incentives to pursue a "compromise" strategy that combines elements of both policy strategies summarized above. As is the case for probabilistic voting with independent voters, under the PPV model parties have electoral incentives to weigh the beliefs of the entire electorate. However, under the PPV model parties are motivated to attach added weight to their own partisans' beliefs compared to the beliefs of rival parties' partisans, a strategy consistent with the logic of deterministic partisan voting. As a result, vote-seeking parties are motivated to present policies that reflect their partisans' beliefs but are shaded somewhat toward the center in order to appeal to the electorate as a whole. Hence, we shall see that under the PPV model parties have incentives to present policies *similar to but less extreme than* their partisans' policy beliefs.

The Dynamics of Voters' Choice Probabilities under the Probabilistic Partisan Model

Figure 6.3 illustrates the dynamics of voters' choice probabilities for the PPV specification given in equation 6.2 for the situation in which parties C and R locate at $c = 5$ and $r = 7$ along the zero to 10 Left-Right continuum, while voter i's preferred position is $x_i = 3$. With the policy salience coefficient set at $s = .05$ and the strength of voters' partisan attachments set at $b = 3$,[8] figure 6.3A shows how the probability $P_i(L)$ that i votes for L (the vertical axis) varies as a function of L's Left-Right position, l. The top slope shows $P_i(L)$ given that i identifies with party L; the middle slope represents $P_i(L)$ given that i is a partisan of C; and the bottom slope gives $P_i(L)$ given that i identifies with R. As expected, i is most likely to vote for L if he or she identifies with L. Furthermore, note that with s set at the "low" value of .05 the voter's likelihood of voting for L is not very responsive to L's positioning. For instance, if i identifies with party L, his or her probability of voting for L remains above 50 percent even if L locates on the extreme right, far from i's left-wing position, $x_i = 3$. This makes intuitive sense, for partisans who place little weight on policies should reliably vote for their party regardless of its ideology. If i identifies with C or R, by contrast, his or her probability of voting for L is below 20 percent even if L locates exactly at i's preferred policy position, $x_i = 3$.

Figure 6.3B illustrates a hypothetical situation identical to the one pictured in figure 6.3A, except that s is now set at the moderate value $s = .15$. With the importance of policies enhanced, voter i's choice probabilities are much more responsive to L's positioning. If L locates on the far right, for instance, $P_i(L)$ falls below 10 percent even if i is a partisan of L. This corresponds to the situation in which partisans who are attentive to party platforms disagree strongly with their parties' policies.

(A)

(B)

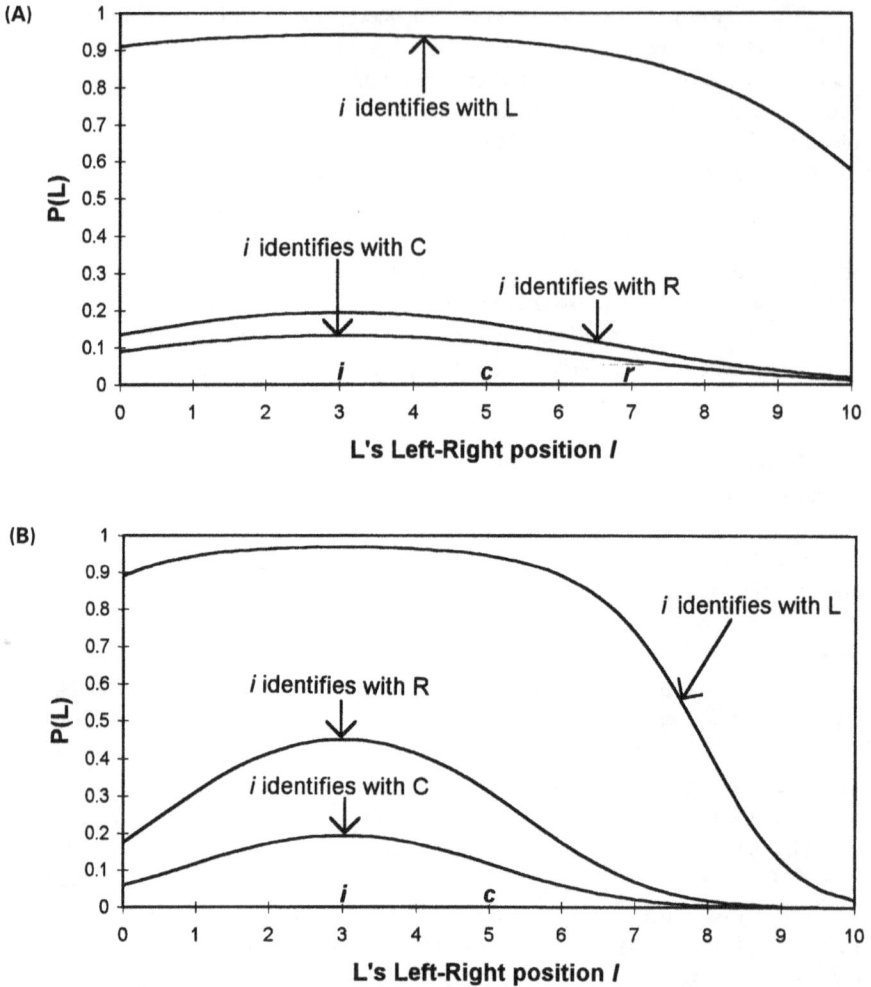

Fig. 6.3. Voter i's probability of voting for party L as a function of L's Left-Right position. Vote probabilities are computed for $b = 3.0$. (A) $P_i(L)$ as a function of party L's Left-Right position for $s = .05$; (B) $P_i(L)$ as a function of party L's Left-Right position for $s = .15$.

One other aspect of figure 6.3 deserves comment. Note that in both figures, as L shifts across the policy spectrum, $P_i(L)$ varies more if i identifies with L than if i identifies with a rival party. In figure 6.3A, for instance, the likelihood that i votes for party L given that i identifies with L varies between 94 percent (when L proposes i's preferred policy $l = 3$) and 58 percent (when $l =$

10)—a difference of 36 percent. If i is a partisan of C, by contrast, $P_i(L)$ varies between 17 and 2 percent, a 15 percent difference; if i identifies with R, $P_i(L)$ varies between 13 and 1 percent, a 12 percent difference. A similar pattern obtains in figure 6.3B. In these examples, therefore, *party L loses more by shifting its policy away from its own partisans than it loses by shifting away from rival parties' partisans.*[9]

The examples illustrated in figure 6.3 therefore suggest that parties gain more votes, on an expected value basis, by presenting policies that appeal to their partisans than they gain by presenting policies that appeal to rival parties' partisans. This implies that when voting is probabilistic vote-seeking parties are motivated to present policies that reflect their partisans' beliefs, the same logic that obtains under the deterministic partisan vote model. However, note that in the above examples party L *does* gain votes (on an expected value basis) by presenting policies that appeal to rival parties' partisans, although this increase is less than the expected gain that accrues from targeting its own partisans. This suggests that in devising their policy strategies vote-seeking parties should consider the views of all voters.

The Tradeoff between Policy Representation and Moderation: How Much Should Parties Moderate Their Policies Compared to Their Partisans' Beliefs?

The preceding analysis suggests reasons why, when voters choose according to the PPV model, vote-seeking parties should present policies similar to but less extreme than their partisans' beliefs. Parties should present policies similar to their partisans' beliefs because they gain more votes, on an expected value basis, by targeting their partisans than they lose by shifting away from rival parties' partisans. Parties should moderate their policies, compared to their partisans' beliefs, because parties do lose some support by deserting rival parties' partisans and hence should attach some weight to these voters' preferences, even as they weight their own partisans' positions more heavily. This raises the question: *how much* should vote-seeking parties moderate their policies compared to their partisans' beliefs?

Using a combination of technical analysis and computer simulations on multiparty spatial competition under the PPV model, Merrill and Adams (2000b) identify several factors that affect vote-seeking parties' motivations to moderate their policies compared to their partisans' beliefs. These include: the number of party identifiers; the degree to which the beliefs of a party's identifiers diverge from the beliefs of the electorate as a whole; and the strength of the policy salience coefficient, s.[10] Specifically, Merrill and Adams conclude that, ceteris paribus, *a party is motivated to shift its policies further away from the center, in the direction of its partisans' beliefs, to the extent that:*

1. The number of voters that identify with the party increases (e.g., large parties are motivated to move further away from the center than small parties are)
2. The party's partisans take extreme positions (e.g., parties supported by extreme partisans have incentives to move further away from the center than do parties supported by moderate partisans)
3. The policy salience coefficient, s, increases (e.g., the greater the emphasis voters place on policies, relative to unmeasured motivations, the greater are parties' incentives to present noncentrist policies)

Each of these conclusions makes intuitive sense. With regard to the strategic implications of the number of partisans, given that vote-seeking parties are motivated to weigh their own partisans' policy preferences more heavily than those of rival parties' partisans, it is logical that the larger the number of voters that identify with a party the more heavily these partisans weigh in the party's strategic calculations and the more the party will shade its position in the direction of these partisans' beliefs. A similar logic applies with respect to the extremity of partisans' beliefs: the more extreme the views of a party's partisans the more strongly these views "pull" the party in the direction of these partisans. Finally, with regard to the policy salience coefficient, s, note that as s increases voters place more weight on policies compared to random, unmeasured motivations and hence the less "random" voters' decisions become. Since we have seen that it is probabilistic or random voting that gives parties incentives to present centrist policies that appeal to the entire electorate, it makes sense that as this random component declines in importance vote-seeking parties will move further away from the center in the direction of their partisans' beliefs.

Figures 6.4 and 6.5 present examples that illustrate the impact of each of the three factors discussed above. Figure 6.4A pictures the voter distribution analyzed earlier for independent probabilistic voting (see fig. 6.1A), but here voters display partisan biases: voters in the policy interval [0,3.5] identify with party L, those located in the right-wing policy interval [6.5,10] are partisans of R, and centrist voters in the interval [3.5,6.5] identify with C. I further assume that the strength of voters' partisan bias is set at $b = 3$, about the value that Endersby and Galatas estimate for voting in the 1992 British general election. Figure 6.4B gives party L's expected vote, EVL(l,s), the vertical axis, as a function of its Left-Right position l, with parties C and R located at the voter mean, 5.0.[11] When the policy salience coefficient, s, is set at the low value $s = .05$, party L maximizes votes by locating at $l^* = 4.5$, a position near the voter mean but shaded in the direction of L's left-wing partisans. When s is increased to $s = .15$, L's vote-maximizing position shifts slightly left to $l^* = 4.4$. Thus, in both cases party L has electoral incentives to propose policies shaded toward its

(A)

(B)

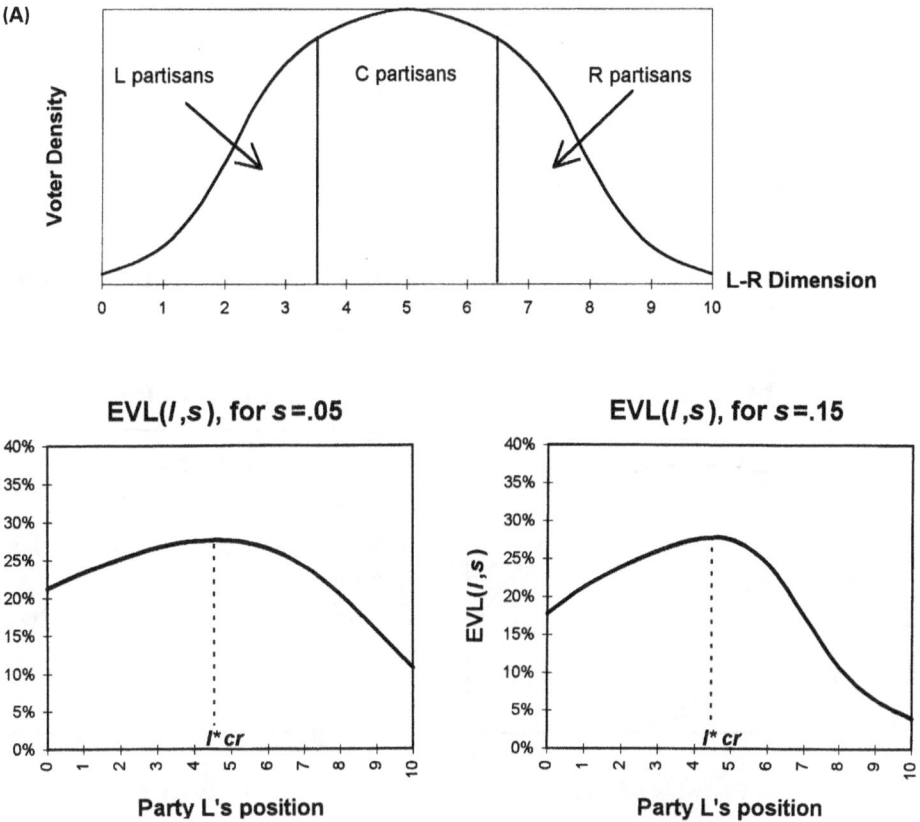

Fig. 6.4. Analysis of party L's policy strategies when voters choose according to the partisan probabilistic vote model. (*A*) Initial policy distribution of voters and parties; (*B*) EVL(*l,s*) as a function of L's position, with C and R located at 5.0 (strength of voters' partisan attachment set at *b* = 3.0).

party's partisans, but, consistent with the Merrill-Adams analysis, this incentive is slightly more pronounced when voters place greater emphasis on policies.

Note that in the above examples party L's computed vote-maximizing positions are quite centrist and thus not particularly representative of its partisans' beliefs. This occurs in part because in figure 6.4A the portion of the electorate that identifies with party L is fairly modest, about 25 percent. In addition, note that, although L's partisans are located in the left-wing policy interval [0,3.5], within this interval these partisans are most heavily concentrated between 2.5 and 3.5, the portion of the [0,3.5] interval nearest the center; thus, the mean position of L's partisans is about 2.60. The Merrill-Adams results suggest that

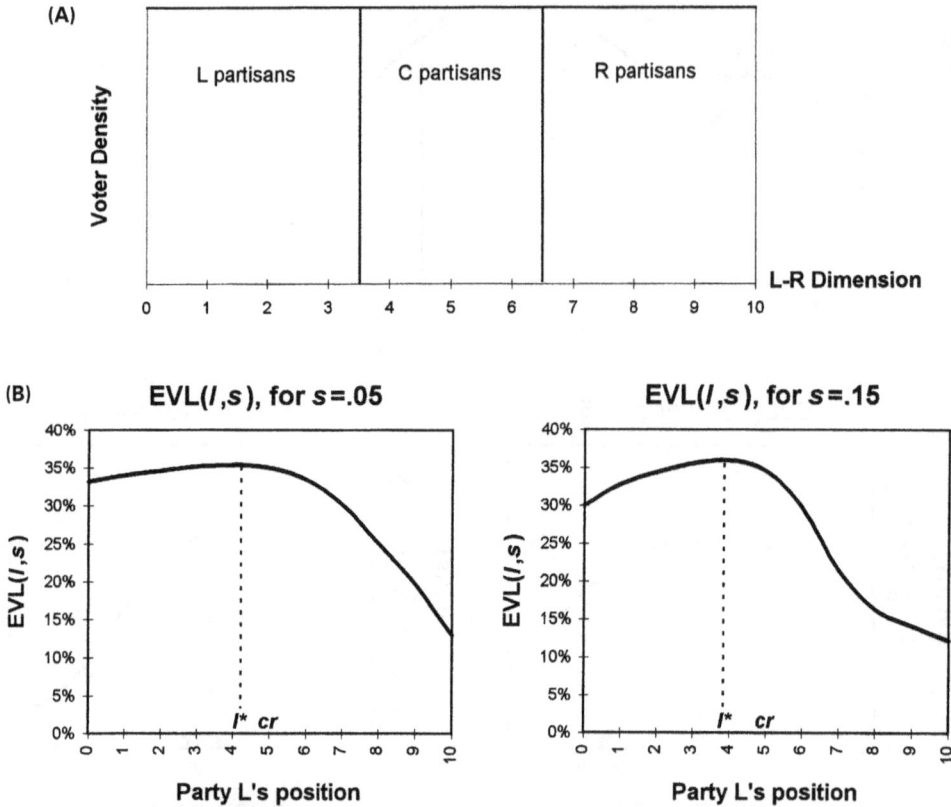

Fig. 6.5. Analysis of party L's policy strategy for an alternative voter distribution when voters choose according to the PPV model. (*A*) Initial policy distribution of voters and parties; (*B*) EVL(*l,s*) as a function of L's position, with C and R located at 5.0.

party L would be motivated to shift its position further left, in the direction of its partisans, if the number of partisans increased and/or if these partisans took more extreme left-wing positions. Figure 6.5 illustrates the strategic implications for party L if *both* of these conditions are satisfied simultaneously. Figure 6.5A pictures a voter distribution in which the partisans of parties L, C, and R are again located in the policy intervals [0,3.5], [3.5,6.5], and [6.5,10], respectively, but in this example the voter distribution is uniform. As a result, C's partisan constituency is larger and more extreme in figure 6.5A than was the case in figure 6.4A.

Figure 6.5B gives party L's expected vote (the vertical axis) as a function of its Left-Right position, with C and R located at 5.0 (for these calculations *b* is again set at $b = 3$). Compared to the results for the voter distribution given in figure 6.4A, here party L's expected vote increases because it now has a larger partisan constituency. More importantly, L's vote-maximizing position shifts to the left, in the direction of its partisans: for $s = .05$, L's optimal location is l^* = 4.1; for $s = .15$, this position is $l^* = 3.9$. Collectively, the examples presented in figures 6.4–6.5 illustrate the Adams-Merrill conclusions that *a vote-seeking party is motivated to shift its policies away from the center in the direction of its partisans' beliefs to the extent that: the party has a large partisan constituency, these partisans take extreme positions, and voters emphasize policy voting compared to unmeasured, nonpolicy motivations.*

6.5. The Existence and Characteristics of Policy Equilibrium under the PPV Model

Although the above analysis of party strategies under the PPV model is suggestive, to this point I have relied on illustrative examples rather than deductive theorems. Here I present two equilibrium results that formalize the intuitions presented above. Theorem 6.2, which is proved in appendix C, obtains provided that each party selects its policy position from a finite set of feasible positions, *and* that for each party K this set of feasible positions includes the position k_m, which maximizes the function TK(k), where[12]

$$\text{TK}(k) = \sum_{i \in V} \left[e^{b_{iK}} / \left(\sum_{J \in \Re} e^{b_{iJ}} \right) \right] [1 - e^{b_{iK}} / \left(\sum_{J \in \Re} e^{b_{iJ}} \right)] [-(x_i - k)^2] \qquad (6.4)$$

THEOREM 6.2: *Assume the vote probability function for partisan voters given in equation 6.2. Then there exists η such that for all $0 < s < \eta$ each party $K \in \Re$'s vote-maximizing policy position is k_m.*

In words, the theorem states that, when the importance of voters' measured policy motivations is sufficiently small relative to their unmeasured motivations, each party maximizes its expected vote by locating at k_m, regardless of rival parties' positions. An immediate corollary to theorem 6.2 is that *when s is sufficiently small the policy configuration $\{a_m, b_m, \ldots, n_m\}$ represents an equilibrium for vote-maximizing parties.* This contrasts with deterministic partisan voting, for which we have seen that equilibrium is problematic.

Two questions arise in relation to theorem 6.2. First, when is the degree of policy voting, s, sufficiently small for theorem 6.2 to hold? Second, what are the characteristics of the policy equilibrium $\{a_m, b_m, \ldots, n_m\}$ specified in the corollary to theorem 6.2? With respect to the first question, I present simulation results in appendix C that suggest that, although theorem 6.2 holds exactly only for small values of s, for larger values of s parties' vote-maximizing positions are quite similar to k_m. It therefore appears that the party configuration given in theorem 6.2 provides a reasonable approximation of the vote-maximizing positions that parties would converge toward in real world elections.

With respect to the second question, note first that the strategic logic of party competition outlined in section 6.4 implies that parties have incentives to weigh all voters' preferences when determining their policy strategies but that they should attach added weight to their own partisans' preferences compared to the preferences of rival parties' partisans. Thus, I suggested that parties are motivated to present policies similar to but less extreme than their partisans' beliefs. Merrill and Adams (2000b) prove the following result:

THEOREM 6.3:   *Assume the vote probability function for partisan voters given in equation 6.2 and that all voters are partisan. Let* x_V *represent the mean voter position and* x_K *the mean position of party K's partisans. Then, in elections involving at least three parties, either* $x_V < k_m < x_K$ *or* $x_K < k_m < x_V$.

The theorem states that when the degree of policy voting is sufficiently low party K's equilibrium position, k_m, is invariably located between the mean voter position and the mean position of K's partisans. Thus, the theorem establishes that, for a sufficiently small s, *vote-seeking parties' equilibrium positions will be similar to but less extreme than the mean position of their partisans.* The tightness of the representational fit between parties and their partisans depends on the factors discussed above: the size of parties' partisan constituencies; the degree to which partisans take extreme positions; and the value of the policy salience coefficient, s.

6.6. Party Equilibria for Historical Elections in Britain and France for the *PPV* Model: Empirical Applications

Previous Research on Multiparty Equilibrium under the PPV Model

Theorems 6.2 and 6.3 establish that when voters choose according to the PPV model then under specified conditions equilibria will exist in which vote-seeking parties present positions similar to but less extreme than the positions of their supporters. This raises the question: do these conditions typically obtain in national elections in contemporary democracies, including those of France and Britain?

To my knowledge, the only existing empirical studies on multiparty-candidate competition that explore the above question using the PPV voting specification are those of Adams and Merrill (1999a, 1999b), which explore policy equilibrium in the 1989 Norwegian Storting election (Merrill and Adams

2000a, 2000b; see also Adams and Merrill 1999a) and analyze the 1988 French presidential election, and Adams (forthcoming a), which focuses on the 1992 American presidential election.[13] Using survey data from the 1989 Norwegian Election Study, Adams and Merrill (1999b) estimate a conditional logit model identical to the specification used in equation 6.2 in that it incorporates the squared Left-Right distance between respondent and party, the respondent's party identification (which is incorporated via a proxy variable, previous vote), and an extreme value random variable. Using the estimated model parameters, the authors carry out simulations on the electoral effects of shifts in parties' Left-Right positions and locate a dispersed policy equilibrium in which each of the seven major Norwegian parties presents a policy similar to but less extreme than the positions of its partisans (see 1999b, table 3). The Adams and Merrill (2000) study on French politics and Adams's (forthcoming a) study on American three-candidate elections, both of which also rely on simulations based upon empirically estimated vote models, also locate equilibria that display these identical properties.[14] Collectively, these results suggest that, given voters' empirically estimated behavior under the PPV model, multiparty equilibria *will* typically exist in which parties present centrist policies that are shaded in the direction of their partisans' beliefs.

Empirical Applications to British Politics

To determine whether a multiparty equilibrium could be located for British elections when voters choose according to the PPV model, I carried out simulations based upon the voter distributions pictured in figures 2.8A and 3.6A, which show the distributions of respondents' self-placements on nationalization of industry as well as their party identifications, as reported in the 1987 and the 1992 British General Election Studies, respectively. Because both sets of simulations yielded similar conclusions on parties' policy strategies, here I report results of simulations based on the 1992 voter distribution.[15] The 1992 electoral context is particularly intriguing because of the conclusion, reported in chapter 3, that the 1992 British voter distribution on nationalization of industry does *not* support a policy equilibrium when voters choose according to the deterministic partisan vote model.

In setting simulation parameters for British voters' behavior under the PPV model, given in equation 6.1, I relied upon parameter estimates reported by Endersby and Galatas, who analyzed voter choices in the 1992 British general election using a logit model that included both respondent party identification and policy distance on nationalization of industry (1997, table 2). The authors estimate partisan parameters of approximately $b = 3.0$ and a policy salience parameter for nationalization of industry of $s = .045$. Using these parameters as the basis for my computations, I initially located the parties at their actual (perceived) positions on the nationalization of industry scale and then proceeded as follows. With the Labour and Liberal Democratic Parties fixed at their actual locations, I calculated the expected vote for the Conservative Party for the set of 101 positions {1.0, 1.1, . . . , 11.0} and then located the Conservatives at their vote-maximizing position.[16] For this new party configuration, I then performed an identical exercise for the Labour Party and in turn for the Liberal Democrats. This process was repeated until no party could improve its expected vote given the positions of its competitors.[17]

Figure 6.6 and table 6.1 show the eventual equilibrium configuration computed for the 1992 British general election based on the PPV vote model: Labour at 5.3, the Liberal Democrats at 5.7, and the Conservatives at 6.1. Figure 6.6 pictures each party's expected vote as a function of position, with the rival parties fixed at their equilibrium positions. Note that, given the low policy salience coefficient $s = .045$, the parties' votes do not vary greatly as a function of their policies but that the parties' expected votes at equilibrium, given in table 6.1, are quite similar to their actual vote shares in the 1992 British general election. Furthermore, as expected, the parties' equilibrium positions are fairly centrist, with each party located near the mean voter position of 5.7. However, the Labour and Conservative Parties are shaded in the direction of their partisans, so that Labour is located to the left, and the Conservatives to the right, of the voter mean. As a result, these parties present positions similar to but less extreme than the positions of their partisans, which are given in table 6.1. These results are consistent with theorems 6.2 and 6.3.

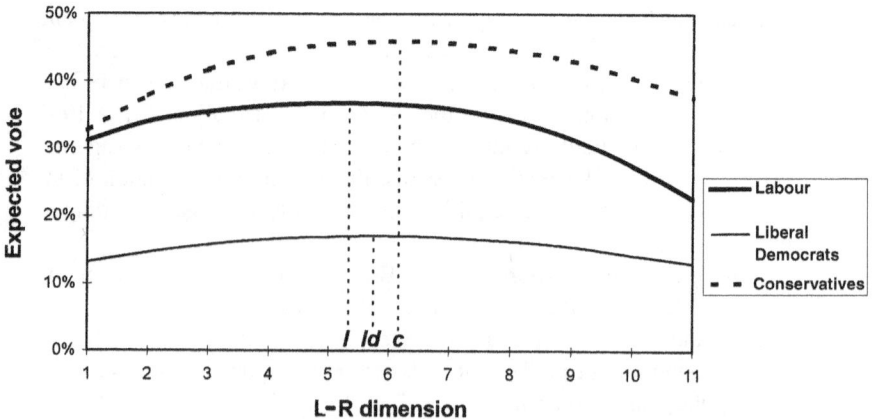

Fig. 6.6. British parties' expected votes with rival parties located at their equilibrium positions (parties' expected votes for $s = .045$). Calculations are based on the 1992 British voter distribution for nationalization of industry pictured in figure 3.6A, with b set at $b = 3.0$.

TABLE 6.1. Equilibrium Configurations on Nationalization of Industry for Varying Degrees of Policy Voting, 1992 British General Election

Degree of Policy Voting, s	Parties' Equilibrium Locations			Parties' Vote Shares[a]		
	Labour	Alliance	Conservatives	Labour	Alliance	Conservatives
$s = .045$[b]	5.3	5.7	6.1	37%	17%	46%
$s = .05$	5.3	5.7	6.1	37	17	46
$s = .10$	5.2	5.7	6.2	38	16	46
$s = .15$	5.1	5.8	6.4	39	15	46
$s = .20$	[	No equilibrium discovered	]	—	—	—
Partisans' mean positions	4.1	5.8	7.0	37[c]	19[d]	44[e]

Note: Calculations are based on the voter distribution pictured in figure 3.6A, with the strength of voters' partisan attachment set at $b = 3.0$.
[a]Parties' vote shares at equilibrium.
[b]Policy salience coefficient estimated in Endersby and Galatas 1996, table 2.
[c]Labour's share of the three-party vote, 1987 British general election.
[d]The Alliance's share of the three-party vote, 1987 British general election.
[e]The Conservatives' share of the three-party vote, 1987 British general election.

Equilibrium for Varying Degrees of Policy Salience

Because the Endersby-Galatas study (1997) incorporated policy dimensions in addition to nationalization of industry, it seems plausible that the authors' parameter estimate of $s = .045$ for nationalization represents a conservative estimate of the electoral impact of policies in the 1992 election. In order to determine whether the equilibrium result obtained for $s = .045$ generalizes to elections in which voters place greater emphasis on policies, I carried out simulations for varying values of s, ranging from $s = .05$ to $s = .20$. In these simulations, the strength of partisan attachment was held constant at $b = 3$. Table 6.1 reports the results of these simulations. They show that when s was less than or equal to .15 equilibria were located in which the Labour and Conservative Parties presented positions similar to but less extreme than the positions of their partisans, while the centrist Liberal Democrats presented positions virtually identical to their supporters' beliefs. These results are consistent with theorem 6.3. In addition, note that the greater the importance of policies (i.e., the higher the value of s) the more the parties' equilibrium positions shift in the direction of their partisans. This supports the Merrill and Adams (2000b) conclusion that increased policy voting motivates parties to shift their policies in the direction of their partisans.

Empirical Applications to French Politics

I next carried out simulations on French elections, with my computations based on the voter distribution pictured in figure 4.3A, which shows the distribution of French respondents' Left-Right self-placements and party identifications as reported in the 1988 French Presidential Election Study. I performed these simulations using both the PPV vote model, given in equation 6.1, and a probabilistic version of the coalition bias model introduced in chapter 5, for which voters' utilities for party K were specified as

$$U_i(K) = b_{iK} + c_{iK} - s(x_i - k)^2 + \mu_{iK} \tag{6.5}$$

with μ_{iK} again specified as an extreme value random variable. Both sets of simulations yielded similar results.[18] However, because empirical analyses of French voting data (see, e.g., Dow 1997b and Adams and Merrill 2000) suggest that French voters do display coalition biases, here I report results based upon this probabilistic coalition bias model.

In setting parameters for French voters' behavior in these simulations, I relied on unpublished results made available to me by Samuel Merrill III, who analyzed voting behavior in the first round of voting for the 1988 French presidential election using the voting specification given in equation 6.5. Merrill estimated a partisan parameter of $b = 2.27$, a coalition bias parameter $c = .26$, and a policy salience coefficient $s = .195$.[19] Given that Merrill's results are based upon an analysis of the same data set that I employ in my simulations, these voting parameters represent an excellent starting point for simulations on French parties' strategies in the 1988 parliamentary elections.

Using the above parameters, I carried out simulations on French parties' policy strategies for four-party competition in the 1988 election.[20] These simulations were based on the same methodology described above for Britain, that is, that the parties were initially located at their actual (perceived) positions along the Left-Right dimension and then they shifted sequentially to their computed vote-maximizing positions, with this process continuing until no party could improve its expected vote.[21] Figure 6.7 and table 6.2 show the equilibrium configuration located for the 1988 French National Assembly election: the Communists at 3.8, the Socialists at 3.6, the UDF at 4.4, and the RPR at 4.5.[22] Also pictured in figure 6.7 is each party's expected vote as a function of its Left-Right position (the vertical axis), with rival parties located at their equilibrium positions. This figure reveals that the traditional left-wing parties, the Communists and Socialists, would suffer severe electoral penalties if they shifted to the right. Conversely, the traditionally right-wing RPR could expect to lose much of its electoral support if it shifted to the left. These conclusions accord with common sense. In addition, each party's expected vote at equilibrium (given in table 6.2) is similar to its actual first-round vote in the 1988 parliamentary election.

Consistent with theorem 6.3, the equilibrium pictured in figure 6.7 finds the French parties presenting relatively centrist policies that are shaded in the

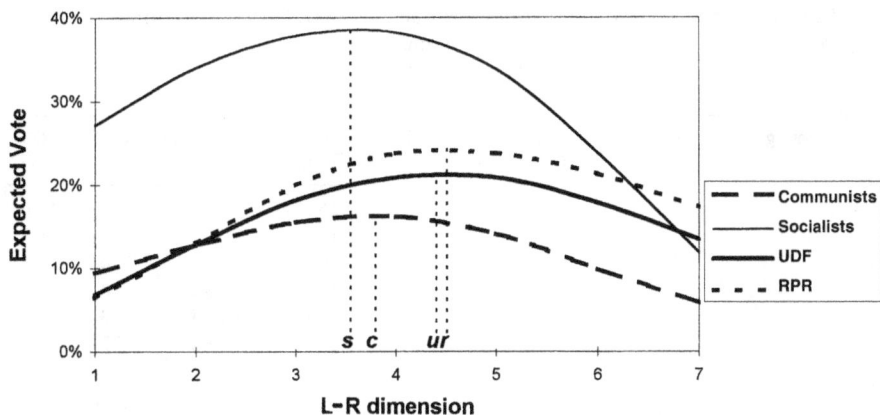

Fig. 6.7. French parties' expected votes with rival parties at their equilibrium positions for four-party competition (parties' expected votes for $s = .195$). Calculations are based on the 1988 French voter Left-Right distribution pictured in figure 4.3A, with b and c set at $b = 2.27$ and $= 0.26$.

direction of their partisans' beliefs, which are reported in table 6.2. In addition, note that at equilibrium the Socialist Party actually presents a more leftist position than do the Communists, despite the fact that the Communists' partisans take more extreme left-wing positions than the Socialists partisans do. The explanation for this result revolves around the strategic logic deduced in the Merrill and Adams (2000b) study, that ceteris paribus large parties are motivated to present more extreme positions than are small parties. Because the Socialist Party has a larger partisan constituency than the Communists, the Socialists are motivated to move further away from the center, in the direction of their partisans.

Equilibrium for Varying Degrees of Policy Salience
I carried out additional simulations on policy competition in France in which I varied the policy salience coefficient, s, while holding the partisan and coalition coefficients constant at $b = 2.27$ and $c = .26$. The results are presented in table 6.2, which reports results for varying values of s, ranging from $s = .10$ (barely half the value of the policy salience coefficient estimated by Merrill) to $s = .50$ (more than twice Merrill's empirical estimate). Columns 2–5 report the equilibrium positions located for the Communists, Socialists, UDF, and RPR, respectively; columns 6–9 report the parties' expected vote shares at equilibrium. Also given in the bottom two rows are the mean positions of each party's partisans and the parties' actual vote shares in the first round of voting in the 1988 parliamentary election. The table shows that party equilibria were located

TABLE 6.2. French Parties' Equilibrium Positions for Four-Party Competition
for Varying Degrees of Policy Voting, 1988 French Election

Degree of Policy Voting, s (1)	Parties' Equilibrium Positions				Parties' Vote Shares[a]			
	Communists (2)	Socialists (3)	UDF (4)	RPR (5)	Communists (6)	Socialists (7)	UDF (8)	RPR (9)
s = .10	3.9	3.7	4.3	4.4	16.5%	38.4%	21.2%	24.1%
s = .195[b]	3.8	3.6	4.4	4.5	16.3	38.5	21.0	24.2
s = .20	3.8	3.6	4.4	4.5	16.3	38.5	21.0	24.2
s = .30	3.7	3.6	4.5	4.6	16.3	38.9	20.8	24.2
s = .40	3.5	3.5	4.7	4.7	16.1	39.1	20.8	24.2
s = .50	3.4	3.4	4.8	4.8	15.7	39.4	20.7	24.1
Partisans' mean positions	2.4	3.1	4.9	5.4				
Parties' actual vote shares[c]					13.1	43.3	21.4	22.2

Note: Simulations are based on the voter distribution pictured in figure 4.3A, with the strength of partisan attachment set at $b = 2.27$ and the strength of voters coalition biases set at $c = .26$.
[a]Parties' vote shares at equilibrium.
[b]Policy salience coefficient estimated for the 1988 French presidential election.
[c]Parties' shares of the four-party first round vote, 1988 parliamentary elections.

for *all* the values of s that were investigated and furthermore that each equilibrium configuration finds the parties presenting centrist positions that are shaded in the direction of their partisans. In addition, note that as the importance voters attach to policies increases the parties' positions shift away from the center in the direction of their supporters. Each of these results is consistent with the strategic logic of party competition outlined earlier in this chapter.

6.7. Incorporating Additional Sources of Voter Bias

Throughout this book, I have focused exclusively on the strategic implications of only one measured source of voter bias, party identification. Although this decision is defensible in that party identification is one of the most widely studied aspects of political behavior, the question nonetheless arises: to what extent do my conclusions on party policy strategies for the PPV model generalize to electorates that are moved by a variety of measured nonpolicy motivations, including group loyalties rooted in class, religion, and geography, economic conditions, and retrospective evaluations of incumbent performance?

To my knowledge, the only studies that bear on the issue of comparative party strategies for the PPV model versus their strategies for more fully specified behavioral vote models are those by Adams and Merrill, who carry out simulations on data from the 1989 Norwegian Election Study and on data from Pierce's 1988 French Presidential Election Study. Using the PPV specification given in equation 6.1, the authors locate a policy equilibrium for the seven major Norwegian parties (see Adams and Merrill 1999b, table 3) and the five major French presidential candidates (see Merrill and Adams 2000a, table 3) that are consistent with the theoretical results reported here in that both equilibria find each competitor presenting a policy similar to but less extreme than the policies of its/his partisans. In a different set of essays (Adams and Merrill 1999a, 2000), the authors locate policy equilibria for these two elections using more fully specified voting models that include additional nonpolicy variables such as the respondent's income, religion, union membership, geographic location, and employment sector. The equilibrium configurations that Adams and Merrill locate for these more fully specified behavioral vote models (Adams and Merrill 1999a, table 2, col. 8; 2000, n. 20) are quite similar to the equilibria they obtain for the basic PPV model.[23] *These results support the conclusion that when additional measured nonpolicy motivations are added to the basic PPV specification inclusion of these variables has a negligible effect on party strategies.* This suggests in turn that my conclusions on party policy strategies under the PPV model generalize to the more fully specified behavioral models that behavioralists employ in their empirical voting studies.

Why do voter biases arising from group-related loyalties rooted in class, religion, union membership, and geography have a negligible impact upon party strategies once the parties have accounted for voter partisanship? The first reason is that when these variables are included in a model with party identification they have relatively small (though statistically significant) effects on the vote compared to the party identification variable. Second, while such voter characteristics as class and union membership correlate with voters' policy preferences, this correlation is weaker than the one between partisanship and policies. Because I have argued throughout this book that voter biases influence party strategies *when these biases correlate with voters' policy preferences,* it is not surprising that biases that are only weakly related to policies exert negligible effects on party strategies.

6.8. Conclusions

The results presented in this chapter suggest that for a wide range of assumptions about the salience of voters' policy motivations the probabilistic partisan vote model supports party equilibria in which parties present policies similar to but less extreme than their partisans' positions. Vote-seeking parties are motivated to present policies similar to their partisans' beliefs because they typically gain more votes, on an expected value basis, by presenting policies that reflect partisans' positions than they gain by taking positions that appeal to rival parties' partisans. This result thereby extends the central strategic logic of party competition under the partisan vote model—namely, that vote-seeking parties are motivated to appeal on policy grounds to voters biased toward them for nonpolicy reasons—from the deterministic to the probabilistic voting setting. However, the introduction of probabilistic voting introduces a new element into parties' strategic calculus in that they are motivated to moderate their policies because they have electoral incentives to weigh *all* voters' beliefs, even as they attach the most weight to their own partisans' preferences.

The degree to which parties are motivated to shift toward the center and away from their partisans depends on several factors, including the size of the parties' partisan constituencies, the extent to which these constituencies take extreme positions, and the degree to which voters emphasize policies compared with unmeasured, nonpolicy factors. I have shown how variations in each of these factors alter the logic of parties' policy strategies, which in turn affects the resulting multiparty equilibrium. What is important is that in empirical applications to historical elections in Britain and France the probabilistic version of the partisan vote model consistently supports policy equilibria given realistic voting model parameters derived from empirical voting studies. This conclusion is further supported by the analytic results presented in theorems 6.1 through 6.3, which guarantee the existence of a policy equilibrium under specified conditions.

My results on party policy competition under the PPV model have mixed implications for responsible party government. On the one hand, the policies that vote-seeking parties pursue under the probabilistic partisan vote model are somewhat more centrist, and less representative, than the policies parties typically pursue for deterministic partisan voting. On the other hand, we have seen that the introduction of probabilistic voting enhances the prospects for stability in that policy equilibria are extremely likely to exist. As a result, compared to the deterministic partisan vote model, probabilistic voting enhances *policy stability* but depresses *policy divergence* and *policy representation.* As a result, when voters display partisan biases but choose probabilistically, vote-seeking parties can be expected to present quite stable policies that are somewhat divergent and reasonably representative of their partisans' beliefs.

CHAPTER 7

Extensions to Two-Party Competition in American Elections: A Sketch of a Partisan Spatial Model with Variable Voter Turnout

7.1. Introduction

Although the central focus of this book is on policy competition in multiparty elections, the question arises: can the partisan spatial model similarly illuminate the temporal patterns of party policies, and mass-elite policy linkages, in two-party systems? This issue is important given that the American party system—arguably the most important political system in the world—is dominated by two parties, the Democrats and the Republicans.

In this chapter, I show that the answer to this question is no. The partisan spatial model explored in chapters 1–6 cannot account for American parties' policy strategies during the postwar period. It can do so, however, if we incorporate a crucial missing link: the voter's turnout decision. Specifically, I show that if we expand the partisan spatial model to incorporate the possibility that voters abstain if neither party is sufficiently attractive—that is, that *voters abstain due to alienation*—then vote-seeking parties in two-party systems have the same strategic motivations as the parties in multiparty elections do under the full-turnout version of the partisan spatial model. In other words, the parties have incentives to present divergent policies that reflect the beliefs of their partisan constituencies. Hence, a turnout-based partisan spatial model—which I abbreviate to the *partisan turnout model*—illuminates important patterns of party competition and political representation in two-party elections. Below I present illustrative arguments, theorems, and simulation results on ANES survey data that suggest that this model can help us understand important features of American elections.

If the partisan turnout model provides insights into American parties' policy strategies as well as political representation, then why do I confine myself to "sketching" the arguments derived from this model near the end of the book? There are two reasons, which relate to scholarly disputes concerning voter turnout and political representation in the United States. With respect to turnout, behavioralists do not fully understand how citizens decide whether to vote in

American elections, with some scholars viewing abstention as motivated by citizens' indifference between the competing candidates or parties (e.g., Sanders 1998) and others implicitly emphasizing alienation (Burden and Lacy 1999; Lacy and Burden 1999; Morgan 1996). Thus, there exists no scholarly consensus that alienation is the motivation that drives nonparticipation in American elections, and for this reason the partisan turnout model I develop here—which specifies that voter abstention is driven by alienation not indifference—rests on a shakier empirical foundation than the full-turnout partisan model (hereafter referred to as the *basic partisan model*) explored in chapters 1–6. The distinction between alienation and indifference is important because, as Erikson and Romero (1990 1120–21) have shown, a partisan turnout model that specifies that abstention is driven by indifference does *not* motivate policy divergence in two-party competitions.

With respect to political representation, as discussed in chapter 1, it is not clear whether the responsible party government model is relevant to mass-elite policy linkages in the United States. Given the greater autonomy of American legislators compared to their European counterparts (Mayhew 1974, 19–28; Fenno 1978), many scholars view political representation in the United States as revolving around the relationship between individual legislators and the geographic constituencies that elect them (see, e.g., Miller and Stokes 1963 and Kuklinski 1978). This model of political representation assigns a distinctly subordinate role to political parties and hence does not emphasize the policy linkages between parties and their supporters that are the particular focus of this book.

These caveats notwithstanding, there are also reasons why the partisan turnout model holds promise for understanding the dynamics of American elections. In the first place, although some behavioralists downplay the relationship between voter alienation and abstention, there is considerable evidence that alienation plays at least *some* role in depressing voter turnout in the United States (e.g., Lacy and Burden 1999), so the arguments I develop about the strategic implications of abstention due to alienation appear to be relevant to party competition. Furthermore, while scholars frequently emphasize the district-legislator representation bond in the United States, others argue that the policy link between American party elites and their supporters is also relevant to representation (see, e.g., Backstrom 1977; Bishop and Frankovic 1981; and Herrera, Herrera, and Smith 1992) or even that in practice policy representation in the United States revolves around parties, not individual legislators (see Ansolabehere, Snyder, and Stewart 1999). For these reasons, it appears worthwhile to sketch the implications of the partisan turnout model for party competition and responsible party government in American elections.

In section 7.2, I review the temporal patterns of American parties' policies, as revealed by the MRG's coding procedures and I show that these patterns— which find the parties presenting dispersed policies that reflect their supporters' beliefs—are inconsistent with the predictions derived from the basic partisan spatial model. This is because in two-party elections under the basic partisan model the parties are motivated to target independent voters, not their partisan supporters, so that vote-seeking parties should converge to similar, centrist platforms.

Section 7.3 expands the partisan spatial model to include abstention from alienation. I present illustrative arguments that, in two-party elections under this partisan turnout model, parties have electoral incentives to present policies that appeal to their partisans. The central reason is that, for realistic model parameters, the parties cannot take their partisans' support for granted since these voters may abstain if they disapprove of the party's platform. By contrast, the parties have little incentive to target rival parties' partisans since these voters are likely to prefer the rival party due to their partisan loyalty, and even when this is not the case these voters may prefer abstention to voting. I also present a theoretical result on American elections that (for certain restrictive assumptions about the voter distribution), if an equilibrium exists, it must find the Democratic Party presenting a more liberal platform than the Republicans.

In section 7.4, I report computer simulations on American National Elections Study data from 1992 and 1996, which support both my theoretical results and my illustrative arguments. These simulations show that when equilibria exist they indeed find the Democrats located to the left of the Republicans and that in the (more common) nonequilibrium scenarios the Democrats consistently locate to the left of the Republicans, so that the parties avoid leapfrogging while presenting positions that reflect the views of their partisan constituencies. These results accord well with the parties' historical behavior, suggesting that the partisan turnout model captures the underlying logic of party strategies in two-party elections.

Finally, I note that, although I employ the language of party competition in this chapter, all of the results I present apply equally to competitions involving candidates. This point is important because American elections revolve around candidates to a greater extent than do elections in most Western democracies, with American candidates frequently staking out positions at odds with their parties' official platforms (witness pro-choice Republican candidates). Hence, my arguments can also illuminate the empirical finding that, candidate variability notwithstanding, Democratic candidates consistently take more liberal positions than their Republican competitors (Ansolabehere, Snyder, and Stewart 1999).

7.2. The Logic of Two-Party Competition under the Basic Partisan Spatial Model: The Pressure for Policy Convergence

Figure 7.1 shows the Left-Right positions of the Democratic and Republican Parties over the period 1956–88 as coded by the Manifesto Research Group. The parties are coded as presenting divergent positions, with the Democrats con-

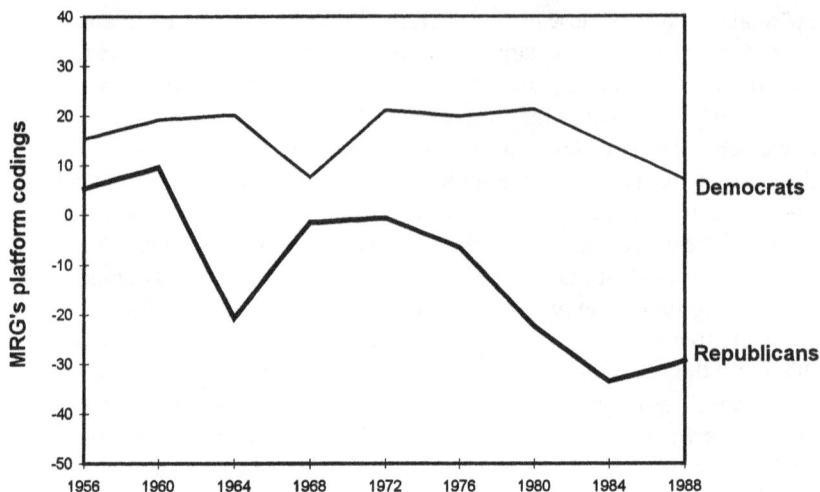

Fig. 7.1.   MRG's coding of the Left-Right trajectories of American political parties, 1956–88.

sistently locating on the left and the Republicans on the right. Furthermore, the
parties vary their positions over time without leapfrogging, and, with the exception of the Republican platforms of 1956–60, which are coded as being (barely)
to the left of center, the parties remain within ideologically delimited sectors
of the policy space. These patterns are similar to those observed in Britain and
France. In the cases of these multiparty systems, we have seen that the basic partisan spatial model accounts well for the MRG's results. Can the model similarly
illuminate the parties' policy trajectories in American two-party elections?

Unfortunately, the answer to the above question is no. The reason is that
in two-party elections under the basic partisan spatial model vote-seeking parties lack the central strategic incentive that drives results in multiparty contests,
namely, the motivation to appeal on policy grounds to voters biased toward
them for nonpolicy reasons. To see this, consider the hypothetical distribution
of American voters and parties along the 1–7 Liberal-Conservative scale pictured in figure 7.2A.[1] In this distribution, like those employed for the illustrative arguments on Britain and France, the voters' party loyalties correlate with
their policy preferences—specifically, all voters on the liberal side of the scale
midpoint (4.0) are Democratic partisans while those on the conservative side
identify with the Republicans. Initially the Democratic and Republican Parties
locate at $d = 4.0$ and $r = 4.0$, respectively, the position of the median voter. In
this party configuration, all voters are indifferent between the parties' policies
and hence the entire electorate votes its party identification.

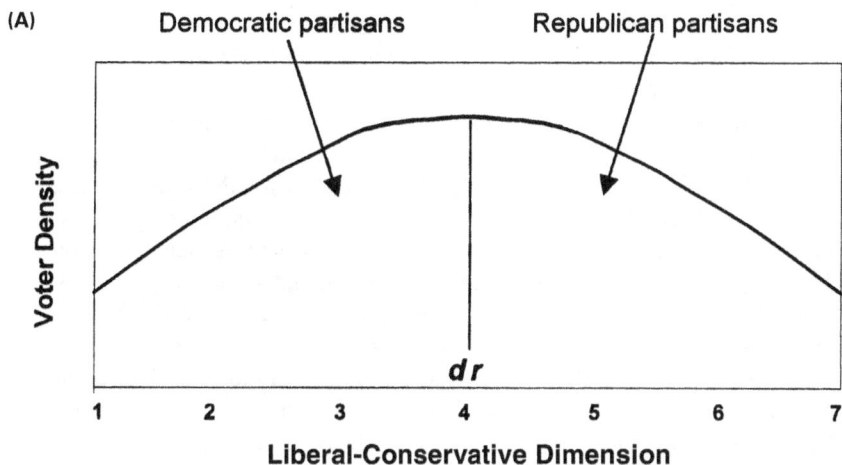

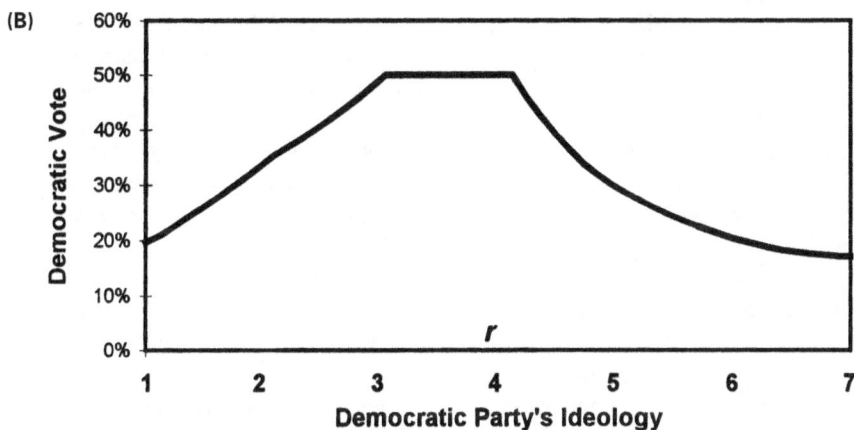

Fig. 7.2. Two-party competition under the partisan spatial model. (*A*) Initial liberal-conservative voter distribution; (*B*) Democratic Party's vote for varying ideological positions.

Now consider the Democrats' strategic calculus when the strength of voters' party identification is set at $b^{1/2} = 1.0$. Given that the Democrats already receive 100 percent of the votes of Democratic partisans, the only way the party can enhance its support is to siphon off voters from the Republican constituency. This precludes shifting to a more liberal position, since this policy change makes the Democratic Party's position less attractive to *all* Republican partisans. This leaves the option of presenting a more conservative stance designed to appeal to Republican partisans. The problem with this strategy, from the Democratic Party's perspective, is that in order to attract significant support from Republican partisans—who prefer their own party on nonpolicy grounds—the Democrats must differentiate their ideology from the Republicans by presenting a strongly conservative position that will alienate their Democratic constituency. Thus, in this example the Democrats can win the votes of conservative Republicans by shifting to $d = 5.0$, a platform significantly different from the Republican position, $r = 4.0$. However, while this Democratic proposal wins the votes of Republican partisans located in the policy interval [5.00,7.00],[2] it simultaneously forfeits the support of the *entire Democratic voting constituency*—a disastrous electoral tradeoff.[3]

This conclusion is illustrated in figure 7.2B, which shows the Democrats' expected vote as a function of their liberal-conservative position, d, with the Republicans located at $r = 4.0$. As long as the Democrats locate in the vicinity of the median voter, they receive a 50 percent vote share since these positions attract support from the entire Democratic constituency but no support from Republican partisans. If the Democrats shift too far toward the liberal end of the scale, they lose votes from centrist Democrats without, of course, attracting compensating support from Republicans. If the Democrats take a conservative position, they attract support from conservative Republicans, but these electoral gains are outweighed by defections from their Democratic constituency. Hence, for this stylized voter distribution the Democrats lack a compelling electoral incentive to present liberal policies—and, by a similar logic, the Republicans lack the motivation to propose a conservative platform.

However, the above example actually *understates* the electoral attraction of the center because it does not consider the implications of independent voters in the electorate. Suppose that the median independent voter has the same policy preference as the median partisan voter, 4.0 (below I show that in the U.S. electorate the mean independent's preference is indeed virtually identical to the mean partisan's preference). In this case, the Democrats *lose* votes by shifting away from the center. This is because, with the Republicans located at the median voter's position, the Democrats necessarily win a minority of the independent vote if they desert the median position and, since we have seen that the Democrats cannot gain additional net partisan votes by shifting their position, such a policy shift must entail a net vote loss. *Hence, the presence of even a miniscule set of independent voters in the electorate motivates the competing parties to present identical, centrist policies*—the same result that obtains under the basic Downsian spatial model. In summary, unlike the multiparty scenario, in two-party elections the basic partisan spatial model does not provide parties with compelling electoral incentives to appeal to their partisan constituencies.

7.3. Extending the Partisan Spatial Model to Encompass Voter Turnout: The Pressure for Responsible Parties

A Partisan Turnout Model of Spatial Competition

To this point, I have explored the implications of the partisan spatial model in an idealized electorate in which all eligible citizens vote. This ignores the fact that in American congressional and presidential elections large proportions of the electorate typically abstain and, especially important from the perspective of party strategies, that parties can potentially affect voter turnout by their choice of policies. Voter turnout is a particularly appropriate modification to introduce in the context of American elections since turnout in U.S. congressional elections barely reaches 50 percent in presidential election years and falls well below 40 percent in midterm elections. These percentages are low in an absolute sense, and also comparatively, since U.S. turnout lags significantly behind that of most other advanced industrial societies.[4]

In recent years, behavioralists have proposed a variety of unified voting models that incorporate abstention as an option along with the choice of voting for a candidate (see, e.g., Burden and Lacy 1999; Lacy and Burden 1999; Sanders 1998; Herron 1998; and Timpone 1998). Here I employ the specification developed by Lacy and Burden (1999) in which voters *abstain due to alienation* if neither party is sufficiently attractive.[5] In this vote model, each voter, i, compares his or her utility, $U_i(A) = a$, for abstention against the utilities $U_i(D)$ for the Democratic Party and $U_i(R)$ for the Republicans. If $U_i(A)$ exceeds $U_i(D)$ and $U_i(R)$, then the voter abstains; otherwise, he or she votes for the preferred party.

Figure 7.3 illustrates how introducing abstention due to alienation changes voters' decisions. The figure shows how democratic partisans' voting decisions vary as a function of liberal-conservative position, with the Democratic Party located at $d = 3.0$ and the Republicans at $r = 5.0$. (For this illustration, I assume that there are Democratic partisans distributed all along the liberal-conservative continuum, not just on the liberal side, as in the previous example.) The strength of partisan bias is set at $b^{1/2} = 1.0$. Figure 7.3A illustrates the basic partisan spatial scenario, which assumes full voter turnout, that is, the utility for abstention is set so low that all eligible citizens will turn out to vote (e.g., $U_i(A) = a = -\infty$). In this situation, all Democratic partisans located in the policy interval [1.00,4.25] vote for the Democrats and those in the interval [4.25,7.00] vote Republican.[6]

Figure 7.3B displays Democratic partisans' decisions under a different scenario, one in which the attraction of abstention has increased. Specifically, I increase the utility for abstention from $a = -\infty$ to $a = -1.0$, while leaving

(A)

(B)

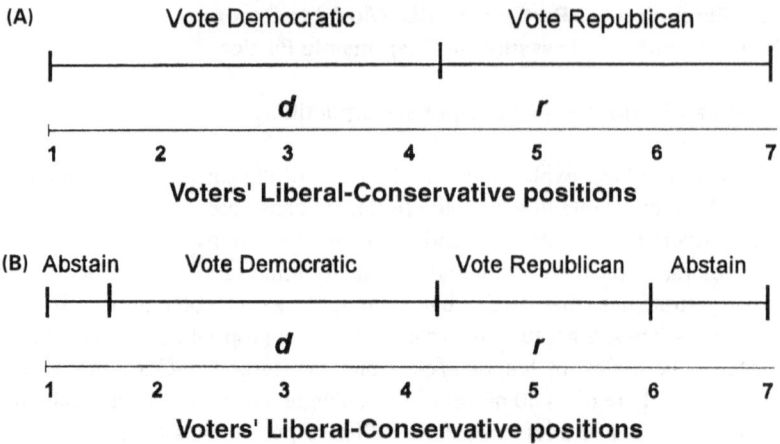

Fig. 7.3. **Voter decisions under the partisan vote model for varying levels of voter turnout (hypothetical examples with the strength of voter partisanship set at $b = 1.0$. (A) Democratic partisans' voting decisions for the partisan vote model with full voter turnout; (B) Democratic partisans' voting decisions for the partisan turnout vote model ($a = -1.0$).**

the values of the remaining parameters (d, r, and b) unchanged. For this specification, Democratic partisans will prefer abstaining to voting Democratic whenever $U_i(D) > U_i(A)$, that is, whenever $[b - (x_i - d)^2] > a$. And Democratic partisans prefer abstention to voting Republican whenever $U_i(R) > U_i(A)$ $\Rightarrow [-(x_i - r)^2] > a$. In this example, the effect of introducing abstention from alienation is to motivate extremely liberal and conservative Democratic partisans to abstain because neither party is sufficiently attractive. Thus, Democratic partisans located in the approximate policy interval [1.00,1.59] abstain rather than voting Democratic;[7] meanwhile, Democratic partisans in the policy interval [6.00,7.00] abstain rather than voting Republican.[8] The remaining voters continue to turn out, and they support the same party as they did under the "basic" partisan spatial model, because the introduction of the abstention option does not change voters' comparative utilities for the Democratic Party versus the Republicans.

One additional feature of this hypothetical example is important. Note that while extremely liberal *and* conservative Democratic partisans abstain due to alienation extreme liberals show a greater willingness to vote Democratic than extreme conservatives show to vote Republican. This is reflected in the fact that on the extreme conservative end of the continuum all voters located in the policy interval [6.00,7.00] abstain, while on the liberal end only those voters located in the narrower interval [1.00,1.59] abstain. This reflects the influence of these voters' partisan biases. Liberal Democrats are prepared to turn out and support their party even in the face of significant policy losses because they grant their party added utility arising from their partisan loyalty and this compensates for their policy losses (for all but the most extreme liberals). Hence, under the partisan turnout model, partisan loyalties help the parties in two ways: first, by motivating partisan loyalists to support their party in preference to its rival, even in situations in which the rival party proposes more attractive policies; and, second, by motivating partisans to turn out for their party in preference to abstaining. The latter feature of the partisan turnout specification captures researchers' empirical finding that party identification tends to increase political participation (Lacy and Burden 1999; Highton and Wolfinger 1998; Sanders 1998).

The Pressure for Responsible Parties under the Partisan Turnout Model

I now consider the question: does the introduction of abstention from alienation modify parties' strategic incentives in spatial competition involving partisan voters? The answer to this question is yes. To see this, consider the election scenario illustrated in figure 7.4A, in which all voters located to the liberal side of the median voter location $x_i = 4$ identify with the Democrats, those to the conservative side of the median are Republican partisans, the strength of the partisan parameter is set at $b^{1/2} = 1$, and the utility for abstention is set at $a = -1$. This election scenario is identical to the one pictured in figure 7.2A *except* that I have replaced the full turnout specification (e.g., $a = -\infty$) with the specification $a = -1.0$. With both parties positioned at the median voter, all voters in the approximate policy interval [2.59,4.00] will vote Democratic, those in the approximate interval [4.00,5.41] will vote Republican, and the rest will abstain due to alienation.[9]

Now consider how this partisan turnout specification alters the Democratic Party's strategic incentives. Recall that for the basic partisan spatial model the Democrats cannot improve their vote by shifting to a more liberal position away from the median voter (see fig. 7.3B). The central reason is that, although such a liberal shift does not forfeit support from moderate Democratic partisans (at least as long as the Democratic Party does not shift too far toward the liberal end of the ideological continuum), neither does it gain *additional* votes from liberal Democrats since these Democratic partisans will vote their party identification even if the Democratic Party locates at the position of the median voter. However, the second part of this proposition—that a liberal shift by the Democratic Party fails to attract additional votes from liberal Democrats—does *not* hold for the partisan turnout specification. With utility from abstention set at $a = -1$, the Democratic Party can indeed attract additional votes by shifting to a more liberal position since such a policy shift will motivate some voters lo-

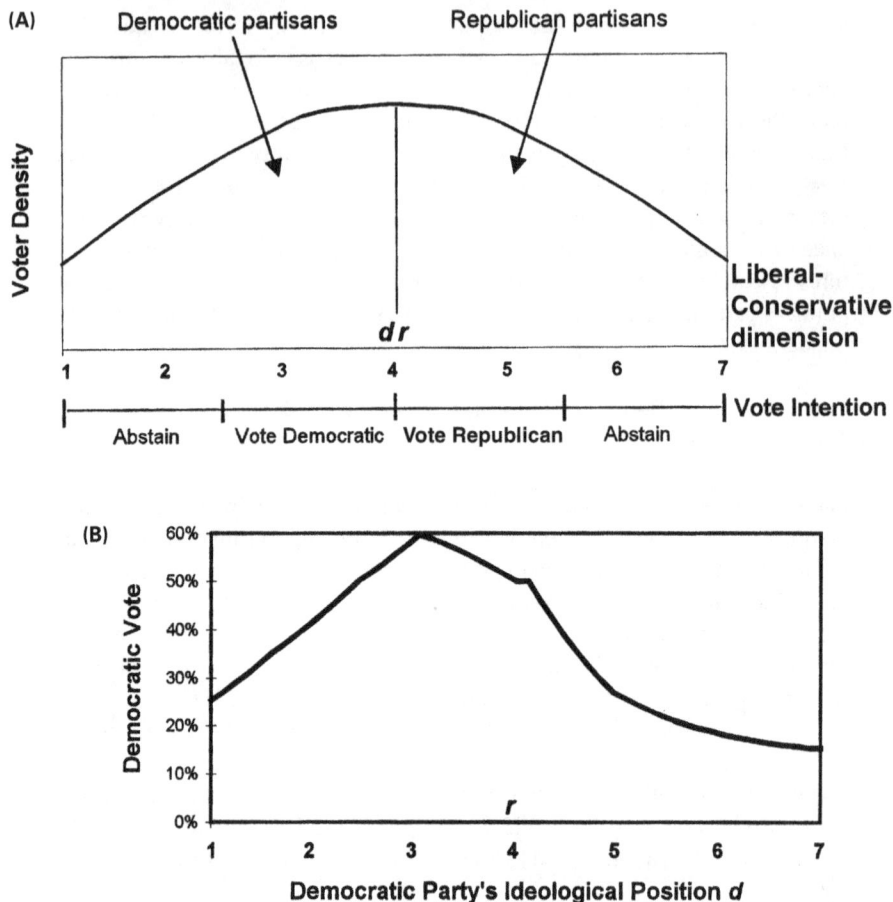

Fig. 7.4.   Two-party spatial competition under the partisan turnout vote model. Strength of voter partisanship is set at $b = 1.0$ and utility of abstention at $a = -1.0$. (A) Initial distribution of voters and parties; (B) The Democratic party's vote for varying ideological positions.

cated on the liberal side of $x_i = 2.59$ to vote Democratic rather than abstain. Furthermore, the Democratic Party can shift to a considerably more liberal position without sacrificing support from moderate Democratic partisans because these voters' partisan loyalties outweigh their policy preference for the Republican Party. Specifically, the Democrats can shift to a position as liberal as $d = 3.0$ without losing the support of moderate Democratic partisans.[10] And, if by shifting left the Democrats can attract additional votes from liberals without sacrificing support from moderates, their strategy is clear: *under this nonpolicy turnout specification the Democratic Party is motivated to present a liberal position that appeals to its partisan constituency.*

Figure 7.4B, which plots the Democratic Party's percentage of the two-party vote as a function of its liberal-conservative position, d (with the Republicans positioned at $r = 4$), shows that the Democrats maximize their share of the two-party vote by locating at the liberal position $d = 3$.[11] In this position, the Democrats win the votes of all Democratic partisans located in the policy interval [1.59,4.00], while the Republicans win votes from the Republican partisans located in the narrower policy interval [4.00,5.41] and the remaining voters abstain. Hence the Democratic Party wins approximately 60 percent of the votes cast. If the Democrats shift to a still more liberal position than $d = 3$, they win additional support from extremely liberal Democrats but they simultaneously lose support from moderate Democrats, who switch their votes to the Republican Party. Hence, the Democratic Party's aggregate vote percentage will decline. Thus, while the presence of liberal Democrats in this hypothetical electorate motivates the Democratic Party to propose a liberal ideology, the presence of moderate Democrats discourages the party from adopting an extremely liberal position.

One other aspect of figure 7.4B is important. Note that while the Democrats win the election under a wide range of liberal policies their support declines precipitously as they shift toward positions on the conservative side of the median voter, in the direction of the Republican Party's voting constituency. This is because Republican partisans prefer their party on nonpolicy grounds. To attract these voters' support, the Democratic Party must present conservative policies that differ substantially from the Republican Party's centrist position. And, while such positioning will motivate conservative Republican partisans to vote Democratic, this positioning simultaneously forfeits the votes of most of the Democrats' own partisan constituency.[12] Hence, in this illustrative example, not only are the Democrats motivated to appeal to their own partisan constituency but they suffer disastrous electoral losses if they desert their constituency in search of support from Republican partisans.

Figure 7.5 shows the unique policy equilibrium that exists for this illustrative example, which finds the Democrats locating at approximately $d = 2.59$ and the Republicans at approximately $r = 5.41$. Also pictured is each party's percentage of the two-party vote as a function of its ideology, with the rival party located at its equilibrium position. Under this policy configuration, the Democrats attract the votes of virtually their entire partisan constituency, with only extremely liberal Democrats abstaining; the same is true for the Republican Party with respect to conservative voters. Thus, under the nonpolicy turnout spatial model, both *parties are motivated to appeal on policy grounds to the constituencies that are attached to them in part for nonpolicy reasons.*

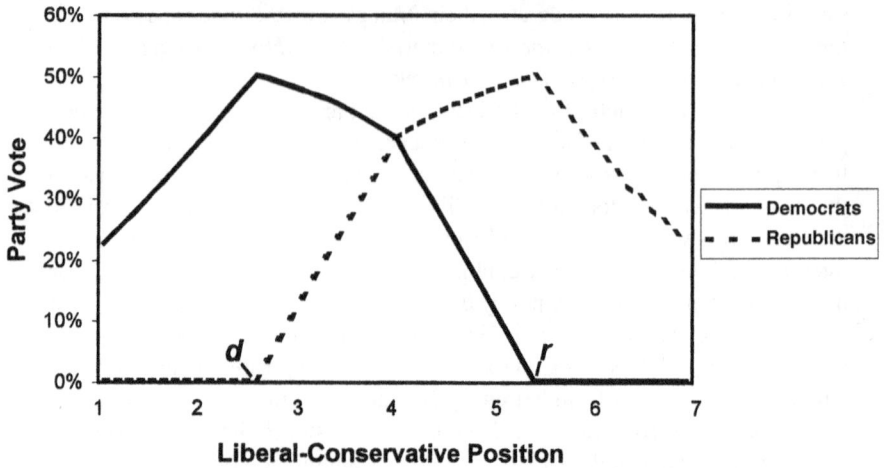

Fig. 7.5. Parties' expected votes, with the rival party at its equilibrium position, for the partisan turnout vote model. Calculations are based on the voter distribution and voting parameters given in figure 7.4.

In summary, this illustrative example shows how a voting model that incorporates turnout effects as well as the nonpolicy motivations that behavioralists find important can illuminate party behavior in the United States. The turnout decision is important because it motivates the parties to appeal to voters located in the wings who would otherwise abstain from voting. Voters' partisan loyalties are important because they ensure that moderate partisans will reliably turn out to support their party, provided it does not present an extreme position. Thus, partisan loyalties allow the parties to shift away from the center in pursuit of additional votes from the more extreme elements among their partisan constituencies.

In appendix D, I prove the following theorem, which obtains providing that the following conditions on the voter distribution are satisfied:

1. The voter distribution is continuous.
2. All voters are either Democratic or Republican partisans, and every Republican partisan is more conservative than every Democratic partisan.
3. The policy intervals that contain the Democratic and the Republican partisans both exceed $(b - a)^{1/2}$ in length.[13]
4. Both parties seek to maximize their percentage of the two-party vote.
5. The partisan salience coefficient, b, is larger than the voters' abstention utility a.[14]

THEOREM 7.1:   *If an equilibrium exists, then at equilibrium the Democratic Party presents a more liberal position than the Republican party does.*

The equilibrium pictured earlier in figure 7.5 illustrates a party configuration consistent with the theorem. However, note that while figure 7.5 pictures a scenario in which the competing parties faithfully reflect their partisans' beliefs the theorem itself merely specifies that when voters choose according to the partisan turnout model all possible equilibria will find the Democrats positioned to the left of the Republicans. Hence, the theorem does not ensure that the parties will provide faithful representations at equilibrium, nor does it ensure that equilibria always exist. Furthermore, both the theorem and the illustrative arguments presented above are based upon the same set of stylized assumptions that I employed in the analyses of British and French politics, namely that all voters are partisans and the spatial distributions of the rival parties' partisan constituencies do not overlap. This raises two questions concerning two-party competition under the partisan turnout model: (1) what are the strategic dynamics of party competition in American elections given the actual distribution of American voters' policy (and partisan) preferences and (2) will party equilibria typically exist, and if not what are plausible patterns of the parties' policy trajectories in the absence of policy equilibrium?

7.4. Empirical Applications to American Politics

To answer these two questions, I simulated policy competition between the Democratic and Republican Parties for voter distributions derived from American National Election Study data. Specifically, I performed simulations based on the 1996 and the 1992 ANES under the assumption that voters chose according to the partisan turnout model. Figures 7.6A and 7.6B show the distributions of self-identified Democratic partisans, Republican partisans, and independent voters along the seven-point liberal-conservative scale for 1996 and 1992, respectively. The mean positions of the partisan constituencies are also shown.[15] As expected, Republican partisans tend to be more conservative than Democrats, but nonetheless there are many conservative Democratic partisans as well as a smaller number of liberal Republicans. As a group, the Republican partisans display a strong conservative bent, with mean positions of 4.92 in 1992 and 5.19 in 1996, which are significantly to the right of the "moderate" designation (4.0) along the 1–7 scale; by contrast, the Democratic partisans are (on average) quite moderate, with mean positions of 3.60 in 1992 and 3.62 in 1996. As a result, the survey populations as a whole display slightly conservative tendencies, with mean ideological self-placements of 4.19 in 1992 and 4.32 in 1996.

(A)

(B)

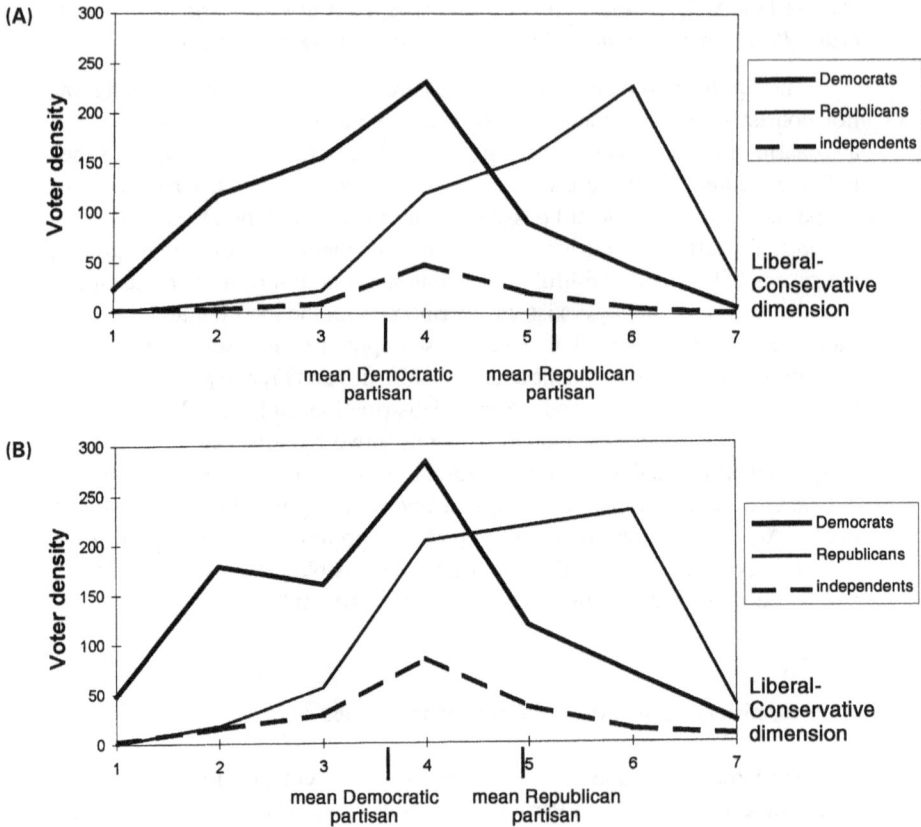

Fig. 7.6. Distributions of respondents' liberal-conservative self-placements in the 1992 and 1996 American National Election Studies. (*A*) 1996
ANES distribution; (*B*) 1992 ANES distribution.

In analyzing party strategies for these voter distributions, we must first
specify the parties' objectives. Spatial modelers interested in two-party/two-
candidate elections with variable turnouts have employed a variety of assumptions, including: (1) that each party maximizes the number of votes it receives
(see, e.g, Enelow and Hinich 1982, 1984); (2) that each party maximizes its plurality, defined as the difference between the number of votes the party receives
and the number of votes the rival party attracts (Lindbeck and Weibel 1987);
and (3) that each party maximizes its proportion of the two-party vote, with a
party's vote proportion defined as the number of votes it receives divided by the
total number of votes cast for the two parties (for simplicity, I will refer to each

party's vote *percentage,* which is equal to its vote proportion multiplied by
100). Because a party's success in electing candidates—either to the Congress
or the presidency—depends on the magnitude of its electoral support *relative*
to its opponent, assumptions 2–3 appear most plausible in the context of American elections, and I therefore performed simulations based upon each of
them.[16] Because the two sets of simulations yielded virtually identical predictions about party strategies, below I report results based on assumption 3, that
each party selected a position that maximized its percentage of the two-party
vote.

The specifications I employed in the simulations were similar to those described for the simulations on French (section 4.3) and British (section 3.4)
election data. First, the parties were placed at the mean voter position along the
liberal-conservative scale.[17] Next I computed the parties' successive vote-per-
centage-maximizing positions for varying assumptions about the strength b of
voter partisanship and the value, a, of voters' utilities from abstention, with each
calculation updated to reflect the rival party's policy shift.[18] Each simulation
was concluded following 100 party policy shifts.

The simulation results I obtained were consistent with both the illustrative
arguments and the theorem presented above. Consistent with theorem 7.1, *in
the cases in which equilibria were located, these equilibria found the Democrats presenting more liberal positions than the Republicans.* Furthermore, in
the (more common) cases in which the simulations failed to locate policy equilibria, *the parties presented policies that were stable but not static, the parties
did not leapfrog, and each party presented ideologies that reflected the beliefs
of its partisan constituency.* These simulation results match the MRG's empirical findings, and they suggest that the partisan turnout spatial vote model illuminates the patterns of mass-elite policy linkages in American elections.

Examples of Party Equilibria

Figure 7.7 presents an example of an equilibrium configuration that was obtained in a simulation based on the 1996 ANES data for the voting specification $b^{1/2} = 1.0$ and $a = -0.5$. The equilibrium finds the Democrats located at
$d = 4.21$, slightly on the liberal side of the mean voter position, 4.32, and the
Republicans presenting the conservative ideological position $r = 5.28$. This
configuration is consistent with theorem 7.1. Also shown are the parties' vote
percentages as a function of their positions, with the rival party located at its
equilibrium position. These support curves show that if the Democrats were
paired with the Republicans (i.e., if we set $d = r = 5.28$), they would win only
about 35 percent of the vote—a disastrous defeat. This is because, as outlined
in the illustrative arguments presented above, a conservative Democratic Party
would not attract votes from Republican partisans—because these voters

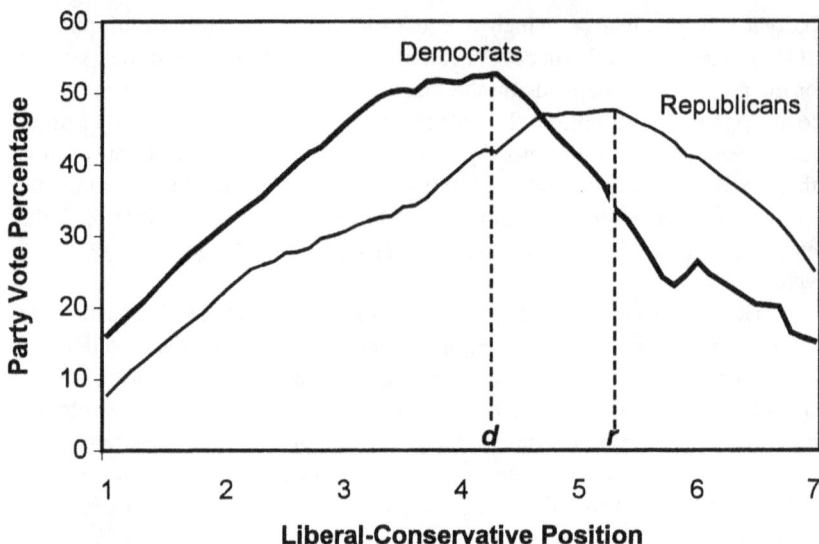

Fig. 7.7. Simulated equilibrium for the partisan turnout model for the voter distribution derived from the 1996 ANES. Parties' support curves are derived given the voting specifications $b = 1.0$ and $a = -0.5$.

would prefer the Republican Party on nonpolicy grounds—while simultaneously alienating liberal Democrats, who would abstain. By a similar logic, the Republican Party would suffer dramatic losses if it matched the Democrats' moderate equilibrium position $d = 4.21$. Finally, note that the Republican Party's equilibrium position ($r = 5.21$) is virtually identical to the mean preference of its partisan constituency ($x_i = 5.19$), while the Democratic Party's equilibrium ideology ($d = 4.21$) is similar to but more conservative than its partisans' mean position ($x_i = 3.62$). Thus, in this example the parties have electoral incentives to present divergent positions that reflect their supporters' ideological tendencies.

Examples of Parties' Policy Trajectories in the Absence of Equilibrium

Although the simulated equilibrium configuration presented above supports theorem 7.1, the majority of the simulations did not locate policy equilibria. Figure 7.8 illustrates the parties' policy trajectories for two of these nonequilibrium outcomes for simulations based on the 1996 ANES voter distribution. In the first, pictured in figure 7.8A, the strength of voters' party identification was set at $b^{1/2} = 1.0$ (the same value specified in the equilibrium illustrated in

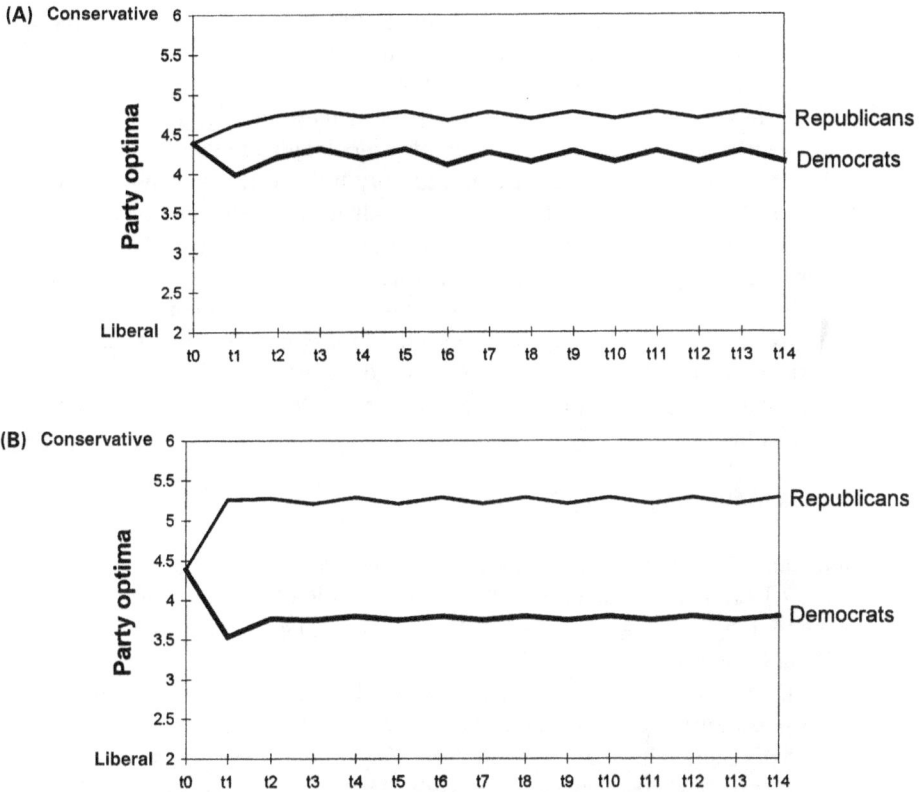

Fig. 7.8. Spatial mappings of the parties' policy trajectories for simulations based on the 1996 ANES voter distribution. Simulations are based on the voter distribution pictured in figure 7.6A. (A) Parties' policy trajectories for $b^{0.5} = 1.0$ and $a = -1.0$; (B) Parties' policy trajectories for $b^{0.5} = 1.75$ and $a = -1.0$.

fig. 7.7) and the utility from abstention was set at $a = -1.0$ (rather than at $a = -0.5$ as in fig. 7.7). For this voting specification, figure 7.8A shows the trajectories of the parties' positions over the first 14 of the 100 successive simulated policy shifts. The figure shows that the Republicans immediately shift to the conservative side of the voter mean $x_i = 4.32$ and consistently present moderately conservative policies, which range from approximately $r = 4.70$ to $r = 4.80$. The Democrats, in contrast, present consistently moderate positions that vary between $d = 3.98$ and $d = 4.28$. Furthermore, the parties do not leapfrog. Thus, in this example the parties present moderately divergent policies whose patterns are largely consistent with the MRG's empirical findings.

Figure 7.8B illustrates the parties' simulated policy trajectories when the partisan salience coefficient is increased from $b^{1/2} = 1.0$ to $b^{1/2} = 1.75$, with the utility from abstention held constant at $a = -1.0$. With the salience of partisanship increased, the parties now present more divergent—and quite stable—positions: the Republicans vary their ideology within the narrow policy interval [5.20,5.28] and the Democrats vary their positions within the interval [3.74,3.79].[19] This result is consistent with our earlier findings on French and British politics, that the greater the strength of voters' partisan biases the greater the policy divergence between parties. Of course, for the British and French multiparty elections this effect occurs even in full-turnout elections, whereas the illustrative arguments presented in section 7.2 suggest that for American two-party contests this effect depends on voters' willingness to abstain. Finally, note that in this example the parties provide excellent representations of their partisan's preferences.

Results for Varying Voting Specifications

Simulation Results on the 1996 ANES Voter Distribution
Table 7.1 summarizes the results of simulations on the 1996 voter distribution pictured in figure 7.6A for varying values of b (ranging from $b = 0$ to $b^{1/2} = 1.75$) and for varying values of a (ranging from $a = -1.0$ to $a = -0.5$).[20] Columns 3–4 give the Democratic and the Republican Parties' mean positions, respectively, over the course of the 100 policy shifts. Column 5 shows the proportion of policy shifts that involve leapfrogging; column 6 shows the percentage of the parties' positions that lie outside their ideological areas (defined as the policy interval [1,4] for the Democrats and [4,7] for the Republicans); and column 7 shows whether an equilibrium was located. For comparison, the mean positions of self-identified Democratic and Republican partisans are also reported, and the last row gives the results of the MRG's historical mapping of the American parties' postwar platforms (pictured in fig. 7.1).

Table 7.1 shows that for all positive values of b the simulations find the parties presenting divergent positions that are shaded in the direction of their partisans' ideologies. As expected, the degree of policy divergence increases with the strength of voters' partisan biases so that when the strength of the partisan coefficient reaches about $b^{1/2} = 1.5$, a value consistent with behavioral researchers' empirical studies on American elections (see note 20), the parties' positions diverge significantly and each party accurately reflects its partisans' beliefs. When voters do not display partisan biases (i.e., $b = 0$), by contrast, the parties do not present divergent positions but instead converge to the similar, centrist locations predicted by the basic Downsian model. In addition, the results presented in column 5 show that the parties do not leapfrog, while column 7 shows that in a majority of the simulation scenarios (10 out of 12) the parties

TABLE 7.1. Patterns of American Parties' Policy Trajectories under the Partisan Turnout Vote Model for the 1996 ANES Voter Distribution

Voting Parameters		Mean Party Positions			Positions	Was
Strength of Partisanship (1)	Abstention Utility (2)	Democrats (3)	Republicans (4)	Leapfrogging Frequency (5)	Outside Ideological Area (6)	Equilibrium Located? (7)
$b^{1/2} = 0.00$	$a = -1.0$	4.12	4.13	0%	50%	NO
$b^{1/2} = 0.00$	$a = -0.5$	4.06	4.06	50	50	NO
$b^{1/2} = 0.50$	$a = -1.0$	4.41	4.71	0	50	NO
$b^{1/2} = 0.50$	$a = -0.5$	4.20	5.50	0	50	NO
$b^{1/2} = 1.00$	$a = -1.0$	4.21	4.73	0	50	NO
$b^{1/2} = 1.00$	$a = -0.5$	4.21	5.28	0	50	YES
$b^{1/2} = 1.25$	$a = -1.0$	4.11	4.90	0	50	YES
$b^{1/2} = 1.25$	$a = -0.5$	4.11	4.90	0	50	NO
$b^{1/2} = 1.50$	$a = -1.0$	4.04	5.10	0	17	NO
$b^{1/2} = 1.50$	$a = -0.5$	3.96	5.07	0	0	NO
$b^{1/2} = 1.75$	$a = -1.0$	3.77	5.24	0	0	NO
$b^{1/2} = 1.75$	$a = -0.5$	3.70	4.95	0	0	NO
Partisans' mean positions		3.62	5.19			
MRG's empirical results				0%	0%	

Note: Simulations are based on the respondent distribution on Liberal-Conservative ideology, using the assumption that the parties maximized their vote percentages.

Column 5 gives the percentages of parties' policy shifts that involve leapfrogging. Column 6 gives the percentages of the parties' policy shifts that fall outside the party's ideological area, defined as the policy interval [1,4] for the Democrats and [4,7] for the Republicans. Column 7 reports whether the parties converged to an equilibrium position over the course of 100 policy shifts.

failed to converge to an equilibrium.[21] Thus, in the simulations the parties present stable, divergent, and representative policies.

The one feature of the simulation results that is inconsistent with the MRG's empirical findings emerged in the simulations in which voters were assigned low to moderate degrees of partisan attachment (roughly $b^{1/2} = 0.5$ to $b^{1/2} = 1.25$). In these simulations, the Democratic Party persistently presented moderate ideologies located in the policy interval [4.10,4.30] along the 1–7 liberal-conservative scale. These positions were more liberal than the mean position of the ANES voters (4.32), but they fell slightly to the conservative side of the center (4.0) of the scale. As discussed earlier, one reason for this result is that Democratic partisans display moderate preferences, so that, although the Democratic Party is frequently positioned on the "wrong" side of the liberal-conservative scale relative to its supporters—which accounts for the fact that column 6 in table 7.1 reports that 50 percent of the parties' positions lie outside their ideological areas, for the simulations in which $b^{1/2} < 1.5$—both the party and its partisans are actually quite moderate.

Simulation Results on the 1992 ANES Voter Distribution
Table 7.2 summarizes the outcomes of simulations based on the 1992 voter distribution (pictured in fig. 7.6B). These results are entirely consistent with the results reported for 1996: in both years, the parties present divergent policies that are shaded in the direction of their partisans' preferences, and for both years the parties' policies grow increasingly divergent—and representative—as the strength, b, of voters' partisan loyalties increases. The close correspondence between the simulated party strategies generated for 1992 and 1996 strongly suggests that these results capture the general patterns of spatial competition that should be expected when American parties compete for support from an electorate that votes according to the partisan turnout model.[22]

7.5. Discussion

Over the past two decades, spatial modelers have proposed several extensions of the basic Downsian model that can potentially illuminate why American parties and candidates do not converge toward the similar, centrist policies that Downs's model implies. These include models that explore the influence of party activists (Aldrich 1983), candidates' policy motivations (Wittman 1983; Groseclose 1999), and party leaders' calculations about the possible entry of new parties (Palfrey 1984). Although these studies present promising avenues for understanding the dynamics of American two-party elections, the results presented in this chapter suggest an extremely simple explanation for American parties' (and candidates') empirical policy divergence: that when voters abstain due to alienation the parties maximize votes by shifting away from the center in the direction of their partisans' beliefs.

The arguments and simulation results presented here are interesting for two additional reasons. The first concerns the implications of these results for the debate over the empirical status of Rabinowitz and Macdonald's (1989) directional voting model vis-à-vis the traditional proximity metric (see also Rabinowitz, Macdonald, and Listhaug 1991; Merrill and Grofman 1999; Westholm 1997, forthcoming; Dow 1997a; and Lewis and King 2000). Supporters of the directional model have argued that the observed behavior of American candidates, who typically present divergent, noncentrist positions (see Powell 1982; and Ansolobehere, Snyder, and Stewart 1999), is compatible with directional theory but not proximity (see Rabinowitz and Macdonald 1989, 110–14). However, I have shown that a proximity-based spatial model can also illuminate American parties' noncentrist positioning, provided that proximity voting is incorporated into a spatial model that incorporates voter abstention along with voters' partisan loyalties.

Second, my results suggest that voter turnout alters political representa-

TABLE 7.2. Patterns of American Parties' Policy Trajectories under the Partisan Turnout Vote Model for the 1992 ANES Voter Distribution

Voting Parameters		Mean Party Positions		Leapfrogging Frequency (5)	Positions Outside Ideological Area (6)	Was Equilibrium Located? (7)
Strength of Partisanship (1)	Abstention Utility (2)	Democrats (3)	Republicans (4)			
$b^{1/2} = 0.00$	$a = -1.0$	4.12	4.13	0%	50%	YES
$b^{1/2} = 0.00$	$a = -0.5$	4.05	4.05	100	50	NO
$b^{1/2} = 0.50$	$a = -1.0$	4.03	4.43	0	50	NO
$b^{1/2} = 0.50$	$a = -0.5$	4.00	4.51	0	25	NO
$b^{1/2} = 1.00$	$a = -1.0$	4.13	4.69	0	50	NO
$b^{1/2} = 1.00$	$a = -0.5$	4.11	4.68	0	25	NO
$b^{1/2} = 1.25$	$a = -1.0$	4.03	4.86	0	25	NO
$b^{1/2} = 1.25$	$a = -0.5$	4.03	4.87	0	25	NO
$b^{1/2} = 1.50$	$a = -1.0$	3.86	4.76	0	0	NO
$b^{1/2} = 1.50$	$a = -0.5$	3.88	4.87	0	0	NO
$b^{1/2} = 1.75$	$a = -1.0$	3.53	4.50	0	0	NO
$b^{1/2} = 1.75$	$a = -0.5$	3.55	4.72	0	0	NO
Partisans' mean positions		3.60	4.94			
MRG's empirical results				0%	0%	

Note: Simulations are based on the respondent distribution on Liberal-Conservative ideology, using the assumption that the parties maximized their vote percentages.

Column 5 gives the percentages of parties' policy shifts that involve leapfrogging. Column 6 gives the percentages of the parties' policy shifts that fall outside the party's ideological area, defined as the policy interval [1,4] for the Democrats and [4,7] for the Republicans. Column 7 reports whether the parties converged to an equilibrium position over the course of 100 policy shifts.

tion in the United States in surprising ways. Many scholars argue that low turnout weakens mass-elite policy linkages in the United States, first, by undermining the legitimacy of elected officials, and, second, by reducing the political influence of low-turnout groups, including the poor and racial minorities (see, e.g., Lijphart 1997; and Highton and Wolfinger 1998). The arguments presented here, that vote-seeking parties should present centrist policies in full-turnout elections but should reflect their partisans' beliefs in elections with abstention, suggest an alternative perspective: that the *threat* of voter abstention motivates parties to faithfully represent their constituencies. Although this thesis does not mitigate the force of the argument that *unequal* turnout damages representation, it does suggest that—to the extent that representation in the United States revolves around the policy links between parties and their supporters—voter abstention can actually *enhance* the quality of representation.

CHAPTER 8

Directions for Future Research

The aim of this book has been to develop a parsimonious model of spatial competition that accounts for parties' actual behavior and empirical patterns of mass-elite policy linkages in postwar democracies. In chapter 1, I asked three questions. First, why is the behavior of political parties in advanced industrial societies characterized by policy stability and differentiation when spatial modeling results imply the opposite conclusions? Second, why is there agreement between the policies that parties propose and the policy beliefs of the voters who support them given behavioral researchers' findings that voters are motivated in large part by nonpolicy considerations? Consideration of these issues led to a third, overarching question: why does responsible party government function reasonably well in contemporary Western democracies when results from spatial modelers and behavioral researchers suggest that it should function poorly?

In exploring these questions, I have analyzed the strategic logic of a model of party competition that combines the perspectives of spatial modeling and behavioral research. From spatial modeling, I take the perspective that parties compete for votes by strategically manipulating their policy images. From behavioral research, I adopt the perspective that, while voters care about policies, they are also moved by considerations that are not necessarily related to policies such as party identification, group-related loyalties rooted in class and religion, and additional, possibly unmeasured motivations. I have argued that, while neither spatial modeling nor behavioral research by itself provides convincing answers to the questions posed in chapter 1, their combined perspectives can succeed where each alone may fail.

Throughout most of this book, I have explored the logic of an extremely simple version of such a behavioral spatial model of elections in which parties seek votes from an electorate moved entirely by a combination of partisan loyalties and policy motivations along a unidimensional continuum. This simple setup has allowed me to isolate the ways in which voter bias alters parties' strategic considerations as they manipulate their policy images in search of electoral advantage. I argue that the central strategic logic that drives party behavior in this context is as follows: that *in situations in which voters' biases correlate with their policy preferences the parties competing in multiparty elec-*

tions have electoral incentives to appeal on policy grounds to voters biased toward them for nonpolicy reasons. Furthermore, chapter 7 established that this identical strategic motivation applies to two-party elections provided that voters are prepared to abstain due to alienation.

Because many of the factors that motivate voter biases, including class, race, and (most importantly) party identification, do in fact correlate with voters' policy preferences, the strategic imperative summarized above motivates policy differentiation, stability, and representation on the part of political parties. Because groups of voters biased toward different parties tend to cluster in different regions of the policy space, parties have electoral incentives to differentiate their policies, with each appealing to its own constituency. Because parties can incur severe electoral penalties if they shift their policies away from their partisans' beliefs, they are motivated to present stable policies. Because parties appeal on policy grounds to voters biased toward them for nonpolicy reasons, they provide faithful policy representations. Thus, this simple model of spatial competition in a partisan electorate implies the three essential features of responsible party government—policy stability, differentiation, and representation. Furthermore, I have shown that the logic that obtains for this simple partisan spatial model extends to more complex (and realistic) scenarios that incorporate such factors as additional policy dimensions, more complex models of voter partisanship, probabilistic voting, and additional sources of voter bias.

As I see it, the central contributions my work makes to scholarship on spatial modeling, voting behavior, and political representation are fourfold.

First, in line with recent scholarship by Merrill and Grofman (1999), Schofield and his coauthors (Schofield, Martin, et al. 1998; Schofield, Sened, and Nixon 1998), Erikson and Romero (1990), Alvarez and Nagler (1995; see also Alvarez, Bowler and Nagler 1996), and Dow (1997c), this work explicitly links the behavioral literature on voting behavior to spatial models of party competition. The specific contribution this book makes is to highlight the ways in which the nonpolicy voting motivations that behavioralists emphasize alter parties' policy strategies. My theoretical results strongly suggest that even if parties cannot manipulate voter biases they should take these biases into account when devising their policy strategies. What I have explored here is how these biases affect party strategies and what the likely outcomes will be.

Second, my empirical applications to Britain, France, and the United States suggest that a spatial model that incorporates voters' non-policy-related biases not only can make theoretical contributions but can account for the policies that political parties have proposed in historical elections. In attempting to explain real world party strategies, I am following in the footsteps of Erikson and Romero (1990), Schofield (Schofield, Martin, et al. 1998; Schofield, Sened, and Nixon 1998), and my own work with Samuel Merrill III (Adams and

Merrill 1999a, 1999b, 2000). With regard to this subject, one innovation I have introduced in this book is to focus on political parties' policy trajectories across time. I have shown that the partisan spatial model accounts well for parties' policy trajectories in postwar Britain, France, and the United States, as measured by the content analyses of party election programs carried out by the Manifesto Research Group.

A third, and related, contribution of this book is to move beyond a focus on equilibrium analysis to explore the dynamic aspects of party policies in the absence of long-run policy equilibrium. In so doing, I contribute to a literature that includes work by Kramer (1977), Kollman et al. (1992), and Jackson (1990), all of whom explore this topic in the context of two-party competition.[1] In extending this approach to the study of multiparty elections, I find that even in the absence of a policy equilibrium parties that compete for votes in a partisan electorate will present reasonably stable policy images and furthermore they will differentiate their policies.[2] To be sure, this "contribution" is a two-edged sword in that in examining dynamic aspects of party competition I rely on illustrative examples and simulation analyses rather than deductive theorems. However, my analyses explain why parties' policies are *stable* yet not *static,* a prediction consistent with the Manifesto Research Group's empirical results and one that is not captured by spatial models that study policy equilibrium for a single election period. While both dynamic and equilibrium perspectives are important, my results suggest that studying the dynamic aspects of multiparty competition can illuminate important features of party policies, which are not considered in most spatial analyses.

The final two contributions this book makes also relate to possible extensions and areas for future research. The first concerns the implications of my results, which are based on a simple model of party objectives for spatial analyses that assume more complex models of party motivations. Throughout this book, I have adopted the most basic view of party goals, that they single-mindedly seek votes. While it is encouraging that this basic assumption, when married to the behaviorist's perspective on voting, can illuminate party behavior and responsible party government in contemporary democracies, it would be worthwhile to explore the implications of more complex party models.[3] In this regard, one of the most important findings in this book is that *when parties compete in a partisan electorate the goals of vote-seeking and policy seeking are largely compatible,* that is, parties maximize votes by proposing policies that plausibly reflect their sincere policy preferences. The reason for this is that parties have electoral motivations to appeal to voters biased toward them for nonpolicy reasons, so that socialist parties win votes by appealing to their own partisans, who are concentrated on the Left; Conservative parties win votes by appealing to voters concentrated on the Right; and so on. While it may appear trite to claim that parties maximize votes by proposing noncentrist positions that reflect their sincere policy beliefs, I emphasize that this argument runs counter to the results presented in all previous spatial analyses of party strategies in historical elections (see, e.g., Erikson and Romero 1990; Dow 1997c; Schofield, Martin, et al. 1998; Schofield, Sened, and Nixon 1998; Alvarez, Bowler, and Nagler 1996; and Alvarez, Nagler, and Willette 1998), which conclude that parties maximize votes by shifting toward similar, centrist positions.[4]

Finally, I hope that this book will convince formal theorists that behavioral researchers' debates about voting have crucial implications for spatial models of party and candidate competition. Here I have focused primarily on the stakes involved in one of these debates, concerning the electoral impact of party identification. I have shown that, *to the extent that party identification influences the vote independently of voters' policy beliefs,* parties will present stable, differentiated policies that reflect their supporters' preferences. Thus, the central argument in this book depends on the assumption that partisanship indeed exercises such an independent effect upon the vote. As I emphasized in chapters 1 and 2, this hypothesis is supported by extensive behavioral research. However, there remains considerable controversy about the empirical status of partisanship, particularly in elections held outside the United States. We have seen here that this behavioral debate is relevant—indeed, central—to our understanding of parties' policy strategies and thus that it is also central to spatial models of multiparty competition.

There remain many additional debates in behavioral research that are relevant to parties' policy strategies. One of these, the empirical question about what motivates voter abstention, was introduced in chapter 7, in which I showed that a turnout-based version of the partisan spatial model can illuminate American two-party competition *provided that voters abstain due to alienation.* Thus, the empirical debate over the motivations behind voter abstention appear to be crucial to understanding party policy competition. In addition, I believe that one of the most promising directions in spatial modeling research involves a systematic study of the implications of alternative behavioral voting models for party policy strategies. Merrill and Grofman's study (1999, chaps. 8–11) of how party strategies vary depending on the relative importance voters assign to proximity, directional, and discounting policy metrics provides a striking example of this approach's potential. Some additional controversies in the behavioral literature that may be important to spatial modeling include debates about the extent to which the electoral salience of policies differs across voters (see, e.g., Rivers 1988; Converse and Pierce 1993; and Glasgow 1999) and the effect of parties' policy ambiguity on voting behavior (Alvarez 1997).

In this book, I have focused on the strategic logic of party competition when parties seek votes from a partisan electorate. I have shown that even modest degrees of partisan attachment change the nature of multiparty policy competition and facilitate responsible party government.

Description of the Simulation Procedures

For the empirical applications of the biased voter model to British and French politics, I employed the following conventions.

1. Generating the voter distributions.   Because respondents were constrained to place themselves at one of only 11 positions along the British nationalization scale (and at one of seven points along the French Left-Right scale), the respondent policy distributions were discontinuous, a condition that probably does not reflect the empirical voter distributions in these countries. For the purposes of the simulations, I therefore assumed that each respondent ideal point, x_r, represented a set of 10 voters, with ideal points located at $x_r - .45, x_r - .35, \ldots, x_r + .45$; furthermore, all 10 voters were assumed to have the same nonpolicy bias as the original respondent. Thus, if a respondent in the BGES study placed himself or herself at 3.0 on the nationalization scale and indicated that he or she felt close to the Labour Party, in the simulations on party strategies this respondent was represented by 10 Labour sympathizers distributed at the points $\{2.55, 2.65, \ldots, 3.45\}$. This transformation created more nearly continuous voter distributions without fundamentally changing the distributions of party sympathizers along the policy scales.

2. Constraints on party positioning.   In the simulations, the parties' vote-maximizing positions were located by varying their positions across the policy scales in intervals of 0.10 or 0.05, depending on the election under review (see below) and calculating their votes for each position. In the simulations on Britain, each party's vote was calculated for the set of 101 positions $\{1.0, 1.1, \ldots, 11.0\}$; in France, each party's vote was calculated for the set of 121 points $\{1.00, 1.05, \ldots, 7.00\}$.

3. The order of party movement.   The simulations reported in the chapter were performed using the assumption that the parties moved sequentially. For Britain, the order of party movement was: (1) Labour, (2) Liberal Democrats, and (3) Conservatives. For France, the order was: (1) Communists, (2) Socialists, (3) UDF, (4) RPR, and (5) National Front. I also replicated these simulations while reversing the order of party movements. The results, which are available from the author upon request, were similar to those reported in the chapter.

On Using Election Surveys to Analyze
Parties' Cross-Time Policy Trajectories

As discussed in section 3.4, the most obvious method for capturing the cross-time evolution of voters' ideologies, as well as their partisan affiliations, during the postwar period would be to analyze voter distributions from a series of national election studies. Thus, one could potentially measure the shifts in the British electorate by analyzing distributions of survey respondents' policy preferences (and party identifications) as reported in a *series* of British general election surveys.

Unfortunately, there are two problems with this approach. The first concerns limitations in the available data, which make it unfeasible to use this method to develop a *general* explanation for party behavior in Western democracies over the entire postwar period and in particular one that will generalize to French politics, which I analyze in chapter 4–5. In many democracies, there is little survey research available prior to the 1980s that provides data on the distribution of policy preferences and partisanship in the electorate. In the case of France, for instance, the only existing national election study that predates 1988 is the 1967–69 study conducted by Pierce and Converse.[1] Even in the case of British politics, which has been the focus of the most sustained survey research effort outside of the United States, detailed national election surveys date back only to 1963, nearly 20 years after the beginning of the postwar era.

Second, due to changes in question wordings with regard to both party identification items (see, e.g., Heath and Pierce 1992; and Sinnott 1998) and policy questions, survey respondents' answers are not always comparable over time, so one cannot conclude that shifts in respondents' reported policy preferences and partisanship, as recorded in different election studies, represent "real" changes in the electorate. With respect to the construction of policy scales, a major change in format between the policy items included in many surveys

---

1. That is, this is the only careful scientific survey of French voters prior to 1988 that provides data on respondents' Left-Right self-placements and their party identifications. Data from the pre-1988 period are available through a number of commercial polls. However, such data are of questionable quality, owing to the lack of quality controls (see, e.g., the discussion in Converse and Pierce 1993).

from the 1960s and early 1970s, compared to those included in more recent surveys, is that the former typically include a small number of carefully described categories, while the latter are usually seven- or 11-point scales for which only the endpoints are described. This is true for the policy scales used in the British General Election Studies as well as in American National Election Study data. Thus, in the 1963–69 versions of the British surveys, the nationalization of industry item provided four distinct response categories (in addition to "no opinion"). These were: (1) A lot more industries should be nationalized; (2) Only a few more industries, such as steel, should be nationalized; (3) No more industries should be nationalized, but industries that are nationalized now should stay nationalized; and (4) Some industries that are nationalized now should be denationalized. However, beginning in 1974 this item was changed, and respondents were instead presented with an 11-point scale, which provided the respondent with definitions of the endpoints only; these were described as (1) Nationalize more industries and (11) Sell off nationalized industries.

Finally, the fact that Western European electorates display relatively stable Left-Right orientations over time (see, e.g., Dalton 1996, 137, fig. 6.4; and Rose and McCallister 1990, 23), suggests another reason why it is problematic to analyze temporal patterns of British parties' policies via analyses based upon data from a series of British election surveys. Given that these surveys do not include Left-Right items, one is forced to rely on responses to other policy questions—such as the nationalization item I employ in chapters 2 and 3—which typically show much greater volatility over time than do Left-Right orientations. Hence, in the case of Britain temporal analysis of successive respondent policy distributions will necessarily overstate the degree of policy change in the electorate, which may lead to mistaken inferences about parties' policy strategies.

Party Policy Strategies and Equilibrium Results for a Generalized Multivariate Probabilistic Voting Model

C.1. Introduction

In this appendix, I develop the implications of a more general spatial model of multiparty probabilistic voting, one in which voters choose over multiple policy dimensions in which their policy evaluations may take any functional form and for which they may be influenced by multiple sources of nonpolicy bias in addition to partisanship. I outline this model in section C.2, and in section C.3 I develop a sufficient condition for the existence of party equilibrium for the generalized vote model. Section C.4 shows that theorems 6.1 and 6.2 presented in chapter 6 follow directly from the equilibrium results presented in the preceding section. In section C.5, I study the effect of voter bias on candidate positioning at equilibrium. I find that when bias is correlated with voters' policy positions—as is the case with party identification—the equilibria are dispersed and locate the parties near groups of voters that have nonpolicy biases in their direction.

C.2. A General Probabilistic Voting Model with Biased Voters

In the model, a set, $V = \{1, 2, \ldots, m\}$, of voters and $\mathfrak{R}$ of parties are located in an n-dimensional policy space. I assume that the cardinality of $\mathfrak{R}$ is greater than two—that is, that the analysis concerns a multiparty election. For each voter $i \in V$, i's location, x_i, is $x_i = \{x_{i1}, x_{i2}, \ldots, x_{in}\}$, where x_{ij} represents i's position along the jth policy dimension. Each party $K \in \mathfrak{R}$ proposes a platform, k_n, which is selected from the set of feasible platforms $L_K = \{k_1, k_2, \ldots, k_p\}$; k_n corresponds to a position in the policy space.

Let each voter i's utility for K's platform be given by the real-valued function $p(x_i, k_n)$. Let s be a nonnegative salience parameter, which varies with the importance voters attach to the parties' platforms. β_{iK} represents i's *bias* toward K and consists of all measured nonpolicy sources of i's utility for K, such as party identification, sociodemographic characteristics, and so on. β_{iK} may be either positive or negative. A voter is said to be biased *in favor* of K if $\beta_{iK} > \beta_{iJ}$ for all $J \in \mathfrak{R} - K$; he or she is biased *against* K if $\beta_{iK} < \beta_{iJ}$ for all $J \in \mathfrak{R} - K$. Let μ_{iK} be a random disturbance term (whose distribution is given below) that represents unmeasured sources of i's utility for K. The voter's utility for candidate K, $U_i(K)$, is given as

$$U_i(K) = \beta_{iK} + s \times p(x_i, k_n) + \mu_{iK} \tag{C.1}$$

$$= V_{iK} + \mu_{iK} \tag{C.2}$$

where $V_{iK} = [\beta_{iK} + s \times p(x_i, k_n)]$ represents i's strict utility for K. I assume that i votes for the candidate that maximizes his or her utility.

Note that equation C.1 generalizes the vote function specified in equation 6.1 in three ways: (1) here voters may choose over multiple policy dimensions; (2) the function $p(x_i, k_n)$ for voters' policy utilities may take any functional form in equation C.1, while in equation 6.1 voters are assumed to have quadratic policy losses; and (3) the nonpolicy bias term β_{iK} in equation C.1 represents all measured nonpolicy sources of voter bias rather than partisanship only.

With respect to the random disturbance terms, μ, I employ the same assumption used in chapter 6, that each μ_{iK} is independently generated from a type I extreme value distribution. As a result, the probability $P_i(K)$ that voter i votes for K is:

$$P_i(K) = e^{V_{iK}} / \left(\sum_{J \in \mathfrak{R}} e^{V_{iJ}} \right) \tag{C.3}$$

Note that the functional form of equation C.3 implies that $P_i(K) > 0$.

C.3. Equilibrium Results

The Existence of Policy Equilibrium

Two additional definitions and an assumption are required for the theorem developed below. First, let $P_i^0(K)$ equal the probability that i will vote for K, given $s = 0$. Thus,

$$P_i^0(K) = e^{\beta_{iK}} / \left(\sum_{J \in \mathfrak{R}} e^{\beta_{iJ}} \right) \tag{C.4}$$

Second, let $EVK(k_n, s)$ equal party $K \in \mathfrak{R}$'s expected vote share over the set V of voters so that

$$\text{EVK}(k_n, s) = \sum_{i \in V} P_i(K) = \sum_{i \in V} \left[e^{V_{iK}} / \left(\sum_{J \in \Re} e^{V_{iJ}} \right) \right] \tag{C.5}$$

ASSUMPTION C.1.   *For each party $K \in \Re$ there exists a unique platform, $k_m \in L_K$, which maximizes the function TK, where*

$$\text{TK}(k_n) = \sum_{i \in V} P_i^0(K) \times [1 - P_i^0(K)] \times p(x_i, k_n) \tag{C.6}$$

THEOREM C.1:   *If parties {A, B, . . . , M} maximize their expected vote, there exists η such that for all $0 < s < \eta$ the locational configuration {a_m, b_m, . . . , m_m} is an equilibrium in dominant strategies.*

PROOF: I denote by ΔTK the difference between TK(k_m) and the "second-highest" value of TK for some $k_h \in L_K - k_m$:

$$\Delta \text{TK} = \text{TK}(k_m) - \max\{\text{TK}(k_h); k_h \in L_K - k_m\}$$

Note that by assumption C.1, ΔTK is strictly positive.

I begin with two observations:

O_1: When $s = 0$, then for all $K \in \Re$, EVK(k_n,s) is independent of the platform K proposes.

I denote EVK_0 as the expected vote for K when $s = 0$.

O_2: At $s = 0$, $\partial \text{EVK}(k_n, s)/\partial s = \text{TK}(k_n)$.

To see this, note that

$$\partial \text{EVK}(k_n, s)/\partial s = \sum_{i \in V} \partial P_i(K)/\partial s = \sum_{i \in V} \partial P_i(K)/\partial V_{iK} \times \partial V_{iK}/\partial s$$

Given that

$$\partial P_i(K)/\partial V_{iK} = P_i(K) \times [1 - P_i(K)]$$

and

$$\partial V_i(K)/\partial s = \partial [s \times p(x_i, k_n) + \beta_{iK}]/\partial s = p(x_i, k_n)$$

it follows that

$$\partial P_i(K)/\partial s = P_i(K) \times [1 - P_i(K)] \times p(x_i, k_n)$$

Therefore, for $s = 0$,

$$\partial \text{EVK}(k_n, s)/\partial s = \sum_{i \in V} P_i^0(K) \times [1 - P_i^0(K)] \times p(x_i, k_n) = \text{TK}(k_n)$$

I use O_1 and O_2 to show that for any party platform $k_h \in L_K - k_m$ there exists η such that, for all $0 < s < \eta$, $\text{EVK}(k_m, s) > \text{EVK}(k_h, s)$. (I note that the strategy I employ is essentially the same as the one used by de Palma et al. [1989, 246–47] to prove the existence of a multiparty equilibrium for unbiased voters.)

To begin, note that

$$\text{EVK}(k_m, s) - \text{EVK}(k_h, s) = \text{EVK}(k_m, 0 + s) - \text{EVK}(k_h, 0 + s)$$

Doing a Taylor expansion of the right-hand side (RHS) of this expression yields

$$\text{EVK}(k_m, s) - \text{EVK}(k_h, s) =$$

$$[\text{EVK}(k_m, 0) + s \times \partial \text{EVK}(k_m, 0)/\partial s + (s^2/2) \times \partial^2 \text{EVK}(k_m, 0)/\partial^2 s$$

$$+ \ldots + (s^q/q!) \times \partial^q \text{EVK}(k_m, 0)/\partial^q s + (s^{q+1}/(q + 1)!)$$

$$\times \partial^{q+1} \text{EVK}(k_m, \alpha \times s)/\partial^{q+1} s] - [\text{EVK}(k_h, 0) + s \times \partial \text{EVK}(k_h, 0)/\partial s$$

$$+ (s^2/2) \times \partial^2 \text{EVK}(k_h, 0)/\partial^2 s + \ldots + (s^q/q!) \times \partial^q \text{EVK}(k_h, 0)/\partial^q s$$

$$+ (s^{q+1}/(q + 1)!) \times \partial^{q+1} \text{EVK}(k_h, \epsilon \times s)/\partial^{q+1} s] \qquad (\text{C.7})$$

where $0 < \alpha, \epsilon < 1$. Note that the difference between the sums of the first two expressions inside of the brackets in equation C.7 yields

$$[\text{EVK}(k_m, 0) + s \times \partial \text{EVK}(k_m, 0)/\partial s] - [\text{EVK}(k_h, 0) + s$$

$$\times \partial \text{EVK}(k_h, 0)/\partial s]$$

$$= [\text{EVK}_0 + s \times \text{TK}(k_m)] - [\text{EVK}_0 + s \times \text{TK}(k_h)]$$

by observations O_1 and O_2 and $\geq s \times \Delta\text{TK}$ by assumption C.1. Substituting this inequality into equation C.7 and dividing through by s yields

$$[\text{EVK}(k_m, s) - \text{EVK}(k_h, s)]/s \geq \Delta\text{TK} + s \times \{(1/2)[\partial^2 \text{EVK}(k_m, 0)/\partial^2 s$$

$$- \partial^2 \text{EVK}(k_h, 0)/\partial^2 s] + \ldots + (s^{q-1}/q!) \times [\partial^q \text{EVK}(k_m, 0)/\partial^q s$$

$$- \partial^q EVK(k_h,0)/\partial^q s] + [s^q/(q+1)!] \times [\partial^{q+1} EVK(k_m,\alpha \times s)/\partial^{q+1} s$$

$$- \partial^{q+1} EVK(k_h,\epsilon \times s)/\partial^{q+1} s]\} \tag{C.8}$$

It is easily seen that, given that s is strictly positive, $[EVK(k_m,s) - EVK(k_h,s)]$ > 0 iff. the RHS of equation C.8 is strictly positive. Let us set

$$\eta = \frac{\Delta TK}{\{(1/2)[\partial^2 EVK(k_m,0)/\partial^2 s - \partial^2 EVK(k_h,0)/\partial^2 s] + \ldots + (s^{q-1}/q!)}$$

$$\times [\partial^q EVK(k_m,0)/\partial^q s - \partial^q EVK(k_h,0)/\partial^q s] + [s^q/(q+1)!]$$

$$\times [\partial^{q+1} EVK(k_m,\alpha \times s)/\partial^{q+1} s - \partial^{q+1} EVK(k_h,\varepsilon \times s)/\partial^{q+1} s]\}$$

$$\tag{c.9}$$

Clearly, for all $0 < s < \eta$, the RHS of equation C.9, and hence $[EVK(k_m,s) - EVK(k_h,s)]$, is strictly positive.

Q.E.D.

Before turning to the nature of this equilibrium configuration, I consider the theorem's relevance to real world party competition and the importance of assumption C.1. The calculation of η given by equation C.9 suggests that the theorem may only apply when s is extremely small, especially when the function TK is flat around its maximum. In this case, theorem C.1 is weak. However, below I present the results of computer-simulated elections that suggest that, while the precise configuration $\{a_m, b_m, \ldots, m_m\}$ is an equilibrium only for rather small values of s, for larger values of s the computed equilibria are quite similar to $\{a_m, b_m, \ldots, m_m\}$. These equilibria hold even for values of s that equal or exceed the parameters behavioral researchers have estimated in empirical voting analyses in historical elections. It therefore appears that theorem C.1 provides a reasonable approximation of the equilibrium configuration vote-maximizing parties would converge toward in real world elections.

Assumption C.1 is analogous to the assumption used for earlier equilibrium results on unbiased multiparty voting, that there exists a unique platform that minimizes the sum of the distances from all voter ideal points (Adam 1998; de Palma et al. 1989; Lin et al. 1999). Indeed, for unbiased voting—that is, for $\beta_{iJ} = 0$ for all $J \in \Re$—$P_i^0(K)$ is constant across voters and k_m represents the "minimum-sum point" identified by Lin et al. (1998) as a convergent equilibrium. Assumption C.1 is necessary because, as I showed in equation C.7, η is proportional to ΔTK, which is the difference between $TK(k_m)$ and the "second-highest" value of TK for some $k_h \in L_K - k_m$. If k_m is not unique, then $\Delta TK = 0$, and hence $\eta = 0$, so a dominant strategy may not exist.

C.4. Theorems 6.1 and 6.2 as Corollaries to Theorem C.1

Theorems 6.1 and 6.2, which apply to situations in which voters display quadratic policy losses and choose over a unidimensional policy continuum, emerge as special cases of theorem C.1. With respect to theorem 6.1, which applies to policy competition in an independent electorate—that is, one in which voters do not display nonpolicy biases—note that when voters are unbiased and their policy loss functions are quadratic the function TK given in equation C.8 can be written as

$$TK(k_n) = \sum_{i \in V} (1/r)(1 - 1/r)[-(x_i - k_n)^2]$$

where $P_i^0(K) = 1/r$ is the probability that an independent voter i votes for party K, given that $s = 0$ and r is the number of parties. Since $P_i^0(K) = 1/r$ is constant across voters, it follows that the function TK is maximized when the sum of all voters' quadratic policy losses is minimized. For each party, this position is the voter mean. Hence, theorem 6.1, which states that for an independent electorate each party's vote-maximizing position is the voter mean (provided that parties choose from a finite set of platforms and s is sufficiently small), is a corollary of theorem C.1.

With respect to theorem 6.2, which applies to situations in which partisanship is the only source of voter bias, note that for this scenario (and again given that voters have quadratic policy losses and are arrayed along a unidimensional policy continuum) equation C.6 can be rewritten as

$$TK(k_n) = \sum_{i \in V} \left[e^{b_{iK}} / \left(\sum_{J \in \Re} e^{b_{iJ}} \right) \right] \left[1 - e^{b_{iK}} / \left(\sum_{J \in \Re} e^{b_{iJ}} \right) \right] [-(x_i - k)^2] \qquad (C.10)$$

where b_{iJ} is a dummy variable that equals b if voter i identifies with party J and equals zero otherwise (the specification investigated in chapter 6). Equation C.10 is identical to equation 6.4. Since I specify that theorem 6.2 obtains provided that each party's set of feasible positions includes the position k_m, which maximizes the function TK given in equation 6.4, it follows that theorem 6.2 is a corollary of theorem C.1.

C.5. Party Equilibria for a Partisan Electorate:
Theoretical Predictions versus Simulation Outcomes

To explore the practical importance of theorem C.1, I derive theoretical equilibria for some simple three-party election scenarios and then compare these equilibria with the results of computerized searches designed to locate equilibria for these situations.[1] Each of the scenarios I analyze involves three vote-maximizing parties, W, Y, and Z, which compete for votes from an electorate uniformly distributed along the policy continuum [0,10]. I assume that each voter $i \in V$ evaluates the policy position k of each party according to quadratic losses and that partisanship is the only measured source of bias, so that each voter has a bias parameter of $b = 0$ with respect to two of the three parties and a parameter $b = 2$ with respect to the remaining candidate (but that different voters are biased in favor of different parties). Thus, each voter i's strict utility, V_{iW}, for party W is given as

$$V_{iW} = s \times [-(x_i - w)^2] + 2$$

if i is a partisan of W and

$$= s \times [-(x_i - w)^2]$$

otherwise, with comparable strict utility functions with respect to Y and Z.

I consider a partisan distribution on [0,10] in which voters in the interval [0,10/3] are partisans of party W, those in the interval [10/3,20/3] are partisans of Y, and those in [20/3,10] are partisans of Z (fig. C.1). I further assume that each party K's set of feasible platforms is given as the set of 101 locations L_K = {0.0, 0.1, . . . , 10.0}.

Theorem C.1 states that under this scenario η exists such that $0 < s < \eta$ implies that, when there exists a unique platform $k_m \in L_K$ that maximizes the function TK given in equation C.10, each party K's dominant strategy is to propose k_m. Given the assumption of quadratic policy losses, it is easily checked that the unique platform $k_m \in L_K$ that maximizes TK is the platform in L_K that minimizes the policy distance to k_0 in the policy space, with k_0 defined as the weighted mean of voters' locations:

$$k_0 = \left\{ \sum_{i \in V} P_i^0(K) \times [1 - P_i^0(K)] x_i \right\} / \left\{ \sum_{i \in V} P_i^0(K) \times [1 - P_i^0(K)] \right\} \qquad (C.11)$$

For party W, w_0 is calculated as follows:

$$P_i^0(W) = e^{b_{iW}} / (e^{b_{iW}} + e^{b_{iY}} + e^{b_{iZ}})$$

$$= e^2 / (e^2 + e^0 + e^0) \cong .787$$

---

1. I have also compared theoretical equilibria versus computed equilibria for four- and five-party election scenarios. These comparisons support the conclusion I report below with respect to three-party elections: that theoretical equilibria are quite similar to computed equilibria, provided that the value of s is not unduly large. In addition, I note that the simulation results reported in Merrill and Adams 1999 also support this conclusion.

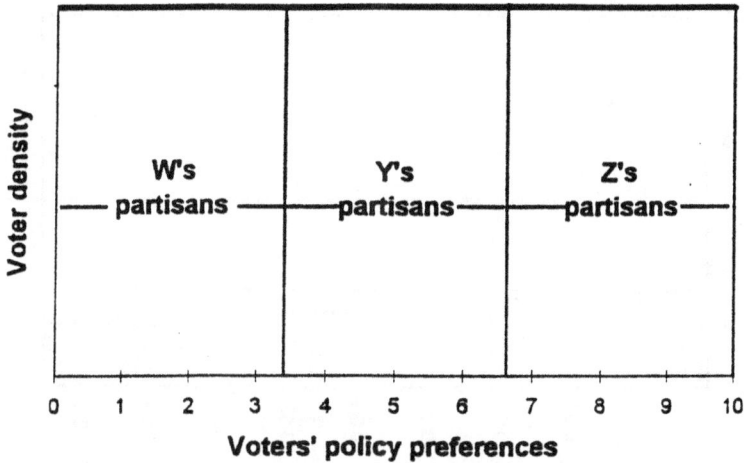

Fig. C.1. Party competition when voter biases correlate with policy positions: Distribution of voters' policy preferences by voter bias

if i is a partisan of W, and

$$= e^0/(e^2 + e^0 + e^0) \cong .107$$

otherwise.

Given the partisan distribution in figure C.1, equation C.11 becomes

$$w_0 \cong \left[\int_0^{10/3} (.787)(1-.787)x_i + \int_{10/3}^{10} (.107)(1-.107)x_i \right] /$$

$$\left[\int_0^{10/3} (.787)(1-.787) + \int_{10/3}^{10} (.107)(1-.107) \right] \cong 4.33$$

This implies that $w_m = 4.3$ since this is the feasible policy nearest 4.33 in the policy space. Using the same approach, y_m and z_m are calculated as 5.0 and 5.7, respectively. Hence, theorem C.1 implies that under this scenario the locational configuration $\{w_m = 4.3, y_m = 5.0, z_m = 5.7\}$ represents an equilibrium for sufficiently small (and positive) s. Note that this configuration is consistent with the intuition developed above, that parties should appeal to voters who have nonpolicy biases in their direction. At equilibrium, party W locates to the left of the voter mean, in the direction of its left-wing partisans; Z locates in the direction of its right-wing partisans; and Y locates at the voter mean, which is the center of its partisans' distribution.

To determine whether this analytically derived equilibrium holds for val-

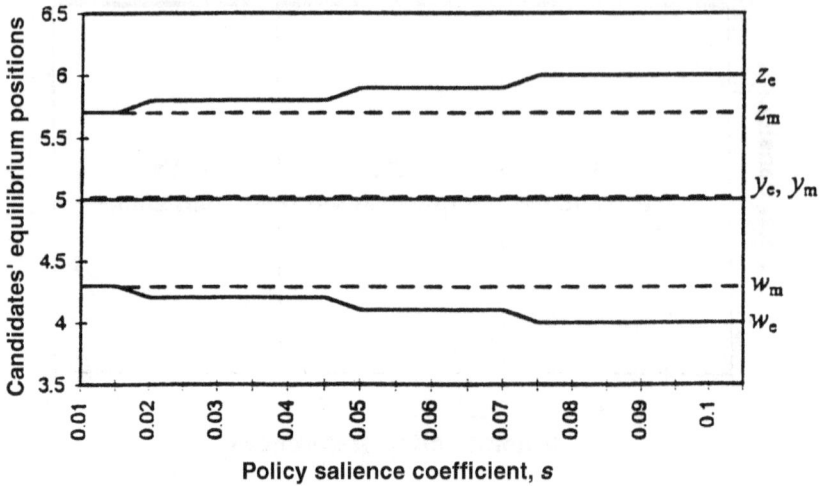

Fig. C.2. Policy equilibria for varying values of s (w_e, y_e, z_e = candidates' computed equilibrium positions for varying values of s; w_m, y_m, z_m = theoretical candidate equilibrium positions for $s \to 0$)

ues of s that differ significantly from zero, I employed computer simulation techniques to locate party equilibria for various values of s for the partisan distribution in figure C.1. The simulation procedure proceeded as follows. First, a value of s was specified and all parties were located at the voter mean 5.0. Next, with the positions of Y and Z fixed, W's expected vote share was calculated at each location from the set of positions $\{0, 0.1, \ldots, 10\}$ and W was then located at its expected vote-maximizing position. Next, with the positions of W and Z fixed, party Y's vote-maximizing policy position was similarly computed.[2] This process continued until the parties reached a Nash equilibrium—defined as a configuration such that no party could increase its expected vote share by relocating.

In the simulations, I varied the value of the policy salience coefficient, s, between $s = 0.1$ and $s = .10$. figure C.2, which shows the simulation results for $.01 \leq s \leq .10$, indicates that equilibria were obtained for all values of s. (Note that figure 6.1B shows only the central region $[3.5, 6.5]$ of the policy continuum along the vertical axis.) For $.010 \leq s \leq .015$, this equilibrium exactly matches the analytically derived configuration $\{w_m = .43, y_m = .50, z_m = .57\}$. For $.020$

---

2. I performed alternative sets of simulations in which the parties were initially located at the extremes of the policy continuum and which varied the order of party policy movement. These simulations produced identical results to those reported here.

$\leq s \leq .045$, I obtain the virtually identical equilibrium configuration $\{w_e = .42,$ $y_e = .50, z_e = .58\}$; for $.050 \leq s \leq .070$, the computed equilibrium is $\{w_e = .41, y_e = .50, z_e = .59\}$; for $.075 \leq s \leq .100$, the equilibrium is $\{w_e = .40, y_e = .50, z_e = .60\}$. Hence, for this scenario the analytical result given by theorem C.1 only holds for $s \leq .015$; however, it provides a very close approximation for $.02 \leq s \leq .10$.

I note that the finding that for the above scenario the analytical result given by theorem C.1 holds "exactly," for $s \leq .015$ is an artifact of the set of feasible platforms specified for each party. Were this set of platforms contracted from the set of 101 points $L = \{0, 0.1, \ldots, 10.0\}$ to a reduced set of platforms— say, $L = \{0, 0.5, \ldots, 10.0\}$—then the equilibrium specified by theorem C.1 would likely hold exactly for higher values of s. Conversely, were the set L expanded to a larger number of points—say, $L = \{0, 0.01, \ldots, 10.00\}$—then the analytical result given by theorem C.1 would extend only to values of s well below .015. Hence, the important conclusion suggested by these simulations does not revolve around the conditions that must obtain in order for the theorem to hold exactly, but the theoretical equilibria specified by theorem C.1 are quite similar to computed equilibria, provided that the value of s is not unduly large.

APPENDIX D

Proof of Theorem 7.1

Theorem 7.1 in chapter 7 reads

THEOREM 7.1.   *If equilibrium exists, then at equilibrium the Democratic Party presents a more liberal position than the Republican Party does.*

PROOF.   The proof consists of demonstrating that any configuration in which the Republicans do not take a more conservative position than the Democrats cannot be an equilibrium. Let x^* be the position such that all voters located to the liberal side of x^* are Democrats and all voters to the conservative side of x^* are Republicans, as in figure D.1A. (Note that the voter distribution is asymmetric in this figure to underscore the point that this proof does not depend on the assumption of a symmetric distribution.) There are five possible configurations, or cases, in which the Republican position, r, is *not* more conservative than the Democratic position, d:

1. $x^* > d\ > r$
2. $x^* > d\ = r$
3. $d\ > x^* > r$
4. $d\ > r\ > x^*$
5. $d\ = r\ > x^*$

By symmetry, it is easily verified that, if a proof exists that equilibria are precluded for case 4, then an analogous proof must exist that equilibria are precluded for case 1, and that, if a proof exists that equilibria are precluded for case 2, then an analogous proof must exist that equilibria are precluded for case 5. Hence, to prove theorem D.1. it is sufficient to prove that equilibria are precluded for cases 1–3.

The strategy I adopt to prove that equilibria are impossible in cases 1–3 is to show that in each case it is possible for the Democratic and Republican Parties to relocate (with the position of the rival party fixed) so that the parties' combined vote shares exceed 100 percent. Since the parties' combined vote shares at equilibrium must equal 100 percent, this result implies that at least one of the parties can improve its vote share by relocating and that the party configuration is therefore not an equilibrium.

(A)

(B)

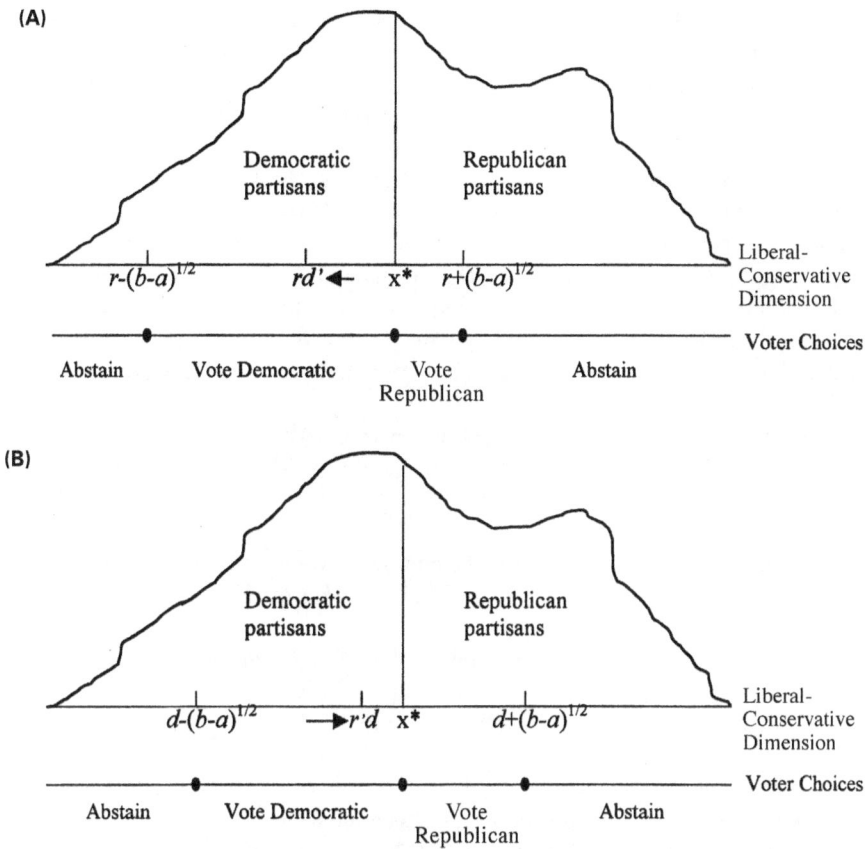

Fig. D.1. Spatial analysis of party strategies for the scenario $x^* > d > r$. (A) Party support when the Democrats shift to the position $d' = r$; (B) Party support when the Republicans shift to the position $r' = d$.

Case 1

In case 1, $x^* > d > r$, the Democrats take a more conservative position than the Republicans and both parties locate to the left of x^* so that their positions lie in the policy interval that contains Democratic partisans. Note, first, that if $[x^* - (b - a)^{1/2}] > r$—that is, if the Republican Party locates to the left of the policy position $[x^* - (b - a)^{1/2}]$ (see fig. 7.1A)—then if the Democratic Party shifts to the position $d' = r$ (i.e., if the Democrats pair with the Republicans) the Democratic Party wins 100 percent of the voters who turn out. This is because under this scenario all Democratic partisans will prefer the Democratic to the Republican Party, while all Republican partisans will prefer abstention to voting for the Republicans.[1] Since the Republican Party can obtain a positive vote percentage by relocating to a position preferred by one of its partisans, it follows that the parties can relocate (with the position of their rival fixed) so as to win a combined vote share of more than 100 percent. Hence no equilibrium is possible when $[x^* - (b - a)^{1/2}] > r$.

We therefore consider the case in which $x^* > d > r > [x^* - (b - a)^{1/2}]$. Given this initial configuration, if the Democratic Party relocates to the position $d' = r$ then the Republicans win the votes of all voters located in the policy interval $[x^*, r + (b - a)^{1/2}]$, the Democrats win the votes of all the voters located in the policy interval $[r - (b - a)^{1/2}, x^*]$, and the remaining voters abstain (see fig. D.1A). Thus, by shifting to the position $d' = r$ the Democrats can win a share of the two-party vote equal to DVS (Democratic vote share):

$$\text{DVS} = \{V[r - (b - a)^{1/2}, x^*]\}/\{V[r - (b - a)^{1/2}, x^*]$$

$$+ V[x^*, r + (b - a)^{1/2}]\}$$

where $V[r - (b - a)^{1/2}, x^*]$ = the number of voters located in the policy
$$\qquad\qquad\qquad\text{interval } [r - (b - a)^{1/2}, x^*]$$
$$\qquad\qquad = VD \ (d' = r)$$
$V[x^*, r + (b - a)^{1/2}]$ = the number of voters located in the policy
$$\qquad\qquad\qquad\text{interval } [x^*, r + (b - a)^{1/2}]$$
$$\qquad\qquad = VR \ (d' = r)$$

Given the initial configuration $x^* > d > r > [x^* - (b - a)^{1/2}]$, if the *Republican* Party relocates to the position $r' = d$ then the Republicans win the votes of all voters located in the policy interval $[x^*, d + (b - a)^{1/2}]$, the Democrats win the votes of all the voters located in the policy interval $[d - (b - a)^{1/2}, x^*]$, and the remaining voters abstain (see fig. D.1B). In this case, the Republican vote share (RVS) of the two-party vote is:

---

1. To see this, note that a Republican voter i's utility differential for voting for the Republican Party versus abstaining is:

$$U_i(R) - U_i(A) = [b - (x_i - r)^2] - a$$

$$= (b - a) - (x_i - r)^2$$

Given $[x^* - (b - a)^{1/2}] > r$ and $x_i > x^*$ (which holds because all Republican partisans are located to the right of x^*), it follows that $(x_i - r)^2 > (b - a)$ and hence $[(b - a) - (x_i - r)^2] < 0$. Therefore, $[U_i(R) - U_i(A)] < 0$, and Republican partisans prefer abstention to voting Republican.

$$\text{RVS} = \{V[x^*, d + (b - a)^{1/2}]\}/\{V[x^*, d + (b - a)^{1/2}]$$

$$+ V[d - (b - a)^{1/2}, x^*]\}$$

where $V[x^*, d + (b - a)^{1/2}] =$ the number of voters located in the interval $[x^*, d + (b - a)^{1/2}]$
$= \text{VD}(r' = d)$
$V[d - (b - a)^{1/2}, x^*] =$ the number of voters located in the interval $[d - (b - a)^{1/2}, x^*]$
$= \text{VR}(r' = d)$

I now show that the sum of the Democratic vote share, given $d' = r$, and the Republican vote share, given $r' = d$, exceeds 1.0. This sum can be written as

$$\text{DVS} + \text{RVS} = \text{VD}(d' = r)/[\text{VD}(d' = r) + \text{VR}(d' = r)]$$

$$+ \text{VR}(r' = d)/[\text{VR}(r' = d) + \text{VD}(r' = d)]$$

Some simple algebra shows that

$$\text{DVS} + \text{RVS} > 1 \Leftrightarrow \text{VD}(d' = r)\, \text{VD}(r' = d)$$

$$> \text{VR}(r' = d)\, \text{VR}(d' = r) \tag{1A}$$

Note first that $\text{VD}(d' = r) > \text{VR}(r' = d)$, since

$$\text{VD}(d' = r) = V[r - (b - a)^{1/2}, d - (b - a)^{1/2}] + V[d - (b - a)^{1/2}, x^*]$$

$$= V[r - (b - a)^{1/2}, d - (b - a)^{1/2}] + \text{VR}(r' = d)$$

Second, $\text{VD}(r' = d) > \text{VR}(d' = r)$ since

$$\text{VD}(r' = d) = V[x^*, r + (b - a)^{1/2}] + V[r + (b - a)^{1/2},$$

$$d + (b - a)^{1/2}] = \text{VR}(d' = r) + V[r + (b - a)^{1/2}, d + (b - a)^{1/2}]$$

Since $\text{VD}(d' = r) > \text{VR}(r' = d)$ and $\text{VD}(r' = d) > \text{VR}(d' = r)$, it follows that the condition in case 1 is satisfied. Hence given $x^* > d > r > [x^* - (b - a)^{1/2}]$, the two parties can unilaterally relocate so as to obtain vote shares that sum to more than 100 percent, and no equilibrium is possible.

Case 2

In case 2, $x^* > d = r$, the Democrats and Republicans present identical positions and both parties locate to the left of x^* so that their positions lie in the policy interval that contains Democratic partisans. In this configuration, the Republicans win no votes from Democratic partisans since these partisans are
indifferent between the parties on policy grounds and prefer the Democratic
Party based on their partisan loyalty. Hence, the Democratic Party wins votes
from all Democratic partisans who prefer voting for the Democrats to abstaining. Now, if the Republican Party shifts rightward from the position $r = d$ to
the position $r = x^*$, it wins additional votes from Republican partisans without
losing votes among Democratic partisans (since the Republican Party did not
win any support from these partisans in the first place). Furthermore, this policy shift cannot increase the number of voters who support the Democrats. To
see this, note that: (1) when $r = x^*$ the Democratic Party wins no votes from
Republican partisans, since all such partisans prefer the Republican Party on
both policy and nonpolicy grounds; and (2) this Republican policy shift does
not increase the number of Democratic partisans who vote for the Democrats,
since for $r = d$ the Democratic Party already attracts the votes of all Democratic partisans who prefer voting Democratic to abstaining. Hence, whenever x^*
$> d = r$, the Republican Party can increase its share of the two-party vote by
shifting to the position $r = x^*$, so any policy configuration such that $x^* > d =$
r cannot be an equilibrium.

Case 3

In case 3, $d > x^* > r$, the Democrats locate to the right of the Republicans, with
the Democratic position lying in the policy interval that contains Republican
partisans and the Republican position lying in the policy interval that contains
Democratic partisans. Note, first, that under this scenario an equilibrium is possible only if the Republicans locate in the policy interval $[x^* - (b - a)^{1/2}, x^*]$
and the Democratic Party locates in the interval $[x^*, x^* + (b - a)^{1/2}]$; otherwise, either party could win 100 percent of the two-party vote by pairing with
its opponent. We therefore consider the case in which $[x^* + (b - a)^{1/2}] > d >$
$x^* > r > [x^* - (b - a)^{1/2}]$.

From here, the proof that equilibria are precluded follows a logic identical to that in the proof presented for case 1. Given an initial policy configuration such that $[x^* + (b - a)^{1/2}] > d > x^* > r > [x^* - (b - a)^{1/2}]$, if the Democratic Party relocates to the position $d' = r$ then the Republicans win the votes
of all voters located in the policy interval $[x^*, r + (b - a)^{1/2}]$, the Democrats
win the votes of all the voters located in the policy interval $[r - (b - a)^{1/2}, x^*]$,

and the remaining voters abstain. Thus, by shifting to the position $d' = r$ the Democrats can win a share of the two-party vote equal to:

$$\text{DVS} = \{V[r - (b - a)^{1/2}, x^*]\}/\{(V[r - (b - a)^{1/2}, x^*]$$

$$+ V[x^*, r + (b - a)^{1/2}]\}$$

where $V[r - (b - a)^{1/2}, x^*]$ = the number of voters located in the policy interval $[r - (b - a)^{1/2}, x^*]$
$$= \text{VD}(d' = r)$$
$V[x^*, r + (b - a)^{1/2}]$ = the number of voters located in the policy interval $[x^*, r + (b - a)^{1/2}]$
$$= \text{VR}(d' = r)$$

Given the initial configuration $[x^* + (b - a)^{1/2}] > d > x^* > r > [x^* - (b - a^{1/2}]$, if the *Republican* Party relocates to the position $r' = d$ then the Republicans win the votes of all voters located in the policy interval $[x^*, d + (b - a)^{1/2}]$, the Democrats win the votes of all the voters located in the policy interval $[d - (b - a)^{1/2}, x^*]$, and the remaining voters abstain (see fig. D.1A). In this case, the Republican share of the two-party vote is:

$$\text{RVS} = \{V[x^*, d + (b - a)^{1/2}]\}/\{V[x^*, d + (b - a)^{1/2}]$$

$$+ V[d - (b - a)^{1/2}, x^*]\}$$

where $V[x^*, d + (b - a)^{1/2}]$ = the number of voters located in the interval $[x^*, d + (b - a)^{1/2}]$
$$= \text{VD}(r' = d)$$
$V[d - (b - a)^{1/2}, x^*]$ = the number of voters located in the interval $[d - (b - a)^{1/2}, x^*]$
$$= \text{VR}(r' = d)$$

From here the proof that the sum of the Democratic vote share (DVS) and the Republican vote share (RVS) exceeds 1.0 is identical to the proof presented for case 1.

Q.E.D.

Notes

Chapter 1

1. The greater party cohesion in legislatures outside of the United States, compared to the American Congress, stems in part from the fact that most democracies are parliamentary systems in which party unity is crucial for maintaining control of the government. In addition, in countries that employ some form of proportional representation—and particularly those in which voters vote directly for party lists—parties necessarily assume an intermediary role in selecting parliamentary representatives so that it makes little sense to focus on the link between a specific parliamentary representative and the voters from some geographic constituency.

While representation research in the United States suggests substantial policy agreement between geographically based constituencies and their legislators (Miller and Stokes 1963; Achen 1975; Page et al. 1988), extensions to other Western democracies find little evidence of this form of policy agreement (Barnes 1977; Converse and Pierce 1986, chap. 22; Farah 1980; Thomassen 1976). For this reason, research on representation in non-American settings has shifted away from this geographically based notion of representation to the responsible party model described below.

2. These conditions are not intended as a complete list of necessary and sufficient conditions for responsible party government. In addition to the conditions presented here, scholars have identified a number of other factors that influence both the links between voters and parties and voters' abilities to influence government policy outputs. These include constitutional features such as the electoral system and the form of government, for example, parliamentary versus presidential democracy (see Powell 1989); clarity of governing responsibility (Powell 1986, 1989); internal party organization (May 1973; Przeworski and Sprague 1986); and features of the party system such as the number of parties (Dalton 1985; Powell 1989). Some of these factors relate directly to the three conditions, cited above, concerning policy stability, policy differentiation, and policy-oriented voters. For instance, the degree of policy differentiation among the competing parties is related to the number of parties in the party system (see Powell 1989), which is in turn influenced by the electoral system (e.g., Duverger 1954; Cox 1997; Dow 1997c; Taagepera and Shugart 1989). In addition, as I outline below, spatial modeling results suggest that the degree to which parties propose stable policy platforms depends on the number of parties, and the degree to which voters are policy oriented is plausibly influenced by the degree to which parties present stable, divergent policy positions.

These considerations suggest that a complete list of factors that enhance the workings of responsible party government plausibly encompasses more than a dozen items.

However, the three conditions I discuss in the text appear to be the most frequently cited features of responsible party government.

3. This condition has received less attention in the literature on responsible party government than the other two requirements cited here. However, it also corresponds to Downs's stipulation that parties must behave "reliably" and "responsibly" with respect to policies.

4. This requirement actually has two related components: first, that voters possess meaningful policy attitudes and/or political ideologies, and, second, that these beliefs influence their voting behavior. Many of the classic works on public opinion argue that, at least on certain kinds of issues, large segments of mass publics do not satisfy the first requirement (e.g., Converse 1964, 1970). However, as I outline below, in this book I focus primarily on the second component.

5. In particular, voters may choose to reward or punish the incumbent parties based upon their performance, with evaluations of performance not directly tied to policy issues (see, e.g., Dalton 1985).

6. An alternative criterion for assessing mass-elite linkages is to assess the *collective correspondence* between the overall distribution of policy beliefs among all parties' elites compared to the distribution of attitudes among the mass public (Weissberg 1978). However, to ensure some degree of responsiveness by elites, they must be electorally dependent on a specific constituency, which is why studies focused upon responsible party government typically imply the dyadic correspondence criterion (see, e.g., Dalton 1985).

7. Much of the spatial modeling literature is couched in terms of competition between candidates, not parties. When this distinction becomes relevant, it will be noted in the text.

8. Spatial modeling theory predicts that in two-party competition over multiple policy dimensions the parties are unlikely to reach a policy equilibrium but will instead cycle their positions endlessly in the policy space (for reviews, see Enelow and Hinich 1984; and Mueller 1989). While such results seemingly imply some degree of policy divergence, recent theoretical work on the "uncovered set" and the "yolk" (see McKelvey 1986; and Shepsle and Weingast 1984) suggest that for most realistic multidimensional settings both parties will select their positions from within an identical, extremely circumscribed policy area near the center of the policy space (see also Feld, Grofman, and Miller 1988; Feld et al. 1987; and Miller 1980). These results imply that the parties will present extremely similar positions, which deny voters a meaningful choice between contrasting policy programs. Thus, the distinction between one-dimensional policy equilibrium and multidimensional disequilibrium notwithstanding, the spatial literature suggests that in both settings the two parties will present extremely similar, centrist policies.

9. Ironically, Downs himself (1957, 107–13) argued that parties are constrained to present consistent policy proposals in order to develop a reputation for trustworthiness, without which voters would not support them in future elections. However, most subsequent spatial modelers have ignored this prohibition against policy change.

10. With respect to policy stability, the analytical results of Eaton and Lipsey (1975), Shaked (1975), and Hermsen and Verbeek (1992) suggest that for any number of parties greater than two, and for any number of policy dimensions, party equilibria among vote-maximizing parties will exist only under extremely unusual or contrived

conditions. With respect to policy divergence, Cox (1990) has shown that when four or more parties compete spatial competition typically exerts some "centrifugal" pressures on parties to propose divergent policies in that the policies of the right-most and left-most parties (in a one-dimensional space) will diverge if an equilibrium exists. However, even under this scenario there remains a strong tendency for policy similarity in that at equilibrium peripheral parties will typically be "paired" with another party that presents identical policies (see, e.g., Eaton and Lipsey 1975; and Lomborg 1996). This pairing implies, for instance, that in a four-party political system the electorate will be offered only two distinct policy alternatives. In chapter 2, I review spatial modeling efforts that attempt to account for the policy divergence observed in many contemporary democracies.

11. The positions of party elites and voters were based upon the mean of respondents' answers to two questions concerning their support for public ownership of industry and government management of the economy (see Iversen 1994b, 166–70).

12. The similarity between the views of party elites and those of their constituencies can be assessed using various statistical measures, which can affect the conclusion one reaches concerning the degree to which elites "represent" their supporters. With respect to Left-Right self-placement, for instance, Dalton (1985, table 3) reports that party elites are extremely *responsive* to the views of their constituents, in that as party constituencies become increasingly right-wing so do the party elites that represent them, but that in terms of absolute similarity of voter and elite opinions elites are systematically more leftist than their constituencies, resulting in a low degree of *centrism*. With respect to the economic issues presented in figure 1.2, elites are both responsive and centrist. Empirical analyses of alternative policy dimensions such as foreign aid, environmental issues, and national defense also reveal high degrees of centrism and responsiveness, except for foreign aid, for which responsiveness is low (see Dalton 1985, table 3; and Iversen 1994, figs. 2–5). For a discussion of alternative measures of representation, see Achen 1978 and Dalton 1985.

13. Two-party models that explore the strategic implications of voter bias include those of Chapman (1967, 1968), Erikson and Romero (1990), and Feld and Grofman (1991), Groseclose (1999), Macdonald and Rabinowitz (1998), and Berger, Munger, and Potthoff (2000). I review multiparty models that incorporate voter bias in chapter 2.

14. As I outline below, there is a heated scholarly debate about the *magnitude* of the electoral effects of voter characteristics such as social class, religion, and partisanship. However, there is a consensus that these characteristics exercise at least some independent electoral influence. As I discuss in the following section, one of the central points of this book is to determine how parties' policy strategies vary depending on the assumptions one makes about the electoral impact of voters' nonpolicy biases compared to their policy motivations.

15. As discussed in chapter 2, the nature of political partisanship—as well as the influence of such group-related factors as class, religion, and race—is a matter of controversy, and some scholars conceptualize these influences in ways that deemphasize the role of affect while emphasizing cognitive motivations that fit more easily into the rational choice framework (see, e.g., Fiorina 1981). However, even in these alternative approaches such factors as partisanship are typically viewed as containing considerations unrelated to the parties' positions on policy issues.

16. As outlined below, there is a heated scholarly debate about the extent to which personal characteristics such as social class, religion, and partisanship influence the vote, *independently* of voters' policy preferences. However, there is a consensus that these voter characteristics exercise at least some independent electoral influence. As I discuss in section 1.5, one of the central points in this book is to determine how parties' policy strategies vary depending on the assumptions one makes about the importance of voters' nonpolicy biases compared to their policy motivations.

17. Indeed, according to certain conceptions of party identification, partisanship summarizes the impact of virtually *all* nonpolicy considerations relevant to the vote, at least in elections involving parties, not candidates. This is the case for Fiorina's notion of partisanship as a "running tally" of the voter's comparative evaluations of the competing parties. An even more extreme position is taken by Achen (1992), who argues that empirical voting models should exclude *all* of the respondents' personal characteristics other than partisanship. Finally, I note that in empirical voting studies on elections held outside the United States, when the effects of partisanship and of other group loyalties relating to social class and religion are estimated simultaneously, partisanship typically emerges as by far the strongest electoral influence (see, e.g., Adams and Merrill 1999b, 1999c; Alvarez and Nagler 1995; Dow 1997b; and Endersby and Galatas 1997).

18. Chapter 2 is based in part on Adams 1998.

19. Chapters 3 and 4 are drawn in part from Adams (forthcoming b).

20. Chapter 6 draws in part on work by Adams (1997, 1998), Adams and Merrill (1999a, 1999b, 1999c), and Merrill and Adams (1999).

Chapter 2

1. This summary of spatial modeling efforts to explain policy stability and divergence focuses on models in which parties can relocate costlessly in the policy space and are fully informed about the policy proposals of their rivals. A large number of alternative explanations have been proposed, starting with Downs's argument (1957, 107–13) that parties must behave responsibly—and therefore present stable policy proposals—in order to develop a reputation for trustworthiness, without which voters would not support them in the future (see also Dow 1997c). Another strand of research considers the uncertainty parties experience with respect to the behavior of rival parties and argues that parties develop relatively simple rules of thumb for coping with this uncertainty. These rules ensure some degree of policy stability in that they typically preclude parties radically changing their policy proposals (see, e.g., Robertsen 1976). Budge (1994) presents a review of such models. Finally, this summary does not include a discussion of studies that rely upon voter policy utility metrics other than proximity, such as Rabinowitz and Macdonald's (1989) directional voting model, Iversen's (1994a) mixed directional-proximity model (see also Merrill and Grofman 1997, 1999; and Adams and Merrill 1999a, 1999b, 2000). Mathews's (1979) version of the directional voting model, and Grofman's (1985) "discounting" model (see also Lacy and Paolino 1998, and Merrill and Grofman 1999, chap. 9). While these policy metrics provide a promising approach for explaining policy divergence, their implications for party policies in multi-

party spatial competition—and in particular for the existence and nature of multiparty equilibria—have not been rigorously derived (but see ibid., chap. 10). For a review of these alternative policy metrics, see ibid., chap. 2.

2. In Adams 1999c, I investigate a related model, in which voters perceive varying degrees of similarity between different pairs of parties. My simulation results on three-party competition suggest that equilibria can exist for which the "least similar" party locates between the two "more similar" ones and wins the election.

3. In addition, I note that several additional studies, including those of Alvarez, Bowler, and Nagler (1996), Alvarez, Nagler, and Willette (1998), and Dow (1997c), locate optimal party positions using probabilistic voting models whose parameters are estimated from survey data. However, these studies do not locate global equilibrium configurations but instead report parties' "one-step" optima, that is, the positions that maximize parties' expected votes with their competitors fixed at their actual locations. In addition, unlike the probabilistic voting studies cited in the text, none of these studies is primarily concerned with the strategic logic of party spatial competition.

4. The spatial modeling literature on policy-seeking parties has been more fully developed in the context of two-party elections (see, e.g., Chappel and Keech 1986; Hansson and Stuart 1984; Petry 1982; and Wittman, 1973, 1983). In addition, I note that theories of political coalitions frequently present policy pursuit as a supplement to, rather than a substitute for, office-seeking motivations (Axelrod 1970; Browne 1973; De Swaan 1973; Laver and Shepsle 1996; Lijphart 1984; Luebbert 1986).

5. In addition, note that several of these models illuminate policy stability but not policy divergence in that they imply a *convergent* equilibrium in which all parties present identical policies (or at most the parties split into a small number of blocs); these include the study by Feddersen et al. (1990) and the probabilistic voting studies (Adams 1998; de Palma et al. 1990; Lin et al. 1999; Schofield, Sened, and Nixon 1998).

6. The psychological basis of partisanship has been conceptualized in various ways, some of which deemphasize the role of affective ties to one's preferred party. Thus, Key's (1966) concept of partisanship as a "standing decision rule" and Fiorina's (1981) notion of a "running tally" of retrospective evaluations of party performance both suggest that partisanship has a cognitive component. While the exact nature of partisanship is imperfectly understood (see, e.g., the discussions in Converse and Pierce 1992a; and Pierce 1995, 31–36), note that for my purposes it does not matter whether partisanship represents an affective attachment, a belief in the superior competence or integrity of the party's leaders, or some other nonpolicy motivation. What is important is that there is a component of partisanship that influences voting independently of political ideology.

7. As I discuss below, it is actually more accurate to state that there is a *component* of party identification that is independent of voters' policy considerations. This qualification is necessary because there is strong empirical evidence that ideology influences partisanship as well as the vote.

8. This summary does not exhaust the methodological issues relevant to debates on the electoral impact of ideology versus partisanship. Two additional controversies concern the impact of question-order effects on responses to party identification questions (see, e.g., Heath and Pierce 1992) and debates over interpretations of responses to open-ended questions designed to probe respondent partisanship (see Converse and Pierce

1986, 1993; and Fleury and Lewis-Beck 1993). For our purposes, the central point is not to explore these methodological issues in detail but to note that the number and complexity of such issues has to this point precluded the emergence of a scholarly consensus on the electoral impact of partisanship.

9. For British voters, party identifiers were defined as those respondents who reported that they generally thought of themselves as Labour, Social Democrat, or Liberal (classified as Alliance partisans) or Conservative as well as those who reported feeling closer to one of these parties. Independents were defined as those who answered "no/none" to both questions. For French respondents, party identifiers were defined as those who thought of themselves as generally feeling closest to the Communists, Socialists, French Democratic Union (UDF), Rally for the Republic (RPR), or the National Front, while those who reported feeling close to "no party" were classified as independents. For Norway, respondents were classified as party identifiers if they stated that they generally thought of themselves as Conservative, Labor, Socialist, Center, Christian People's, Progress, or Liberal and were classified as independents if they did not consider themselves close to any of the parties. For each country, these analyses exclude respondents who reported feeling close to one of the minor parties.

10. These results might appear at first glance to be inconsistent with recent scholarship that suggests that electorates are becoming progressively less partisan (Dalton et al. 1984; McCallister 1992; Holmberg 1994). However, note that at this point I am simply counting the number of respondents who classified themselves as partisans in recent national elections surveys, *without* making assumptions about how strongly partisanship influences the vote. I consider the latter question below.

11. To see this, note that, given $l = 4.5$, $c = 5.5$, and $b = 1.0$, for a partisan of party C the utility differential for L over C is:

$$U_i(L) - U_i(C) = L_{iL} - (b + L_{iC})$$

$$= -(x_i - 4.5)^2 - [1 - (x_i - 5.5)^2]$$

$$= 9 - 2x_i$$

so that $[U_i(L) - U_i(C)] > 0 \Rightarrow (9 - 2x_i) > 0 \Rightarrow x_i < 4.5$, that is, all of C's partisans to the left of 4.5 prefer party L to party C.

12. However I show below that this generalization does not apply to spatial competition on electorates that include independent voters.

13. Note that this equilibrium is also stable in the face of an additional potential source of instability: the fact that, for the party configurations pictured in figures 2.4 and 2.5, party R can shift anywhere in the policy interval [6.5,7.5] without losing votes. To see this, suppose that party R shifts its policy position to the right. This change would motivate C to shift to the left, in order to capture some of the left-wing C partisans who currently vote for party L; this is because, with R now located at a greater distance from C's right-wing partisans, C can shift some distance left without sacrificing the support of any of these partisans. However, as soon as C shifts leftward, R is motivated to shift back toward the left in order to capture the right-most C partisans, who are now "vulnerable" to capture due to C's leftward shift. This, in turn, will motivate C to move

right—back toward its original position—in order to protect its right flank. Hence, the equilibrium is "self-correcting" in the face of policy changes by R.

14. To be technically accurate, the probabilistic studies by Adams (1999a), Lin et al. (1999), and de Palma et al. (1989, 1990) conclude that parties receive equal *expected* vote shares at equilibrium because at equilibrium all parties propose identical policies. In addition, as noted in section 2.2, these probabilistic models in certain cases can accommodate "dispersed" policy equilibria, although such equilibria are possible only for rather narrow ranges of values for the variance of the unobserved components in voters' party utilities (see, e.g., Merrill and Adams 2000a; and Schofield, Sened, and Nixon 1998). These dispersed equilibria could conceivably accommodate election outcomes in which different parties have different expected vote shares, although I am unaware of any studies that explore this issue.

15. Condition 1 states that no party can choose a policy such that all of its partisans fall within its "region of invulnerability." Condition 2 precludes situations in which a large clump of voters locates within a very narrow policy interval; this condition is necessary in order to eliminate certain (unrealistic) voter distributions, which can accommodate equilibrium configurations that do not satisfy theorem 2.1.

16. While theorem 2.2 implies that C faces a serious strategic disadvantage in spatial competition with partisan voting, recall that it is nonetheless possible for C to win a plurality of the popular vote, as is the case in figure 2.4.

17. In 1988, the Liberals and the Social Democrats formally merged to form the Liberal Democratic Party.

18. The 1987 BNES did not include items on respondents' Left-Right, or liberal-conservative, orientations. I have selected the nationalization item for study here, first, because of this issue's importance in the 1987 general election (see Crewe and Harrop 1989); second, because it appears plausible that voters' opinions on this issue correlate with their political ideologies; and, third, because the distribution of respondent self-placements on this issue (see fig. 2.8A) was on average quite centrist, which again appears to plausibly approximate the distribution of British voters' political ideologies.

The other issues included in the 1987 BGES related to national defense, the Phillips curve, taxation, redistribution, crime, and welfare. In addition to the analyses reported here, I analyzed party strategies for each of these alternative policy scales except for defense and crime, which appear tangential to Left-Right ideology. Results on redistribution and welfare—the other dimensions that appear most closely related to political ideology—were quite similar to those I report below on nationalization. Results on the Phillips curve and taxation were different in that no party equilibria were located. This occurred because the distribution of responses on each of these dimensions was polarized in that responses were skewed quite sharply toward the extremes. Because the distribution of British voters' Left-Right orientations is presumably fairly centrist, the results for nationalization, redistribution, and welfare are probably more indicative of what an analysis based upon Left-Right ideology would show, were this item available for British politics.

19. For the empirical distribution, partisans were defined as those who thought of themselves as Labour, Conservative, or Liberal–Social Democrat (who were classified as Alliance partisans) as well as those who reported feeling closer to one of these parties. Independents were those who answered "no/none" to both questions. Respondents

who replied "don't know" or did not answer these questions are excluded from this analysis, as are respondents who identified with one of the smaller parties. The total number of respondents thereby excluded is less than 10 percent of the survey sample.

20. Note that all results in this section are based on a computer-simulated party competition in which all parties were initially placed at their actual (perceived) positions along the nationalization scale. (Simulations that initially placed the parties at the extremes of the policy scale yielded identical results.) For a specified degree of partisan attachment, $b^{1/2}$, each party's vote-maximizing location was then calculated and the parties were moved sequentially to their respective vote-maximizing positions. Party movement continued until an equilibrium configuration was reached. If, for a given level of $b^{1/2}$, no equilibrium configuration was reached after each party moved 40 times, the search for an equilibrium was discontinued. The set of feasible positions investigated for each party was the set of 201 points $\{1.0, 1.05, 1.10, \ldots 11.0\}$. For purposes of presentation, party vote shares at equilibrium are rounded. Further details of the simulation procedures, relating to assumptions on the voter distribution, are given in appendix A.

21. Endersby and Galatas (1997, tables 2–3) report estimates in the range of $b^{1/2}$ = 3.0, while Bartle's (1998, table 1) results suggest that $b^{1/2}$ is approximately equal to 2.5. Both of these estimates were based on analyses of 1992 BGES data. However, other scholars who have analyzed British elections question the electoral impact of partisanship (e.g., Alt 1984; Rose and McCallister 1990), albeit without reporting statistical results in a form that allows one to directly compare the effects of partisan and policy voting. In toto, the conflicting results reported in studies on British voting suggest that the "true" value of b lies at or below $b^{1/2}$ = 3.0. Note that the values of b I infer from the empirical studies cited above reflect the ratios of the estimated partisan coefficients relative to estimated coefficients for voters' policy preferences. In the case of the Endersby-Galatas study of the 1992 election, for instance, the reported parameters for Conservative and Labour identification are 2.8 and 3.5, respectively, while many of the parameters for respondent self-placement on the various policy dimensions are in the range of .18 to .30 (see Endersby and Galatas 1997, tables 2 and 3). Thus, the ratio of the partisan coefficients to the policy coefficients is in the range of 10 to one which suggests that $b \approx 10$ and therefore $b^{1/2} \approx 3$.

I am unaware of any analyses of voting in the 1987 British election that estimate the electoral impact of party identification, relative to policies. Both Alvarez and Nagler (1998) and Alvarez, Bowler, and Nagler (1996) report maximum likelihood estimates based on 1987 BGES data, but these analyses do not incorporate partisanship variables.

22. I note that the equilibrium located for $b^{1/2}$ = 1.5 is something of a fluke in that additional simulations for values of $b^{1/2}$ that were very close to 1.5 did not yield policy equilibria. However, equilibria emerged consistently for simulations in which $b^{1/2}$ was set larger than 1.8.

23. Three additional studies that explore situations similar to the one posited by Feld and Grofman are Rabinowitz and Macdonald 1998; Groseclose 1999; and Berger, Munger, and Potthoff 2000.

24. One of the most important differences is that, while my model assumes that the vote is a deterministic function of the voter's partisanship and policy preferences, Snyder assumes that the outcome of each district-level election is probabilistic from the political parties' perspectives.

Chapter 3

1. The Manifesto Research Group, under the direction of Ian Budge, commenced work in 1979 and has published the following reports: Budge, Robertsen, and Hearl, eds., *Ideology, Strategy, and Party Change in 19 Democracies* (1987); Laver and Budge, eds., *Party Policies and Government Coalitions* (1992); and Klingemann, Hofferbert, and Budge, *Parties, Policies, and Democracy* (1994).

2. The countries for which parties' policies have been mapped over the entire postwar period include the United States, Canada, Australia, New Zealand, Ireland, the United Kingdom, Spain, Italy, France, Germany, Austria, Luxembourg, Belgium, the Netherlands, Denmark, Norway, Sweden, Iceland, Israel, and Japan (see Budge 1994, table 1). In addition, I note that the coding frame devised by the MRG has been applied to more than 50 countries in all.

3. See Budge, Robertsen, and Hearl 1987, 458–67, for complete details on these coding procedures.

4. Laver and Budge 1992, 27 (also quoted in Budge 1994, 457–58). Budge argues that the Left-Right dimension is the one axis that generalizes across countries.

5. The instances of leapfrogging are as follows: (1) the Liberals leapfrog and Conservatives between 1945 and 1950; (2–3) the Liberals leapfrog the Conservatives and the Liberals leapfrog Labour between 1959 and 1964; (4) the Liberals leapfrog Labour between 1964 and 1966; and (5) Labour leapfrogs the Liberal Democrats between 1992 and 1997.

6. It would be desirable to compare the MRG's results on temporal patterns of party policies with those generated from alternative methods of estimating party policies such as the use of expert judgments (see, e.g., Castles and Mair 1984; de Swaan 1973; Huber and Inglehart 1995; Laver and Hunt 1992; Laver and John 1998; and Ware 1996), analysis of legislative roll calls (e.g., MacRae 1967), analyses of elite survey data (Dalton 1985; Iversen 1994b), and analyses of mass survey data on voters' perceptions of party positions (e.g., Adams and Merrill 1999a; Alvarez and Nagler 1998; Dow 1997c). However, while these alternative methodologies have been applied to selected historical elections, the MRG's methodology is the only one that has been applied to all major parties in all Western democracies over the entire postwar period. Furthermore, those alternative methodologies that have been applied to parties over a substantial time period— such as the Taylor-Laver scales and the de Swaan scales, both of which employ expert judgments of parties' positions over the period 1945–71—locate the parties on ordinal scales with the parties ranked from left to right. This permits the analyst to determine the locations of the parties relative to *each other,* and hence to identify cases of leapfrogging, but it does not permit conclusions about the extent to which parties vary their policies over time. Finally, I note that, while alternative methodologies occasionally generate party placements at odds with those reported by the MRG, in most cases different methods yield similar party placements (see, e.g., the comparisons presented in appendix B of Laver and Schofield 1990). This suggests that the temporal policy patterns I seek to explain here—that parties vary their policies over time but typically locate within ideologically delimited areas of the policy space and that leapfrogging behavior is rare and typically involves contiguous parties—represent "real" patterns of party policies rather than artifacts of the MRG's methodology.

7. In fact, using the method outlined in note 8, one can calculate L's vote-maximizing location more precisely as $l \approx 5.62$.

8. To see this, note that given $l = 5.0$ and $c = 5.6$, and with the strength, b, of voters' partisan attachments set at $b^{1/2} = 1.0$, for party C's partisans the utility differential for party C versus L is given by equation 2.2 as:

$$U_i(C) - U_i(L) = b + [-(x_i - 5.6)^2 - -(x_i - 5)^2]$$

$$= 1.0 + (1.2x_i - 6.36)$$

$$= 1.2x_i - 5.36$$

so that $U_i(C) - U_i(L) > 0 \Leftrightarrow (1.2x_i - 5.36) > 0 \Leftrightarrow x_i > 4.47 \approx 4.50$, that is, all of C's partisans to the right of 4.50 prefer C to L.

In fact, given $l = 4.5$ and $b^{1/2} = 1$, one can calculate the right-most location c that will ensure support from all of C's partisans located to the right of 4.5 as follows:

$$U_i(C) - U_i(L) > 0 \Rightarrow 1.0 + [-(4.5 - l)^2 - -(4.5 - 5)^2] > 0$$

$$\Rightarrow -l^2 + 9l - 19 > 0$$

$$\Rightarrow l < (4.5 + 5^{1/2}/2) \approx 5.62$$

that is, when C locates at approximately 5.62 it attracts the votes of all of its partisans to the right of 4.5.

9. That all of C's partisans located in the policy interval [6.7,7.0] will vote for R, given $c = 5.6$, $r = 7.0$, and $b^{1/2} = 1.0$, can be verified using the approach outlined in note 8.

10. One might think that party L could do better by leapfrogging both rival parties, thereby locating to the right of party R. However, the fact of voters' partisan loyalties precludes such a strategy. To see this, note that, because all voters to the right of 7.5 are partisans of R, party L would have to differentiate its policies from those of R in order to attract these voters' support. Specifically, with R located at 7.0, L maximizes its support on the right by locating at 8.0, thereby attracting support from all voters to the right of 8.0. However, it is easily seen that this position is less electorally attractive than the location $l = 4.6$.

11. To see this, note that, given $c = 6.15$, $r = 6.6$, and $b^{1/2} = 1.0$, the utility differential for C over R, for partisans of party C, is given by equation 2.2 as:

$$U_i(C) - U_i(R) = b + [-(x_i - 6.15)^2 - -(x_i - 6.6)^2]$$

$$= 1.0 + (5.73 - 0.9x_i)$$

$$= 6.73 - 0.9x_i$$

so that $U_i(C) - U_i(R) > 0 \Leftrightarrow 6.73 - 0.9x_i > 0 \Leftrightarrow x_i < 7.48 \approx 7.50$, that is, all of C's partisans located to the left of 7.50 prefer C to R. A similar approach demonstrates that by shifting to 6.15 C loses the support of the voters in the interval [4.60,5.05].

12. The principal investigators for the 1992 BGES were Anthony Heath, Roger Jowell, John K. Curtice, Jack A. Brand, and James C. Mitchell. The data analyzed here were made available through a computer file produced by Social and Community Planning Research, Colchester, England, and distributed through the Inter-university Consortium for Political and Social Research, Ann Arbor, Michigan.

13. The other issues included in the 1992 BGES relate to national defense, women's rights, the European Community, taxation, tradeoffs between unemployment and inflation, welfare, and redistribution. In addition to the analyses reported here, I analyzed party policy strategies for the latter four policy variables, which presumably tap the Left-Right economic dimension. Results for the redistribution and taxation variables were quite similar to the results I report for nationalization; results for unemployment/inflation and welfare were different, presumably because the survey responses were skewed sharply to the left on these two items. Because the distribution of British voters' Left-Right orientations is presumably not skewed to the left, the results for nationalization, redistribution, and taxation are probably more indicative of what an analysis based upon the Left-Right dimension would show. These analyses are available from the author upon request.

14. Recall from chapter 2 that in 1988 Liberals and the Social Democrats merged to form the Liberal Democratic Party.

15. For the empirical distribution, party sympathizers were defined as those who thought of themselves as Labour, Conservative, or Liberal Democrat as well as those who reported feeling closer to one of these parties. Independents were those who answered "no/none" to both questions. Respondents who replied "don't know" or did not answer these questions are excluded from this analysis, as are respondents who identified with one of the smaller parties. The total number of respondents thereby excluded is fewer than 100.

16. This spatial mapping arises given that the parties move sequentially, with the Conservatives moving first, followed by Labour and then the Liberal Democrats. Spatial mappings based upon alternative orders of party movement produced similar results to those reported here.

17. In figure 3.7, there are 10 instances in which the policy trajectories of two parties cross each other. Thus, at time $t1$, and again at $t2$, the Liberal Democrats' position crosses over the position of Labour, at $t4$ the Liberal Democrats' position again crosses Labour's, and so on.

18. Note that the results reported for $b^{1/2} = 3$ in table 3.2 are slightly different from those given in the preceding paragraph, which were calculated based upon only the 14 policy shifts illustrated in figure 3.7 rather than the full 100 shifts computed for the simulations.

19. The decision to vary the voter distribution after four party policy shifts was made based on the fact that the average length of time between general elections during the postwar period in Britain has been about four years. Since election results provide parties with fresh information about voters' policy preferences and partisanship, it seems

a reasonable approximation to assume that party leaders have relatively stable perceptions of the voter distribution in the period between elections and update these perceptions based upon the next election. In addition, I note that alternative simulations that varied the number of times that parties shifted for a given voter distribution produced results quite similar to those reported here.

20. In particular, the proportions of each party's partisans varied significantly for different distributions, with the percentage of Conservatives varying between 46 and 35 percent and the percentage of Labourites varying between 31 and 39 percent. The mean voter position was much more stable and varied only between 5.72 and 6.03. Both features of these random distributions—that partisan proportions were variable but that the mean voter position was stable—are consistent with British survey data from the postwar period (see, e.g., Dalton 1996, chap. 6; Rose and McCallister 1990, 23; and Sinnot 1998).

21. I note that this pattern extends over the entire 100 moves of the simulation, during which there are only seven instances of a party proposing the same policy during two successive intervals. Of course, this conclusion depends on the criterion that a party's policy is the "same" for two successive periods only if the party's positions agree to one decimal place. However, the essential point that emerges from the simulations, that the parties vary their positions over time but without leapfrogging, does not depend on this criterion.

22. Two factors account for the simulation result that party policies are rarely static. The first is that, while the full 1987 voter distribution admits a policy equilibrium, some of the 200-voter subsamples do not, so there are certain four-move sequences during which the parties cannot possibly converge toward a policy equilibrium. Second, given that each voter distribution is altered after only four moves, any party equilibrium is necessarily short-lived.

Chapter 4

1. As I discuss below, both the UDF and the RPR were founded only in the 1970s; however, both parties are the "descendants" of earlier parties or political movements, so the policy behavior of these two political movements can be traced back continuously at least to the late 1950s.

2. In fact, the RPR can move some distance to the left or right of $r = 8.2$ without any change in its vote share and without disrupting the policy equilibrium.

3. Examples of the formation of new parties during this period include the Poujadists (in 1956) and Pierre Mendes-France's Republican Front. With respect to the changing basis of parties' appeals, the major example is the successive incarnations of the Gaullist Party (see Pierce 1995, chap. 3).

4. The two-stage plurality system used in elections to the National Assembly stipulates that all candidates receiving at least 12.5 percent of the popular vote in the first round are eligible to advance to the second, with the winner being the candidate who receives a plurality in second-round voting. This system was changed on a one-time basis in 1986 to a form of proportional representation. The system used to elect the president, adopted in 1962, stipulates that if no presidential candidate receives a majority of valid votes cast at the first ballot the top two vote getters advance to the second ballot.

5. In fact, the UDF is itself a federation of several smaller parties. In addition, both the RPR and the UDF are the direct "descendants" of earlier political parties: the RPR descends from the Gaullist Party—which was itself later renamed the Union for the New Republic and then the Union for the Defense of the Republic—while the forerunners of the UDF include the Popular Republican Movement, the Democratic Center, the Center for Democracy and Progress, and Progress and Modern Democracy (see Safran 1998, 80–81).

6. The specific form this electoral coordination takes is that alliance partners strategically withdraw candidates during the second round of voting in order to enhance the electoral prospects of their coalition partner's candidate. In the case of the Socialists and Communists, for instance, in each electoral district the weaker of these parties' candidates, based upon the first round of voting, withdraws after round 1 and instructs his or her supporters to transfer their votes to the alliance partner's candidate in round 2. This coordination ensures that Socialist and Communist candidates avoid splitting the left-wing vote on the decisive ballot, which could allow a candidate from the rival coalition to win the election. The RPR and the UDF have a similar electoral pact. This strategic logic of two-stage plurality systems prompted Maurice Duverger (1954) to postulate that second-ballot systems are associated with multiparty systems with electoral alliances—precisely the pattern we observe in France.

An additional factor that has promoted cooperation between parties with similar ideologies is that the second rounds of French presidential elections have typically matched a Socialist candidate against either a centrist or a right-wing candidate, thereby creating incentives for political parties to merge into opposing blocs for the purpose of electing the presidential candidate of their political stripe (see Safran 1998, chap. 4).

7. For instance, one plausible alternative to vote maximization is that party leaders could instead maximize the *combined* votes of all parties that share their ideological *tendance,* reasoning that this strategy enhances their prospects of membership in the governing coalition (see, e.g., Adams, Merrill, and Grofman 1999). With respect to the strategic logic of electoral alliances, some analysts have argued for the opposite conclusion: that in certain circumstances parties are motivated to siphon off electoral support from their alliance partner, even at some sacrifice to their own aggregate support (see, e.g., Tsebelis 1990, chap. 7). If either logic is correct, then parties are not primarily concerned with attracting votes.

An additional factor that may complicate spatial analysis of French parties' policy strategies in parliamentary elections is that these parties also nominate candidates who compete in presidential elections and, to the extent that parties' election platforms constrain presidential candidates, they must select these platforms with an eye on presidential elections as well.

8. As discussed in appendix B, the only detailed scholarly surveys of voting behavior in French postwar elections are the Converse-Pierce survey of 1967–69, the SOFRES surveys of voting in the presidential elections of 1988 and 1995, and Pierce's 1988 Presidential Election Study. Of these, the Converse-Pierce and Pierce surveys are preferable because they incorporate party identification items comparable to those used in American election surveys and these question wordings are less subject to the criticism frequently directed at the party identification items used in most election surveys outside the United States, that such items actually tap current vote intention (see section

204   Notes to Pages 87–94

2.3; also see Converse and Pierce 1993). I employ Pierce's 1988 survey because it includes data on respondents' party identifications with the National Front, which is required in some of the simulations I report below.

9. Note that in this distribution I have deliberately excluded respondents who
identified with the National Front. I will include these respondents when I report simulations on five-party spatial competition that include the National Front.

10. In the simulations, each party's expected vote was calculated for the set of 61
points $\{1.0, 1.1, \ldots, 7.0\}$. All of the simulated party policy trajectories reported in this
section were obtained using the assumption that parties shifted their policies in the sequence Communist, Socialist, UDF, and RPR. Simulations based on alternative party
sequences produced comparable results.

11. Below I explain why these simulations examined 120 shifts rather than 100, as
in the British simulations.

12. In computing the proportion of cases involving leapfrogging for these four-
party simulations, I took as the unit of observation each possible pair of parties (six pairs
in all). For each policy shift, I then recorded whether each pair of parties leapfrogged
each other and used these results as my measure of the frequency of leapfrogging behavior. For the spatial mapping pictured in figure 4.3B, for instance, note that in the transition from time $t1$ to time $t2$ the RPR leapfrogs the UDF. Thus, this party pair is recorded
as a case of leapfrogging. However, none of the five remaining party pairs (Communist-
Socialist, Communist-UDF, Communist-RPR, Socialist-UDF, and Socialist-RPR) involves leapfrogging, so during the transition from time $t1$ to $t2$ the frequency of leapfrogging behavior was one out of six or about 17 percent. I obtained the overall frequency
of leapfrogging by averaging the frequency of leapfrogging over all transitions from tn
to $tn + 1$. I thank Samuel Merrill III for suggesting this approach to me.

13. To see this, note that out of each 100 randomly selected respondents, on average we expect to select 18 independents and 82 partisans. With each independent's voting weight multiplied by 4.0, the expected ratio of partisans to independents is 82 partisans to $4 \times 18 = 72$ independents, so the expected proportion of partisans in the
randomly selected voter distribution is $82/(82 + 72) \approx .53$.

14. As in the case of the simulations on British politics, the decision to vary the distribution of French voters after four party policy shifts was based on the fact that the average length of time between parliamentary elections in France during the period 1958–
88 was about four years. I note that alternative simulations that varied the number of
computed policy shifts for each voter distribution (between two and 10) yielded results
substantially the same as those reported here.

15. In fact, the end partisan frequency of 82 percent slightly exceeds the frequency
that Converse (1969) calculated for mature party systems, which he estimated at approximately 70 percent. However, note that here I am focusing only on voters who can
also self-place on the Left-Right scale, for which the partisan frequency can be expected
to be somewhat higher.

16. One interesting difference between the simulation results for an evolving distribution, compared to the simulations on a stable distribution, concerns the degree of
mass-elite correspondence when $b^{1/2} = 0.5$, that is, when voters have quite weak policy motivations. For the simulations on an evolving distribution, the parties' mean positions for $b^{1/2} = 0.5$ are much more moderate than those of their partisans, while in the

simulations on a stable distribution the parties' positions are quite similar to those of their partisans. This difference occurs because in the simulations on evolving distributions the independent voters are weighed more heavily and, since independents are disproportionately located at the center of the 1–7 scale (see fig. 4.3A), these voting distributions feature higher concentrations of centrist voters. This voter centrism, when it is coupled with weak partisan attachments, motivates parties to moderate their positions.

17. In addition, Strom summarizes a third model, that of the *office-seeking party,* which maximizes its likelihood of membership in the governing coalition. As he notes, this model of party motivation is typically included in formal models as a supplement to either the vote-seeking or the policy-seeking party model (see, e.g., Schofield and Parks 1997; Laver and Shepsle 1995; and Schofield and Parks 1997). I note that the argument that parties can exercise policy leadership without sacrificing votes has also been advanced by Iversen (1994b), who argues for a "representational policy leadership" (RPL) model in which voters prefer parties that present policies similar to but more extreme than the voters' policy beliefs. For an analysis that integrates the RPL model and voters' partisan attachments, see Adams and Merrill 1999b.

18. I insert the qualification that vote-maximizing policies "largely" reflect party leaders' sincere preferences because, in the case of the French Communists, the simulation results reported in this chapter suggest that the party does best by presenting Center-Left policies (see tables 4.1 and 4.2) that are presumably more moderate than the party elites' true preferences. However, the computed vote-maximizing positions for the Socialists, the UDF, and the RPR plausibly match these parties' sincere policy preferences.

19. I note that under the assumption of proximity motivations *and* probabilistic voting parties may also converge to noncentrist positions even when the electorate is nonpartisan, a point emphasized by Lomborg (1996, 16–17; see also de Palma et al. 1990, figs. 2, 3, and 7).

Chapter 5

1. In elections to the French National Assembly, all candidates that win at least 12.5 percent of the vote at round 1 are eligible to compete in round 2.

2. See also table 5.2, below, which reports the mean self-placements on Left-Right ideology and immigration for the partisans of each of the five major French parties, as reported in Pierce's 1988 French Presidential Election Study. For Socialist and Communist partisans, these mean self-placements are 2.4 and 3.1, respectively, on ideology, and 2.7 and 3.0, respectively, on immigration. For RPR and UDF partisans, the mean Left-Right self-placements are 4.9 and 5.4, respectively, and the immigration means are 3.8 and 4.3.

3. To avoid confusion, I mean that the results of simulations on both evolving and stable distributions yielded the conclusion that voters' coalition-based biases provide additional incentives for parties to present stable policy trajectories compared to situations in which voters choose according to the basic partisan model. However, as was the case for the simulations reported in chapter 4, here I found that parties' policy trajectories were slightly less stable for the evolving distribution than for the stable distribution.

4. As was the case for the simulations reported in figure 4.2, in these simulations each party was initially located at its actual (perceived) position and parties were then successively moved to their computed vote-maximizing positions. Each simulation proceeded over 120 successive party policy shifts, and the parties shifted their policy positions according to the sequence Communists, Socialists, UDF, and RPR. Simulations based upon alternative party sequences yielded similar conclusions.

5. Note that $c = b/4$ implies that $c^{1/2} = (b^{1/2}/2)$, which is why, for $b^{1/2} = 0.5$, I specify $c^{1/2} = 0.25$.

6. With respect to French politics, both Adams and Merrill (2000, table 3) and Pierce (1995, 135, table 7.4) report maximum likelihood estimates based upon analyses of voting data from Pierce's 1988 French Presidential Election Study, which suggest that Left-Right ideology influenced voters to a greater extent than did the three alternative policy dimensions (immigration policy, the public sector, and church schools) included in this survey,

7. Indeed, the collapse of the Fourth Republic in 1958 revolved primarily around foreign policy disputes relating to Algeria. In addition, religious issues have at times played a prominent role in French politics (see, e.g., Pierce 1995).

8. The National Front was founded in 1972 by Jean-Marie Le Pen and first attained a substantial electoral following in French municipal elections in 1983 and in elections to the European Parliament in 1984. It followed up these performances by attracting nearly 10 percent of the first-ballot vote in the 1986 National Assembly elections. In all subsequent parliamentary elections (1988, 1993, and 1997), the National Front has attracted between 9 and 16 percent of the first-round vote.

9. Note that this vote model incorporates the simplifying assumption that French voters attach equal weights to each policy dimension, a specification at odds with the results reported in studies on French voting behavior, which suggest the Left-Right dimension is of paramount importance (see, e.g., Adams and Merrill 2000, table 3; and Pierce 1995, table 7.4). Of course, to the extent that the Left-Right dimension dwarfs other dimensions in electoral impact, the unidimensional model we have employed up to this point captures the dynamics of spatial competition in France. However, I note that in addition to the simulations based on equation 5.2, which I summarize below, I performed additional simulations on French voting data based on alternative vote models that assigned greater weight to Left-Right ideology. These simulations produced conclusions concerning parties' policy trajectories similar to the ones reported below.

10. In addition, I performed simulations based on an alternative two-dimensional voter distribution derived from the 1988 French Presidential Election Study, constructed by cross-tabulating respondents' Left-Right self-placements and their self-placements on an item relating to government subsidies for religious schools, another issue that plausibly crosscuts Left-Right ideology. These simulations yielded conclusions on party strategies similar to the conclusions based on immigration policy.

11. Simulations based on alternative party sequences yielded similar conclusions concerning parties' policy behavior. In addition, I note that, unlike the earlier simulations involving a single dimension—see appendix A—in these simulations the respondent distribution was not "smoothed" so as to be continuous over each dimension. Instead it was given by table 5.2—that is, the voters were located from 1 to 7 along each dimension at intervals of 1.0. Hence, there were 49 (7×7) voter locations in all. Fur-

thermore, due to computational constraints, the parties had to adopt positions along each dimension from the set of 13 points $\{1.0, 1.5, \ldots, 7.0\}$, so each party's position was selected from a 13×13 grid (169 possible positions in all). I performed a limited number of simulations in which parties moved over a finer grid (25×25), and these simulations produced similar results.

12. In support of this interpretation, I note that Lomborg (1996, 24–29) reports simulation results on multiparty spatial competition in two dimensions for nonpartisan voters, which show that when the voter distribution is more polarized on one of the two dimensions vote-seeking parties' positions tend to converge on the less polarized dimension. This supports my hypothesis that the French parties' ideological convergence in my two-dimensional simulations is related to the fact that voters are polarized on the immigration dimension.

13. I do not address the incidence of leapfrogging behavior here because the concept of leapfrogging is problematic in multidimensional policy space. For the policy shifts illustrated in figure 5.2D, for instance, the Communist and Socialist Parties shift their policies so that they leapfrog on Left-Right ideology but not on immigration policy. In terms of the spatial representation of these policy shifts, the parties' spatial positions do not appear to "cross" each other, so in one sense they do not leapfrog. Yet, because the parties switch sides on ideology, they *do* leapfrog according to the definition employed for the one-dimensional simulations. Given this ambiguity, in tables 5.3 and 5.4 (below) I do not report the incidence of leapfrogging in simulations on two-dimensional policy competition. However, I note that, using the definition of *leapfrogging* employed for the unidimensional simulations, that is, that it occurs whenever parties' Left-Right positions cross, the incidence of leapfrogging in the two-dimensional simulations is similar to the results reported in tables 4.1 and 5.1 for the one-dimensional simulations.

14. In the party trajectories illustrated in figures 5.3A through 5.3F, this generalization holds for the Socialists and Communists, but there are occasions when the policies of the UDF and RPR do not tightly converge. This occurs because the presence of the right-wing National Front—a party that was not incorporated into the simulations on unidimensional competition—alters to some extent the strategic calculations of the UDF and RPR.

Chapter 6

1. The policy salience coefficient s is necessary for this probabilistic voting formulation because the random term μ_i is specified below as having a fixed variance (see note 2). Without s, the relative importance of voters' policy motivations vis-à-vis unmeasured motivations would be constant. Note that the importance of partisanship compared to unmeasured motivations (and also compared to policies) is captured by the value of b, the strength of partisan attachment.

2. The distribution for a type I extreme value distribution is $F(x) = \exp[-\exp(-x)]$. The distribution has a variance of $\pi^2/6$. The type I EV is a special case of the generalized extreme value (GEV) distribution. For logit, each μ is independent, with a univariate extreme value distribution. For GEV, the marginal distribution of each μ is univariate EV, but they may be correlated with each other (See Train 1986, 53–54, 65–70).

The assumption of independently distributed random terms implies the strong behavioral property of independence of irrelevant alternatives (IIA), that is, that the ratio of the probabilities that a voter votes for any two parties does not depend on the presence of other parties in the choice set. This assumption has been criticized on both theoretical and empirical grounds by Alvarez and Nagler (1995, 1998), who argue that the IIA assumption misspecifies voters' decision processes in situations in which voters perceive different degrees of similarity between different pairs of parties. To my knowledge, however, all existing analytical results on multiparty spatial competition rely upon the IIA assumption (see, e.g., Adams forthcoming a; Merrill and Adams 2000a, 2000b; de Palma et al. 1990; and Lin et al. 1999), although there exist numerous simulation studies that relax this assumption (Adams 1999c; Alvarez and Nagler 1995; Dow 1997c; Schofield et al. 1998a). In addition, I note that the simulation studies by Adams (1999c) and Adams and Merrill (1998) specifically investigate the effects of relaxing the IIA assumption. The Adams study suggests that when voters are motivated exclusively by policies plus unmeasured (random) motivations—that is, when voters are nonpartisan—the IIA assumption can significantly alter vote-seeking parties' policy strategies compared to alternative distributional assumptions. However, the Adams-Merrill simulation results, which are based on simulations on the same French data set I employ in this book, suggest that, when voters choose according to the behaviorist's full multivariate vote model, parties' vote-maximizing policy strategies are similar for vote models that assume IIA and those that relax this assumption.

3. This expected vote is calculated as the sum of individuals' vote probabilities, that is,

$$\text{EVC}(c, s) = \sum_{i \in V} P_i(C),$$

where V represents the set of all voters in the electorate.

4. Adams 1997, 1259–60 presents a fuller development of this issue.

5. For alternative proofs of this corollary to theorem 6.1, see Lin et al. 1999 and de Palma et al. 1990. An obvious question that arises is: when is the degree of policy voting sufficiently small for theorem 6.1 to hold and thus is this corollary to theorem 6.1 of any practical importance? While the answer to this question depends on the number of parties and the distribution of voters' policy preferences, simulation studies by Adams (1999a) and de Palma et al. (1989, 1990) suggest that convergent equilibria obtain even for values of s that exceed the parameter estimates that behavioral researchers have estimated for policy voting in various historical elections. Furthermore, even when the degree of policy voting is too "high" to support a completely convergent equilibrium, alternative equilibria are likely to exist in which the parties cluster into opposing blocs, each of which contains at least two parties proposing essentially identical platforms (see, e.g., de Palma et al. 1989, figs. 2–6). To my knowledge, the only empirically based studies of multiparty equilibrium for unbiased probabilistic voting are Schofield, Sened, and Nixon's (1998) analysis of the 1992 election to the Israeli Knesset and Merrill and Adams's (2000a, table 3A) analysis of the 1988 French presidential election. Schofield et al. locate several possible equilibrium configurations, in all of which the parties do *not* converge to the voter mean but instead cluster into two opposing blocs, because, as the authors suggest, the Israeli voter distribution in 1992 was to some extent bimodal.

Merrill and Adams also located alternative policy equilibria, including a convergent equilibrium in which all candidates presented identical, centrist positions.

6. Indeed, results presented by Eaton and Lipsey (1975) establish that for the voter distribution pictured in figure 6.1A—and indeed for any voter distribution that has a single peak (here at the voter mean 5.0)—equilibrium is precluded for elections involving *any* number of parties greater than two.

7. For this exercise, I calculated $EVC(c,s)$ for the set of 101 points $\{0, 0.1, \ldots, 10.0\}$.

8. These specifications are similar to the empirical estimates that Endersby and Galatas (1997, table 2) report for voting in the 1992 British general election.

9. Adams and Merrill (1999c) present analytical results indicating that when s is sufficiently small this intuition generalizes to all multiparty electoral contexts.

10. I note that the Merrill-Adams study focuses specifically on parties' *equilibrium* positions, so the authors' conclusions bear on the issue of how such factors as the number of party partisans, the extremity of these partisans' positions, and the value of the policy salience coefficient, s, affect parties' vote-maximizing positions, given that all rival parties locate at their own optimal positions.

11. Recall that for this configuration of parties and voters, then, when the electorate is independent party L maximizes votes by locating at the voter mean, given $s = .05$ or $s = .15$ (see fig. 6.2).

12. The function $TK(k)$ represents the mean voter position, with each voter's position weighted by the factor $P_i(K)[1 - P_i(K)]$, where $P_i(K)$ is given for $s = 0$, that is, when voters have no policy motivations. Adams and Merrill (1999c) give a substantive interpretation for this equation.

13. I note that the Adams-Merrill essays are largely concerned with the strategic implications of a *mixed directional-proximity voter metric,* which combines aspects of the traditional proximity vote model along with the directional model proposed by Rabinowitz and Macdonald (1989). The strategic implications of the mixed model are explored in more detail in Merrill and Grofman 1999 and Iversen 1994a.

In addition, Schofield, Sened, and Nixon (1998) have reported equilibrium results for party competition in Israel that are based upon vote models derived from conditional logit analyses of Israeli survey data. However, these models do not include respondent-specific nonpolicy variables such as party identification. This also holds for Dow's (1997c) analysis of party strategies in historical elections in Canada, France, Holland, and Israel. Finally, I note that Alvarez, Nagler, and their coauthors (Alvarez and Nagler 1995; Alvarez, Bowler, and Nagler 1996; Alvarez, Nagler, and Willette 1998) have reported computations of parties' "one-step" vote-maximizing positions for historical elections in the United States, Britain, and Canada using vote models whose parameters were estimated from historical elections. The Alvarez-Nagler models typically do not include party identification (except for the American model), but they do include respondent sociodemographic characteristics (class, income, and religion) that correlate with voters' policy beliefs. The vote-maximizing party positions that the authors report typically find the parties presenting policies similar to but less extreme than the positions of the parties' partisans—the pattern outlined in section 6.4.

14. Adams's (forthcoming a) analysis of equilibrium in the three-candidate American election of 1992 relies on voting parameter estimates reported by Alvarez and

Nagler (1995), based upon statistical analysis of 1992 ANES (American National Election Study) data. In addition, I note that the Adams study relies upon a hypothetical voter distribution designed to capture the strategic context of policy competition in the 1992 election.

15. Recall from chapter 2 that the British General Election Studies do not include questions on Left-Right or liberal-conservative self-placement, which is why I analyze respondent views on nationalization of industry, an issue that plausibly correlates with respondents' Left-Right ideologies. Note that I carried out additional sets of simulations based on respondent distributions on alternative questions included in the 1992 BGES relating to taxation, welfare, and income redistribution. Each of these simulations yielded equilibrium results that were similar to the ones I report below for nationalization of industry.

16. The Conservative Party's expected vote is calculated as the sum of respondents' vote probabilities, that is

$$\text{EVC}(c,s) = \sum_{i \in V} P_i(C)$$

where V represents the set of all respondents in the voter distribution and $P_i(C)$ is given by equation 6.2.

17. I carried out alternative simulations in which the set of possible party positions was expanded to the set of 501 positions $\{1, 1.02, \ldots, 11.0\}$. These simulations yielded equilibrium configurations virtually identical to those reported here. In addition, alternative simulations that varied the order of party movement produced identical results to those reported below. Finally, I note that convergence to equilibrium by this process was quite rapid, with the parties converging to equilibrium in just three "moves" each.

18. The fact that simulations based on probabilistic versions of the partisan vote model and the coalition vote model yielded similar results is due to the fact that in the simulations based on coalition voting the coalition parameter was set near zero, reflecting Merrill's empirical estimates (reported below).

19. I note that Merrill's empirical estimates for b and s are similar to those reported by Merrill and Adams (2000a, table 1) in their conditional logit analysis of voting in the first round of the 1988 French presidential election.

20. I also carried out simulations that included the National Front. These simulations produced similar conclusions concerning both the existence and the configuration of policy equilibria. Compared to the results on four-party equilibrium reported below, the French five-party equilibria found the UDF and RPR locating slightly nearer the center and the Communists and Socialists taking more left-wing positions.

21. In these simulations, each party's expected vote was calculated over the set of 61 positions $\{1, 1.1, \ldots, 7.0\}$. The sequence of party policy shifts was Communist, Socialist, UDF, and RPR. Alternative simulations that expanded the set of feasible party positions, and altered the order of party policy shifts, produced similar results.

22. This configuration is extremely similar to the five-candidate equilibrium that Merrill and Adams (2000b, table 1) locate for the 1988 French presidential election,

which finds the five candidates positioned as follows (the candidates' party affiliations are given in parentheses): Lajoinie (Communist), 3.69; Mitterrand (Socialist), 3.52; Barre (UDF), 4.24; Chirac (RPR), 4.44; and Le Pen (National Front), 4.23.

23. Thus, on the 1–11 Norwegian Left-Right scale, none of the seven parties' equilibrium positions differs by more than 0.35 units between the two models; on the 1–7 French Left-Right scale, none of the candidates' positions differs by more than 0.2 units between the two models. I note that the Adams-Merrill studies on Norway employ previous vote as a proxy for party identification. In addition, in the authors' investigation of parties' policy strategies for the fully specified behavioral vote model, they included policy dimensions in addition to Left-Right self-placement, while their study on the basic PPV model incorporated only Left-Right self-placement. The fact that the policy equilibria obtained for these two models were so similar, in spite of the differences in the model specifications, strengthens the conclusion that partisanship is *the* crucial nonpolicy variable for explaining party strategies.

Chapter 7

1. I employ the terminology *liberal-conservative* rather than *Left-Right* because the former are the terms used in the questions asked in the American National Election Study surveys with respect to the respondents' ideological self-placements (and their party placements). Of course, the arguments I present below apply equally to spatial competition along the Left-Right dimension.

2. To see this, note that that, given $r = 4$, $d = 5$, and $b^{1/2} = 1$, a Republican partisan i's utility differential for the Republican versus the Democratic Party is

$$U_i(R) - U_i(D) = [b - (x_i - r)^2 - [-(x_i - d)^2]$$

$$= [1 - (x_i - 4)^2 - [-(x_i - 5)^2]$$

$$= 10 - 2x_i$$

This implies that $[U_i(R) - U_i(D)] < 0$ for $x_i < 5$ and hence that all Republican partisans to the right of 5.0 will vote for the Democrats.

3. That all Democratic voters prefer the Republican Party, given $r = 4$, $d = 5$, and $b^{1/2} = 1$, can be verified using the approach outlined in note 2.

4. See, for instance, table 3.2 in Dalton 1996, 45, which shows that the U.S. turnout rate ranks twenty-third in a comparison of 24 advanced industrial societies and falls more than 20 percent below the average turnout over these 24 countries. In comparison, turnout rates in Britain and France are typically above 70 percent and fall near the 24-nation average.

5. As noted above, alternatively some scholars model abstention as being due to indifference (see, e.g., Sanders 1998; and Erikson and Romero 1990, 1120–21).

6. To see this, note that that, given $r = 5$, $d = 3$, and $b^{1/2} = 1$, a Democratic partisan i's utility differential for the Democrats versus the Republicans is

$$U_i(D) - U_i(R) = [b - (x_i - d)^2 - [-(x_i - r)^2]$$

$$= [1 - (x_i - 3)^2 - [-(x_i - 5)^2]$$

$$= 17 - 4x_i$$

This implies that $[U_i(D) - U_i(R)] < 0$ for all x_i such that $17 - 4x_i > 0 \Rightarrow x_i < 4.25$, and hence all Democratic partisans located to the liberal side of 4.25 will vote for the Democrats.

7. To see this, note that that, given $r = 5$, $d = 3$, $b^{1/2} = 1$, and $a = -1$, a Democratic partisan i's utility differential for voting Democratic versus abstaining is

$$U_i(D) - U_i(A) = [b - (x_i - d)^2] - a$$

$$= [1 - (x_i - 3)^2] - (-1)$$

$$= -x_i^2 + 6x_i - 7$$

Hence, $[U_i(D) - U_i(A)] < 0$ for all x_i such that $[-x_i^2 + 6x_i - 7] < 0$. For voters who are more liberal than the Democratic Party (i.e., for all voters i such that $x_i < 3.0$), this condition is satisfied whenever $x_i < (3 - 2^{1/2})$. Since $(3 - 2^{1/2}) \approx 1.59$, this implies that all Democratic partisans located in the approximate interval [1.00,1.59] will abstain.

8. This result can be verified using the approach outlined in note 9.

9. To see this, note that that, given $r = 4$, $d = 4$, $b^{1/2} = 1$, and $a = -1$, a Democratic partisan i's utility differential for voting Democratic versus abstaining is

$$U_i(D) - U_i(A) = [b - (x_i - d)^2] - a$$

$$= [1 - (x_i - 4)^2] - (-1)$$

$$= -x_i^2 + 8x_i - 14$$

Hence, $[U_i(D) - U_i(A)] > 0$ for all x_i such that $(-x_i^2 + 8x_i - 14) > 0$. For the Democratic partisans located in the policy interval [1,4], this condition is satisfied whenever $x_i > (4 - 2^{1/2})$. Since $(4 - 2^{1/2}) \approx 2.59$, this implies that all Democratic partisans to the conservative side of the approximate location $x_i = 2.59$ will vote for the Democrats, while those to the liberal side of $x_i = 2.59$ will abstain. A similar argument shows that the Republican partisans located in the approximate interval [4.00,5.41] will vote Republican and that more conservative Republican partisans will abstain.

10. To see this, note that, given $r = 4.0$, $d = 3.0$, and $b^{1/2} = 1.0$, a Democratic voter i's utility differential for the Democrats versus the Republicans is:

$$U_i(D) - U_i(R) = 1 - (x_i - d)^2 - [-(x_i - r)^2]$$

$$= 1 - (x_i - 3)^2 - [-(x_i - 4)^2]$$

$$= 8 - 2x_i$$

This implies that $[U_i(D) - U_i(R)] > 0$ for all $x_i < 4$, and, since all Democratic partisans in our illustrative example are located in the policy interval [1.00,4.00], it follows that all Democratic partisans prefer the Democrats to the Republicans.

11. Some spatial models with variable voter turnout emphasize the competing parties' *vote margins*—defined as the difference between a party's vote total and the vote total of its opponent—rather then the parties' *vote percentages,* as given in figure 7.4B. In this example the Democrats' margin-maximizing position is $d = 3$, the same as their percentage-maximizing position. Below I report simulation results suggesting that, for American two-party competition under the partisan turnout model, margin and percentage-maximizing motivations typically motivate quite similar spatial strategies.

12. For instance, given $r = 4.0$, $b^{1/2} = 1.0$, and $a = -1.0$, the Democrats maximize their support among Republican partisans by locating at a position somewhat more conservative than $d = 5.0$. However, for such positioning the Democrats receive *no* votes from Democratic partisans since all such partisans will then prefer the Republicans to the Democrats.

13. Condition 3 states that if either party locates outside of the policy interval that contains its partisans then some of these partisans would have a higher utility for abstention than for voting for the party.

14. Condition 5 states that a partisan voter will prefer to vote for his or her preferred party rather than abstaining, provided that the party's position is identical to the voter's position. If this condition is not satisfied, no voters will turn out, the parties' positions have no impact on the election outcome, and any party configuration is in equilibrium.

15. The distributions are given for all respondents who could place themselves and both parties on the liberal-conservative scales. In these distributions, the respondents who classified themselves as Democratic and Republican Party "leaners" were classified as partisans.

16. I also performed a limited number of simulations based on the first assumption, that each party maximized the number of votes it received. In these simulations, the parties presented somewhat less centrist positions than they did in the simulations based on assumptions 2–3. However, for simulations based upon all three assumptions the parties presented divergent positions that reflected their partisans' beliefs (in fact, this result held to a greater extent for the simulations based on assumption 1 than for those based on assumptions 2–3). Hence, the central conclusions I report below, on spatial competition between parties that maximize their percentages of the two-party vote, extend to each of these alternative assumptions about party motivations.

17. Alternative simulations, in which the parties were initially located at their mean perceived positions, produced virtually identical results.

18. In the simulations, each party's vote percentage was computed for the set of 601 points {1.00, 1.01, . . . , 7.00}. This differs from the specification used in the simulations on Britain and France, in which the parties were permitted to move in increments of .05 along the policy continuum, not .01. All of the simulation results reported in this section were obtained using the assumption that the Democratic Party moved first; simulations based on the alternative assumption that the Republicans moved first produced extremely similar results. In all other respects, the procedure employed for the simulations on ANES data were identical to those described in appendix A *except* that, instead of assuming that each respondent ideal point x_i represented a set of 10 voters with ideal

points located at $x_i - 0.45, x_i - 0.35, \ldots, x_i + 0.45$—the assumption used for the simulations on Britain and France—I assumed that each respondent ideal point x_i represented a set of 101 voters with ideal points located at $x_i - 0.05, x_i - 0.49, \ldots, x_i + 0.50$. This resulted in a voter distribution that more nearly approximated the assumption of continuity that spatial modelers typically employ. (I note that it was possible to explore this more complex voter distribution for U.S. elections, and to investigate party optima while allowing parties to select from a larger number of policy positions, because the computations of party optima for American two-party elections were significantly faster than those for the British three-party elections and the French four-party and five-party contests.)

19. One other interesting feature of figures 7.8A and 7.8B is that in both figures each party eventually converges to a pattern in which it oscillates between exactly two positions. Thus, in figure 7.8A, starting at time $t4$, the Democrats switch back and forth between the locations $d = 4.14$ and $d = 4.28$ and the Republicans alternate between $r = 4.69$ and $r = 4.77$; in figure 7.8B, starting at time $t3$, the Democrats alternate between the locations $d = 3.74$ and $d = 3.79$ and the Republicans alternate between $r = 5.20$ and $r = 5.28$. I have no theoretical explanation for this pattern, which emerged repeatedly in the simulations.

20. With respect to the partisan salience parameter, b, the empirical estimates reported by Lacy and Burden (1999, table 3) for the 1992 American presidential election and by Morgan (1996, tables 1–2) for the 1980 and the 1984 presidential elections suggest that realistic values for b in the partisan turnout model are in the range of $b^{1/2} = 1.25$ to $b^{1/2} = 1.5$. It is more difficult to determine realistic parameters for a since the limited number of empirical studies that explore turnout-based voting specifications typically incorporate numerous variables relevant to voters' abstention utilities (see, e.g., Sanders 1998; Lacy and Burden 1999; Morgan 1996; and Erikson and Romero 1990, table 1, column 5). Given the values of a used in the simulations, simulated voter turnout (with the parties located at their vote-maximizing positions and with b set at $b^{1/2} = 1.25$ or $b^{1/2} = 1.5$, values consistent with Lacy and Burden's empirical results) was typically in the range of 70 to 80 percent. Although such simulated turnout rates are significantly higher than actual turnout rates for the 1996 presidential and congressional elections, they are consistent with the 77 percent turnout rate that ANES respondents reported for the 1996 presidential election.

21. Note that equilibria were not located for the simulations in which the voters had no partisan biases (i.e., $b = 0$), although the parties' mean positions were virtually identical in these simulations. This result is an artifact of the constraints on party positioning in the simulations; in a set of alternative simulations in which the parties were permitted to choose their positions from among the set of 6.001 locations {1.000,1.001,7.000}, the parties did converge to equilibria.

22. I conducted additional simulations on voter distributions drawn from the 1988 and 1994 ANES, which reproduced the results reported for 1992 and 1996 in every respect, which further supports this contention.

Chapter 8

1. Indeed, much of the seminal work on the instability of two-person voting games (e.g., McKelvey 1976; Plott 1967; Schofield 1978) can be seen as relevant to the question of party or candidate policy trajectories in two-party elections.

2. The only other study of which I am aware that explores party policy trajectories within a spatial modeling framework, and that considers multiparty systems, is Budge's (1994) analysis of the MRG's cross-time data on party policies. However, Budge's study does not incorporate analytical results but measures the degree of empirical support for alternative decision rules that parties might use to choose policies in electoral environments characterized by extreme uncertainty.

3. For important recent work that integrates complex models of party motivations into spatial models of multiparty competition, see Austen-Smith and Banks 1988, Schofield and Sened 1998, and Schofield and Parks 1997.

4. To clarify, this summary applies to spatial analyses that employ the Downsian assumption that voters evaluate parties according to policy proximity. In recent years, a number of alternative models of policy voting have been proposed (e.g., Grofman 1985; Mathews 1979; Iversen 1994a; Rabinowitz and Macdonald 1989), for which parties typically maximize votes by taking noncentrist positions. For analyses of party strategies for these alternative voting models, see Merrill 1993; Merrill and Grofman 1999, chaps. 8–11; Rabinowitz, Macdonald, and Listhaug 1991; and Adams and Merrill 1999a, 1999b, 2000.

References

Aardal, Bernt. 1990. "The Norwegian Parliamentary Election of 1989." *Electoral Studies* 9:151–58.

Aardal, Bernt, and Henry Valen. 1997. "The Storting Elections of 1989 and 1993: Norwegian Politics in Perspective." In *Challenges to Political Parties: The Case of Norway,* ed. Kaare Strøm and Lars Svåsand, 61–76. Ann Arbor: University of Michigan Press.

Achen, Christopher. 1975. Mass Political Attitudes and the Survey Response. *American Political Science Review* 69:1218–31.

Achen, Christopher. 1978. "Measuring Representation." *American Journal of Political Science* 22:475–510.

Achen, Christopher. 1992. "Social Psychology, Demographic Variables, and Linear Regression: Breaking the Iron Triangle in Voting Research." *Political Behavior* 14:195–211.

Adams, James. 1997. "Condorcet Efficiency and the Behavioral Model of the Vote." *Journal of Politics* 59:1252–63.

Adams, James. 1998. "Partisan Voting and Multiparty Spatial Competition: The Pressure for Responsible Parties." *Journal of Theoretical Politics* 10:5–31.

Adams, James, 1999a. "Multiparty Spatial Competition with Probabilistic Voting." *Public Choice* 99:259–74.

Adams, James. 1999b. "Policy Divergence in Multicandidate Probabilistic Spatial Voting." *Public Choice* 100:103–22.

Adams, James. Forthcoming (a). "Multicandidate Equilibrium in American Elections." Forthcoming in *Public Choice.*

Adams, James. Forthcoming (b). "A Theory of Spatial Competition with Biased Voters: Party Politics Viewed Temporally and Comparatively. Forthcoming in *British Journal of Political Science.*

Adams, James, and Samuel Merrill III. 1998. "A Downsian Model of Candidate Competition in the 1988 French Presidential Election." Paper presented at the 1998 annual meeting of the Western Political Science Association, Los Angeles, March 19–21.

Adams, James, and Samuel Merrill III. 1999a. "Party Policy Equilibrium for Alternative Spatial Voting Models: An Application to the Norwegian Storting." *European Journal of Political Research* 36:235–55.

Adams, James, and Samuel Merrill III. 1999b. "Modeling Party Strategies and Policy Representation in Multiparty Elections: Why Are Strategies So Extreme?" *American Journal of Political Science* 43:765–91.

217

Adams, James, and Samuel Merrill III. 1999c. "A Model of Multicandidate Spatial Competition with Biased Voters and Probabilistic Voting." Typescript.

Adams, James, and Samuel Merrill III. 2000 "Spatial Models of Candidate Competition and the 1988 French Presidential Election: Are Presidential Candidates Vote-Maximizers?" *Journal of Politics* 62:729–56.

Adams, James, Samuel Merrill III, and Bernard Grofman. 1999. "Do Vote-Seeking, Coalition-Seeking, and Policy-Seeking Parties Behave Similarly? A Spatial Model with Applications to Norway." Paper presented at the annual meeting of the American Political Science Association, Atlanta, September 1999.

Aldrich, John. 1983. "A Downsian Spatial Model with Party Activism." *American Political Science Review* 77:974–90.

Alt, James. 1984. "Dealignment and the Dynamics of Partisanship in Britain." In *Electoral Change in Advanced Industrial Societies,* ed. R. Dalton, S. Flanagan, and P. Beck, 50–62. Princeton: Princeton University Press.

Alvarez, R. Michael. 1997. *Information and Elections.* Ann Arbor: University of Michigan Press.

Alvarez, R. Michael, Shaun Bowler, and Jonathan Nagler. 1996. "Issues, Economics, and the Dynamics of Multiparty Elections: The 1997 British General Election." Social Science Working Papers, no. 949. California Institute of Technology, Pasadena.

Alvarez, R. Michael, and Jonathan Nagler. 1995. "Economics, Issues, and the Perot Candidacy: Voter Choice in the 1992 Presidential Election." *American Journal of Political Science* 39:714–44.

Alvarez, R. Michael, and Jonathan Nagler. 1998. "When Politics and Models Collide: Estimating Models of Multiparty Elections." *American Journal of Political Science* 42:55–96.

Alvarez, R. Michael, Jonathan Nagler, and Jennifer Willette. 1998. "The Relative Impact of Issues and the Economy in Canada (with Comparisons to the Netherlands, the U.S., and Britain). Paper presented at the 1998 conference on Economics and Elections in Denmark.

Ansolabehere, Stephen, James Snyder, and Charles Stewart. 1999. "Candidate Positioning in U.S. House Elections." Manuscript.

Austen-Smith, David, and Jeffrey Banks. 1988. "Elections, Coalitions, and Legislative Outcomes." *American Political Science Review* 82:405–22.

Axelrod, Robert. 1970. *Conflict of Interest.* Chicago: Markham.

Backstrom, Charles. 1977. "Congress and the Public: How Representative Is One of the Other?" *American Politics Quarterly* 5:411–35.

Baker, Kendall, Russell Dalton, and Kai Hildebrandt. 1981. *Germany Transformed: Political Culture and the New Politics.* Cambridge: Harvard University Press.

Banks, Jeffrey, and John Duggan. 1998. "Stationary Equilibria in a Bargaining Model of Social Choice." University of Rochester. Typescript.

Barnes, Samuel. 1977. *Representation in Italy.* Chicago: University of Chicago Press.

Bartle, John. 1998. "Left-Right Position Matters, but Does Social Class? Causal Models of the 1992 British General Election." *British Journal of Political Science* 28:501–29.

Berelsen, Bernard, Paul Lazerfield, and William McPhee. 1954. *Voting.* Chicago: University of Chicago Press.

Berger, Mark, Michael Munger, and Richard Potthoff. 2000. "With Uncertainty, the Downsian Model Predicts Divergence." *Journal of Theoretical Politics* 12, no. 2 (April).

Bishop, George, and Kathleen Francovic. 1981. "Ideological Consensus and Constraint: Party Leaders and Followers in the 1978 Election." *Micropolitics* 2:87–111.

Boy, Daniel, and Nonna Mayer, eds. 1993. *The French Voter Decides.* Ann Arbor: University of Michigan Press.

Browne, Eric C. 1973. *Coalition Theories: A Logical and Theoretical Critique.* Beverly Hills: Sage.

Brynan, Malcolm, and David Sanders. 1997. "Party Identification, Political Preferences, and Material Conditions." *Party Politics* 3:53–77.

Budge, Ian. 1994. "A New Theory of Party Competition: Uncertainty, Ideology, and Policy Equilibria Viewed Comparatively and Temporally." *British Journal of Political Science* 24:443–67.

Budge, Ian, Ivor Crewe, and Dennis Farlie, eds. 1976. *Party Identification and Beyond: Representations of Voting and Party Competition.* London: Wiley.

Budge, Ian, Ivor Crewe, David McKay, and Ken Newton. 1998. *The New British Politics.* New York: Addison Wesley Longman.

Budge, Ian, and Dennis Farlie. 1977. *Voting and Party Competition.* Chilchester: Wiley.

Budge, Ian, David Robertsen, and D. J. Hearl, eds. 1987. *Ideology, Strategy, and Party Change: Spatial Analyses of Post-war Election Programmes in 19 Democracies.* Cambridge: Cambridge University Press.

Burden, Barry, and Dean Lacy. 1999. "The Vote-Stealing and Turnout Effects of Third-Party Candidates in U.S. Presidential Elections, 1968–1996. Paper presented at the annual meeting of the American Political Science Association, Atlanta, Aug. 29–Sept. 2.

Butler, David, and Donald Stokes. 1969. *Political Change in Britain: Forces Shaping Electoral Choice.* New York: St. Martin's.

Cahoon, Lawrence, Melvin H. Hinich, and Peter C. Ordeshook. 1978. "A Statistical Multidimensional Scaling Model Based on the Spatial Theory of Voting." In *Graphical Representation of Multivariate Data,* ed. P. C. Wang. New York: Academic Press.

Campbell, Angus, Philip E. Converse, Warren E. Miller, and Donald E. Stokes. 1960. *The American Voter.* New York: Wiley.

Castles, Francis, and Peter Mair. 1984. "Left-Right Political Scales: Some Expert Judgments." *European Journal of Political Research* 12:73–88.

Chapman, David. 1967. "Models of the Working of a Two-Party Electoral System—I." In *Papers in Non-market Decision-Making,* 19–38.

Chapman, David. 1968. "Models of the Working of a Two-Party Electoral System—II." *Public Choice* 1:19–38.

Chappel, Henry W., and William R. Keech. 1986. "Policy Motivation and Party Differences in a Dynamic Spatial Model of Party Competition." *American Political Science Review* 80:881–99.

Converse, Philip. 1964. "The Nature of Belief Systems in Mass Publics." In *Ideology and Discontent,* ed. D. Apter, 206–61. New York: Free Press.

Converse, Philip. 1966. "The Normal Vote." In *Elections and the Political Order,* ed. A. Campbell et al., 9–39. New York: Wiley.

Converse, Philip. 1969. "Of Time and Partisan Stability." *Comparative Political Studies* 2:139–71.

Converse, Philip. 1970. "Attitudes and Nonattitudes." In *The Quantitative Analysis of Social Problems,* ed. E. Tufte. Reading MA: Addison-Wesley.

Converse, Philip. 1990. "Popular Representation and the Distribution of Information." In *Information and Democratic Processes,* ed. J. Ferejohn and J. Kuklinski, 131–55. Urbana: University of Illinois Press.

Converse, Philip, and Georges Depeux. 1966. "Politicization of the Electorate in France and the United States." In *Elections and the Political Order,* ed. Angus Campbell et al., chap. 14. New York: Wiley.

Converse, Philip, and Roy Pierce. 1986. *Political Representation in France.* Cambridge: Harvard University Press.

Converse, Philip, and Roy Pierce. 1992a. "Measuring Partisanship." *Political Methodology* 8:143–66.

Converse, Philip, and Roy Pierce. 1992b. "Partisanship and the Party System." *Political Behavior* 14:239–59.

Converse, Philip, and Roy Pierce. 1993. "Comment on Fleury and Lewis-Beck." *Journal of Politics* 55:1110–17.

Coughlin, Peter. 1992. *Probabilistic Voting Theory.* Cambridge: Cambridge University Press.

Coughlin, Peter, and Samual Nitzan. 1981. "Electoral Outcomes with Probabilistic Voting and Nash Social Welfare Maxima." *Journal of Public Economics* 15:113–22.

Cox, Gary. 1984. "An Expected-Utility Model of Electoral Competition." *Quality and Quantity* 18:337–49.

Cox, Gary. 1990. "Centripetal and Centrifugal Incentives in Electoral Systems." *American Journal of Political Science* 34:905–35.

Cox, Gary. 1997. *Making Votes Count.* Cambridge: Cambridge University Press.

Crewe, Ivor. 1986. "On the Death and Resurrection of Class Voting." *Political Studies* 34:620–38.

Crewe, Ivor, and M. Harrop, eds. 1989. *Political Communications: The General Election Campaign of 1989.* Cambridge: Cambridge University Press.

Dalton, Russell. 1985. "Political Parties and Political Representation." *Comparative Political Studies* 17:267–99.

Dalton, Russell. 1996. *Citizen Politics: Public Opinion and Political Parties in Advanced Western Democracies.* Chatham, NJ: Chatham House.

Dalton, Russell, Scott Flanagan, and Paul Beck, eds. 1984. *Electoral Change in Advanced Industrial Societies: Realignment or Dealignment?* Princeton: Princeton University Press.

de Palma, Andre, Victor Ginsberg, Martine Labbe, and Jacques-Francois Thisse. 1989. "Competitive Location with Random Utilities. *Transportation Science* 23:244–52.

de Palma, Andre, Gap-Seon Hong, and Jacques-Francois Thisse. 1990. "Equilibria in Multiparty Competition under Uncertainty." *Social Choice and Welfare* 7:247–59.

De Swaan, Abram. 1973. *Coalition Theories and Cabinet Formation.* Amsterdam: Elsevier.

Debreu, Gerard. 1960. Review of R. Duncan Luce, *Individual Choice Behavior. American Economic Review* 50:186–88.

Dodd, L. C. 1976. *Coalitions in Parliamentary Government.* Princeton: Princeton University Press.

Dow, Jay. 1997a. "Voter Choice and Strategies in French Presidential Elections: The 1995 First Ballot Election." Paper presented at the 1997 annual meeting of the Midwest Political Science Association, Chicago, April.

Dow, Jay. 1997b. "A Comparative Spatial Analysis of Majoritarian and Proportional Elections." Paper presented at the 1997 annual meeting of the American Political Science Association, Washington, DC, Sept. 1–4.

Dow, Jay. 1998. "Directional and Proximity Models of Voter Choice in Recent U.S. Presidential Elections. *Public Choice* 96:259–70.

Dow, Jay. Forthcoming. "A Spatial Analysis of the 1989 Chilean Presidential Election." Forthcoming in *Electoral Studies.*

Downs, Anthony. 1957. *An Economic Theory of Democracy.* New York: Harper.

Duverger, Maurice. 1954. *Political Parties.* New York: Wiley.

Eaton, B., and C. Lipsey. 1975. "The Principle of Minimum Differentiation Reconsidered: New Developments in the Theory of Spatial Competition." *Review of Economic Studies* 42:27–49.

Endersby, James, and Steven Galatas. 1997. "British Parties and Spatial Competition: Dimensions of Party Evaluation in the 1992 Election." Paper presented at the annual meeting of the Public Choice Society, San Francisco, March 21–23.

Enelow, James, and Melvin Hinich. 1981. "A New Approach to Voter Uncertainty in the Downsian Spatial Model." *American Journal of Political Science* 25:483–93.

Enelow, James, and Melvin Hinich. 1982. "Non-spatial Candidate Characteristics and Electoral Competition." *Journal of Politics* 44:115–30.

Enelow, James, and Melvin Hinich. 1984. *The Spatial Theory of Voting.* Cambridge: Cambridge University Press.

Erikson, Robert, and David Romero. 1990. "Candidate Equilibrium and the Behavioral Model of the Vote." *American Political Science Review* 84:1103–26.

Eulau, H. 1987. "The Congruence Model Revisited.: *Legislative Studies Quarterly* 7:171–214.

Farah, Barbara. 1980. *Political Representation in West Germany.* Ph.D. diss. University of Michigan.

Feddersen, Timothy, Itai Sened, and Stephen Wright. 1990. "Rational Voting and Candidate Entry under Plurality Rule." *American Journal of Political Science* 34:1005–16.

Feld, Scott, and Bernard Grofman. 1991. "Voter Loyalty, Incumbency Advantage, and the Benefit of the Doubt." *Journal of Theoretical Politics* 3:115–37.

Feld, Scott, Bernard Grofman, R. Hartley, Marc Kilgour, Nicholas Miller, and N. Noviello. 1987. "The Uncovered Set in Spatial Voting Games." *Theory and Decision* 23:129–56.

Feld, Scott, Bernard Grofman, and Nicholas Miller. 1988. "Centripetal Forces in Spatial Voting: On the Size of the Yolk." *Public Choice* 59:37–50.

Fenno, Richard. 1978. *Home Style* Boston: Little, Brown.

Fiorina, Morris. 1981. *Retrospective Voting in American National Elections.* New Haven: Yale University Press.

Fleury, Christopher, and Michael Lewis-Beck. 1993. "Anchoring the French Voter: Ideology Versus Party." *Journal of Politics* 55:1100–09.

Franklin, Mark, Tom Mackie, and Henry Valen, eds. 1992. *Electoral Change*. New York: Cambridge University Press.

Gilljam, Mikael. 1997. "The Directional Theory under a Magnifying Glass: A Reappraisal. *Journal of Theoretical Politics* 9:5–12.

Glasgow, Garrett. 1999. "Heterogeneity in Issue Salience in the American Electorate." Typescript.

Grofman, Bernard. 1985. "The Neglected Role of the Statue Quo in Models of Issue Voting." *Journal of Politics* 47:230–37.

Groseclose, Tim. 1999. "Character, Charisma, and Candidate Location: Downsian Models When One Candidate Has a Valence Advantage." Manuscript.

Hansson, Ingemar, and Charles Stuart. 1984. "Voting Competition with Interested Politicians: Platforms Do Not Converge to the Preferences of the Median Voter." *Public Choice* 44:431–41.

Harmel, Robert, and Kenneth Janda. 1982. *Parties and Their Environments*. New York: Longman.

Heath, Anthony, and Roy Pierce. 1992. "It Was Party Identification All Along: Question Order Effects on Reports of Party Identification in Britain." *Electoral Studies* 11:93–105.

Hermsen, Hanneke, and Anders Verbeek. 1992. "Equilibria in Multiparty Systems." *Public Choice* 73:147–66.

Herrera, Cheryl, Richard Herrera, and Eric Smith. 1992. "Public Opinion and Congressional Representation." *Public Opinion Quarterly* 56:185–205.

Herron, Michael. 1998. "Voting, Abstention, and Individual Expectations in the 1992 Presidential Election." Northwestern University. Manuscript.

Highton, Benjamin, and Raymond Wolfinger. 1998. "The Political Implications of Higher Turnout." Presented at the Annual Meeting of the American Political Science Association, Boston, MA, September 3–6.

Hinich, Melvin, and Michael Munger. 1994. *Ideology and the Theory of Political Choice*. Ann Arbor: University of Michigan Press.

Holmberg, Søren. 1989. "Political Representation in Sweden." *Scandinavian Political Studies* 12: 1–35.

Holmberg, Søren. 1994. "Party Identification Compared across the Atlantic." In *Elections at Home and Abroad,* ed. M. K. Jennings and T. Mann, 122–53. Ann Arbor: University of Michigan Press.

Huber, John. 1989. "Values and Partisanship in Left-Right Orientations: Measuring Ideology." *European Journal of Political Research* 17:599–621.

Huber, John, and Ronald Inglehart. 1995. "Expert Interpretations of Party Space and Party Location in 42 Societies." *Party Politics* 1:73–111.

Hug, Simon. 1995. "Third Parties in Equilibrium." *Public Choice* 82:159–80.

Inglehart, Ronald. 1977. "The Silent Revolution. Princeton: Princeton University Press.

Inglehart, Ronald, and Hans-Dieter Klingemann. 1987. "Party Identification, Ideological Preference, and the Left-Right Dimensions among Western Mass Publics." In *Ideology, Strategy, and Party Change,* ed. Ian Budge, David Robertsen, and David Hearl, 160–81. Cambridge: Cambridge University Press.

Iversen, Torben. 1994a. "Political Leadership and Representation in Western European

Democracies: A Test of Three Models of Voting." *American Journal of Political Science* 38:45–74.

Iversen, Torben. 1994b. "The Logics of Electoral Politics: Spatial, Directional, and Mobilization Effects." *Comparative Political Studies* 27:155–89.

Jackson, John. 1990. "Endogenous Voter Preferences and Party Strategies." University of Michigan. Typescript.

Janda, Kenneth Robert Harmel, Christine Edens, and Patricia Goff. 1995. "Changes in Party Identity: Evidence from Party Manifestos." *Party Politics* 1:171–96.

Jennings, Kent. 1992. "Ideological Thinking among Mass Publics and Political Elites." *Public Opinion Quarterly* 56:419–41.

Kaase, Max. 1976. "Party Identification and Voting Behavior in the West German Election of 1976." In *Party Identification and Beyond: Representations of Voting and Party Competition,* ed. Ian Budge, Ivor Crewe, and Dennis Farlie, 71–99. London: John Wiley and Sons.

Keane, Michael. 1992. "A Note on the Identification of the Multinomial Probit Model." *Journal of Business and Economic Statistics* 10:193–200.

Key, V. O., Jr. 1966. *The Responsible Electorate.* New York: Vintage.

Klingemann, Hans-Deieter, Richard I. Hofferbert, and Ian Budge. 1994. *Parties, Policies, and Democracy.* Boulder: Westview.

Kollman, Kenneth, John Miller, and Scott Page. 1992. "Adaptive Parties in Spatial Elections." *American Political Science Review* 86:929–37.

Kramer, Richard. 1977. "A Dynamic Model of Political Equilibrium." *Journal of Economic Theory* 16:310–34.

Kuklinski, James. 1978. "Representativeness and Elections." *American Political Science Review* 72:165–77.

Lacy, Dean, and Barry Burden. 1999. "The Vote-Stealing and Turnout Effects of Ross Perot in the 1992 U.S. Presidential Election." *American Journal of Political Science* 43:233–55.

Lacy, Dean, and Philip Paolino. 1998. "Downsian Voting and the Separation of Powers." *American Journal of Political Science* 42:1180–99.

Lancelot, Alain. 1986. "L'orienation du Comportement Politique." In *Traite de Science Politique,* ed. Madeleine Grawitz and Jaen Leca, 3:367–428. Paris: Presses Universitaires de France.

Laver, Michael, and Ian Budge, eds. 1992. *Party Policy and Government Coalitions in Western Europe.* London: Macmillan.

Laver, Michael, and Ben Hunt. 1992. *Policy and Party Competition.* London: Routledge.

Laver, Michael, and Garry John. 1998. "Estimating Policy Positions from Party Manifestos." Paper presented at the European Center for Political Research, Joint Sessions, University of Warwick.

Laver, Michael, and Norman Schofield. 1990. *Multiparty Government.* Oxford: Oxford University Press.

Laver, Michael, and Kenneth Shepsle. 1996. *Making and Breaking Governments.* Cambridge: Cambridge University Press.

Lewis, Jeffrey, and Gary King. 2000. "No Evidence on Directional versus Proximity Voting." *Political Analysis* 8:21–34.

Lewis-Beck, Michael. 1988. *Economics and Elections.* Ann Arbor: University of Michigan Press.

Lijphart, Arend. 1984. *Democracies.* New Haven: Yale University Press.

Lijphart, Arend. 1994. *Electoral Systems and Party Systems: A Study of Twenty-seven Democracies, 1945–1900.* New York: Oxford University Press.

Lijphart, Arend. 1997. Unequal Participation: Democracy's Unresolved Dilemma." *American Political Science Review* 91:1–14.

Lin, Tse-Min, James Enelow, and Han Dorussen. 1999. "Equilibrium in Multicandidate Probabilistic Spatial Voting." *Public Choice* 98:59–82.

Lindbeck, A., and J. Weibull. 1987. "Balanced-Budget Redistribution as the Outcome of Political Competition." *Public Choice* 52:273–97.

Lipset, S. M., and Stein Rokkan, eds. 1967. *Party Systems and Voter Alignments.* New York: Free Press.

Listhaug, Ola. 1989. *Citizens, Parties, and Norwegian Electoral Politics, 1957–85.* Trondheim: Tapir.

Listhaug, Ola. 1997. "The Decline of Class Voting." In *Challenges to Political Parties: The Case of Norway,* ed. Kaare Strøm and Lars Svåsand, 77–90. Ann Arbor: University of Michigan Press.

Lomborg, Bjorn. 1996. "Adaptive Parties in a Multiparty, Multidimensional System with Imperfect Information." Manuscript.

Luce, Duncan. 1959. *Individual Choice Behavior.* New York: Wiley.

Luebbert, Gregory M. 1986. *Comparative Democracy: Policy-Making and Governing Coalitions in Europe and Israel.* New York: Columbia University Press.

Macdonald, Stuart, and George Rabinowitz. 1998. "Solving the Paradox of Non-convergence: Valence, Position, and Direction in Democratic Politics." *Electoral Studies* 17:281–300.

MacRae, Duncan. 1967. *Parliament, Parties, and Society in France, 1946–58.* New York: St. Martin's.

Markus, Gregory, and Philip Converse. 1979. "A Dynamic Simultaneous Equation Model of Electoral Choice." *American Political Science Review* 73:1055–70.

Mathews, Steven. 1979. "A Simple Direction Model of Electoral Competition." *Public Choice* 34:141–56.

May, John. 1973. "Opinion Structures of Political Parties: The Special Law of Curvilinear Disparity." *Political Studies* 21:135–51.

Mayhew, David. 1974. *Congress: The Electoral Connection.* New Haven: Yale University Press.

McCallister, Ian. 1992. *Political Behavior: Citizens, Parties, and Elites in Australia.* Melbourne: Longman Cheshire.

McDonald, Michael, Ian Budge, and Richard Hofferbert. 1998. "American Party Platforms and Dynamic Representation: Responsiveness, Choice, and Rationality." Paper presented at the annual meeting of the American Political Science Association, Boston, September 2–6.

McFadden, Daniel. 1978. "Modeling the Choice of Residential Location." In *Spatial Interaction Theory and Planning Models,* ed. A. Karquist et al., 112–57. Amsterdam: North-Holland.

McKelvey, Richard. 1976. "Intransitivities in Multidimensional Voting Models and Some Implications for Agenda Control." *Journal of Economic Theory* 12:472–82.

McKelvey, Richard. 1986. "Covering, Dominance, and Institution-Free Properties of Social Choice." *American Journal of Political Science* 30:283–314.

Merrill, Samuel, III. 1993. "Voting Behavior under the Directional Spatial Model of Electoral Competition." *Public Choice* 77:739–56.

Merrill, Samuel, III. 1994. "A Probabilistic Model for the Distribution of Party Support in Multiparty Elections." *Journal of the American Statistical Association* 89:1190–99.

Merrill, Samuel, III, and James Adams. 2000a. "An Algorithm to Compute Nash Equilibria in Probabilistic, Multiparty Spatial Models with a Nonpolicy Component." Manuscript.

Merrill, Samuel, III, and James Adams. 2000b. "Centripetal, Centrifugal, and Directional Incentives in Multicandidate Elections." Typescript.

Merrill, Samuel, III, and Bernard Grofman. 1997. "Directional and Proximity Models of Voter Utility and Choice." *Journal of Theoretical Politics* 9:25–48.

Merrill, Samuel, III, and Bernard Grofman. 1999. *A Unified Theory of Voting: Directional and Proximity Models.* Cambridge: Cambridge University Press.

Michelat, Guy, 1993. "In Search of Left and Right." In *The French Voter Decides,* ed. Daniel Boy and Nonna Mayer, 65–90. Ann Arbor: University of Michigan Press.

Miller, Nicholas. 1980. "A New 'Solution Set' for Tournaments and Majority Voting." *American Journal of Political Science* 24:68–96.

Miller, Warren, and Donald Stokes. 1963. "Constituency Influence in Congress." *American Political Science Review* 57:45–56.

Morgan, William. 1996. "A Unified Model of Turnout and Vote Choice." Paper presented at the annual meeting of the American Political Science Association, San Francisco, August 28–September 1.

Mueller, Dennis. 1989. *Public Choice, II.* Cambridge: Cambridge University Press.

Muller, Wolfgang, and Kaare Strøm, eds. 1999. *Policy, Office, or Votes: How Political Parties in Western Europe Make Hard Decisions.* Cambridge: Cambridge University Press.

Page, Benjamin, and Calvin Jones. 1979. "Reciprocal Effects of Policy Preferences, Party Loyalties, and the Vote." *American Political Science Review* 73:1071–89.

Page, Benjamin, Robert Shapiro, Paul Gronke, and Robert Rosenberg. 1988. "Constituency, Party and Representation in Congress." *Public Opinion Quarterly* 48:741–56.

Palfrey, Thomas. 1984. "Spatial Equilibrium with Entry." *Review of Economic Studies* 51:139–56.

Petry, François. 1982. "Vote-Maximizing Versus Utility-Maximizing Candidates: Comparing Dynamic Models of Bi-party Competition." *Quality and Quantity* 16:507–26.

Pierce, Roy. 1995. *Choosing the Chief: Presidential Elections in France and the United States.* Ann Arbor: University of Michigan Press.

Pierce, Roy, 1996. French Presidential Election Survey, 1988. computer file, ICPSR version. Roy Pierce, University of Michigan, producer (1995). Inter-university Consortium for Political and Social Research, distributor (1996).

Plott, Charles. 1967. "A Notion of Equilibrium and Its Possibility under Majority Rule." *American Economic Review* 57:787–806.

Powell, G. Bingham. 1982. *Contemporary Democracies.* Cambridge: Harvard University Press.

Powell, G. Bingham. 1986. "American Voting Turnout in Comparative Perspective." *American Political Science Review* 80:17–44.

Powell, G. Bingham. 1989. "Constitutional Design and Citizen Electoral Control." *Journal of Theoretical Politics* 1:107–30.

Przeworski, Adam, and John Sprague. 1986. *Paper Stones: A History of Electoral Socialism.* Chicago: University of Chicago Press.

Rabier, Jean, and Ronald Inglehart. 1980. *Eurobarometer II.* Ann Arbor: Interuniversity Consortium for Political and Social Research.

Rabinowitz, George, and Stuart Macdonald. 1989. "A Directional Theory of Issue Voting." *American Political Science Review* 89:93–121.

Rabinowitz, George, and Stuart Macdonald. 1997. "Valence, Position, and Direction in Democratic Politics." Paper presented at the annual meeting of the American Political Science Association, Washington, DC, August 28–31.

Rabinowitz, George, and Stuart Macdonald. Forthcoming. "On Attempting to Rehabilitate the Proximity Model: Sometimes the Patient Just Can't Be Helped." Forthcoming in the *Journal of Politics.*

Rabinowitz, George, Stuart Macdonald, and Ola Listhaug. 1991. "New Players in an Old Game: Party Strategy in Multiparty Systems." *Comparative Political Studies* 24:147–85.

Ranney, Austin. 1962. *The Doctrine of Responsible Party Government.* Urbana: University of Illinois Press.

Rivers, Douglas. 1988. "Heterogeneity in Models of Electoral Choice." *American Journal of Political Science* 32:737–58.

Robertsen, David. 1976. *A Theory of Party Competition.* Chichester: Wiley.

Rose, Richard, and Ian McAllister. 1990. *The Loyalties of Voters: A Lifetime Learning Model.* London: Sage.

Safran, William. 1998. *The French Polity.* Menlo Park, CA: Addison Wesley Longman.

Sanders, Mitchell. 1998. "Unified Models of Turnout and Vote Choice for Two-Candidate and Three-Candidate Elections." *Political Analysis* 7:89–116.

Sani, G., and G. Sartori. 1983. "Polarization, Fragmentation, and Competition in Western Democracies." In *Western European Party Systems,* ed. Hans Daalder and Peter Mair, 307–40. London and Beverly Hills: Sage.

Sartori, Giovanni. 1968. "Representational Systems." *International Encyclopedia of the Social Sciences* 13:470–75.

Schofield, Norman. 1978. "Instability of Simple Dynamic Games." *Review of Economic Studies* 45:575–94.

Schofield, Norman. 1997a. "A Comparison of Majoritarian and Proportional Electoral Systems Based on Spatial Modeling and "Rational" Politicians." Paper presented at the conference Constitutional Issues in Modern Democracies, Messina, Italy, September 25–27.

Schofield, Norman. 1997b. "Multiparty Electoral Politics." In *Perspectives in Public Choice,* ed. Dennis Mueller, 119–47. Cambridge: Cambridge University Press.

Schofield, Norman. 1998. "The Heart and the Uncovered Set." Political Economy Working Papers, no. 199. Washington University, St. Louis.

Schofield, Norman, Andrew Martin, Kevin Quin, and Andrew Whitford. 1998. "Multiparty Competition in the Netherlands and Germany: A Model Based on Multinomial Probit." *Public Choice* 97:257–93.

Schofield, Norman, and Robert Parks. 1997. "Nash Equilibrium in a Spatial Model of Coalition Bargaining." Manuscript.

Schofield, Norman, and Itai Sened. 1998. "Political Equilibrium in Multiparty Democracies." Political Economy Working Papers, no. 202. Washington University, St. Louis.

Schofield, Norman, Itai Sened, and David Nixon. 1998. "Nash Equilibrium in Multiparty Competition with 'Stochastic' Voters." *Annals of Operations Research* 84:3–27.

Shaked, Avner. 1975. "Non-existence of Equilibrium for the Two-Dimensional Three-Firms Location Problem." *Review of Economic Studies* 42:51–56.

Shanks, J. Merrill, and Warren Miller. 1990. "Policy Direction and Performance Evaluations: Complementary Explanations of the Reagan Elections." *British Journal of Political Science* 20:143–235.

Shanks, J. Merrill, and Warren Miller. 1991. "Partisanship, Policy, and Performance." *British Journal of Political Science* 21:129–97.

Shepsle, Kenneth, and Barry Weingast. 1984. "Uncovered Sets and Sophisticated Voting Outcomes with Implications for Agenda Control." *American Journal of Political Science* 28:49–74.

Sinnott, Richard. 1998. "Party Attachment in Europe: Methodological Critique and Substantive Implications." *British Journal of Political Science* 28:627–50.

Snyder, James. 1990. "Resource Allocation in Multiparty Systems." *American Journal of Political Science* 34:59–73.

Stimson, James, Michael MacKuen, and Robert Erikson. 1995. "Dynamic Representation." *American Political Science Review* 89:543–65.

Stokes, Donald. 1963. "Spatial Models of Party Competition. *American Political Science Review,* 57:368–77.

Strøm, Kaare. 1990. "A Behavioral Theory of Competitive Political Parties." *American Journal of Political Science* 34:565–98.

Strøm, Kaare, and Lars Svasånd, eds. 1997. *Challenges to Political Parties: The Case of Norway.* Ann Arbor: University of Michigan Press.

Taagepera, Rein, and Matthew Shugart. 1989. *Seats and Votes: The Effects and Determinants of Electoral Systems.* New Haven: Yale University Press.

Thomassen, Jacques. 1976. *Kiezers en Gekozenen in een Representatieve Demokratie.* Alphen an den Rijn: Samson.

Thomassen, Jacques. 1994. "Empirical Research into Political Representation." In *Elections at Home and Abroad,* ed. M. K. Jennings and T. Mann, 26–51. Ann Arbor: University of Michigan Press.

Timpone, Richard. 1998. "Structure, Behavior, and Voter Turnout in the United States." *American Political Science Review* 92:145–58.

Tsebelis, George. 1990. *Nested Games: Rational Choice in Comparative Politics.* Berkeley: University of California Press.

Train, Kenneth. 1986. *Qualitative Choice Analysis.* Cambridge: MIT Press.

Ware, Alan. 1996. *Political Parties and Party Systems.* London: Wiley.

Weissberg, Robert. 1978. "Collective versus Dyadic Representation in Congress." *American Political Science Review* 72:535–47.

Westholm, Anders. 1997. "Distance versus Direction: The Illusory Defeat of Proximity Theory." *American Political Science Review* 91:865–83.

Westholm, Anders. Forthcoming. "On the Return of Epicycles: Some Crossroads in Spatial Modeling Revisited." Forthcoming in *Journal of Politics.*

Whitten, Guy, and Glen Palmer. 1996. "Heightening Comparativists' Concern for Model Choice: Voting Behavior in Great Britain and the Netherlands." *American Journal of Political Science* 40:231–60.

Wittman, Donald. 1973. "Parties as Utility Maximizers." *American Political Science Review* 67:490–98.

Wittman, Donald. 1983. "Candidate Motivation: A Synthesis of Alternatives." *American Political Science Review* 77:142–57.

Index

9 780472 087679